D0086322

Text Review Guide

for

ECONOMICS
U$A

Seventh Edition

Text Review Guide

for

ECONOMICS U$A

Seventh Edition

EDWIN MANSFIELD and **NARIMAN BEHRAVESH**

Revised by

DEBORAH PAIGE

SANTA FE COMMUNITY COLLEGE

W. W. NORTON & COMPANY • NEW YORK • LONDON

Copyright © 2005, 2001, 1998, 1995, 1992, 1989, 1986
   by W. W. Norton & Company, Inc.
All rights reserved.
Printed in the United States of America.
Layout and composition by Roberta Flechner Graphics.

ISBN 0-393-92607-9 (pbk.)

W. W. Norton & Company, Inc., 500 Fifth Avenue, New York, N.Y. 10110
                    www.wwnorton.com

W. W. Norton & Company Ltd., Castle House, 75/76 Wells Street, London W1T 3QT

1 2 3 4 5 6 7 8 9 0

Contents

Preface

As with many subjects, the key to learning economics is continual practice with and application of the concepts. The *Text Review Guide* for *Economics U$A,* Seventh Edition, was written to provide students with the opportunity to review and test their understanding of the text material. Questions proceed in order from the easier to the more difficult, and answers are provided to enable students to build confidence and competence as they work through the material.

Each lesson has a summary of the main points of the corresponding text chapter and presents a list of the key concepts with which students should be familiar. Questions and problems are then provided that cover the full range of the material from basic knowledge to mastery. Those at the end of the lessons are rigorous enough to challenge even excellent students. Finally, open-ended discussion questions are included to provoke thought or classroom interaction.

At the end of each unit, a case study is given to show real-world applications:

1. Council of Economic Advisers (1997), "Does the Consumer Price Index Overstate Increases in the Cost of Living?"

2. Council of Economic Advisers (2000), "The End of the Business Cycle?" plus Deborah Paige (2004) "The End of the Business Cycle Revisited"

3. (2004), "Microsoft versus the Department of Justice"

4. Roland Cousins (1992), "The Well-Paid Receptionist"

5. Council of Economic Advisers (2000), "The Benefits of a Global Economy"

It has been gratifying to update the study guide for a text I have long respected and used. With thanks to the staff at W. W. Norton for their assistance, my family for their patience, and in memory of Dr. Edwin Mansfield.

DJP
2004

Text Review Guide

for

ECONOMICS
U$A

Seventh Edition

Economic Problems: A Sampler

Chapter Profile

Economics is of relevance for the examination of common real-world issues, such as the productivity of labor and economic growth, unemployment and inflation, economic development in emerging economics, and poverty.

Labor productivity refers to the output made by labor per hour; if labor is more productive, then firms are willing to pay higher wages and countries can make more goods and supply more services. This economic growth raises the standard of living for countries as well as workers. In general, U.S. workers have become more and more proficient at producing goods and services over time, but that growth path has not been smooth. The United States has seen labor productivity gradually slow in the 1960s, rapidly slow in the 1970s, slowly improve in the 1980s, and finally rapidly improve in the 1990s. In fact, our biggest productivity concern recently has been that productivity growth has been so high it slowed job creation. The growth of U.S. output and wages was strongly influenced by this trend.

Unemployment and inflation are the fundamental economic problems our economy keeps facing, and they often move against each other. Policies that lower unemployment may raise inflation. Unemployment devastates communities and households and can cause people to lose their savings, homes, and businesses. Inflation eats away at the purchasing power of people's income and savings, particularly striking those on fixed and low incomes. Economists are divided on the target levels of unemployment and inflation that the economy can sustain and the policies to achieve these targets.

While the gap has widened between the richest and poorest economies in the world, some countries have been able to develop more rapidly and close the gap between their economies and ours. These emerging market economies, such as Singapore, Hong Kong, Chile, and Mexico, have experienced a rapid rise in national output and standards of living. This economic growth has not been without cost, as many of the emerging economies have struggled with financial crises in currency exchange, banking, and debt, as well as issues of human rights, corruption, and pollution. Education, free trade, and stable, well-regulated financial and legal systems appear to be key factors in fostering economic growth.

Even a rich developed economy with a high average standard of living will have a spread between those at the bottom and those at the top, and some individuals will live below an income considered acceptable—in poverty. Although one of the most prosperous economies in the world, the United States has a greater degree of inequality and more individuals living below the poverty level than most wealthy countries. Economists, politicians, and citizens strongly disagree over the causes and solutions to this problem.

Concepts for Review

labor productivity   unemployment   inflation
emerging market economies   poverty

Questions for the Prologue are in the Chapter 1 review.

CHAPTER 1

What Is Economics?

Chapter Profile

According to one standard definition, economics is concerned with the way resources are allocated among alternative uses to satisfy human wants. A resource is a thing or service used to produce goods or services that can satisfy wants. Not all resources are scarce. Free resources, such as air, are so abundant that they can be obtained without charge.

Those resources that are scarce are called *economic resources.* The test of whether a resource is an economic resource or a free resource is price: Economic resources command a nonzero price but free resources do not. Economists often classify economic resources into three categories: land, labor, and capital.

Since economic resources are scarce, only a limited amount of goods and services can be produced from them, and the necessity for choice arises. For example, if an isolated town has a certain amount of resources, it must choose how much of each good it will produce from these resources. If it increases the amount produced of one good, it must reduce the amount produced of another good. The opportunity cost (or alternative cost) of using a resource to increase the production of one good is the value of what the resource could have produced had it been used in the best alternative way.

Economists are particularly concerned with four basic questions regarding the working of an economic system, ours or any other. These questions are

1. What determines what and how much is produced?
2. What determines how it is produced?
3. What determines how the society's output is distributed among its members?
4. What determines the rate at which the society's per-capita income will grow?

Economists often distinguish between positive economics and normative economics. Positive economics contains descriptive statements, propositions, and predictions about the world; normative economics contains statements about what ought to be or what a person, organization, or nation ought to do. In normative economics, the results you get depend on your basic values and preferences; in positive economics, the results are testable, at least in principle, by an appeal to the facts.

The methodology used by economists is much the same as that used in any other kind of scientific analysis. The basic procedure is the formulation and testing of models. A model, in general, must simplify and abstract from the real world. Its purpose is to make predictions concerning phenomena in the real world, and in many respects the most important test of a model is how well it predicts these phenomena. To test and quantify their models, economists gather data and use various statistical techniques.

Concepts for Review

economics	free resources	human wants
model	economic resources	choice
*production possibilities curve	land	opportunity cost
*capital goods	labor	alternative cost
*consumer goods	capital	positive economics
resources	technology	normative economics
Adam Smith	direct relationship	inverse relationship

Completion Questions†

1. The true cost of going to college is considerably (higher, lower)

   _____ than the out-of-pocket expenses because one

   can obtain _____ by working rather than attending
   school.

2. The growth of output has not been steady or uninterrupted; instead, output has

   tended to fluctuate and so has _____.

3. The level of _____ may tend to rise when we reduce the

   level of unemployment. In other words, _____ may occur.

4. Although relatively few people in the United States lack food desperately, about

   _____ people, about _____
   of the population, in the United States live in what is officially designated as
   poverty.

5. Economic problems generally involve _____. There are
   often a number of alternative ways to handle a problem, and the question is

   which is _____.

6. A characteristic of many economic problems is that, to choose among a number

   of feasible solutions, one must _____ what will
   occur if each solution is adopted. This emphasis on the future necessarily

   entails some _____.

7. Economic resources are sometimes classified into the three categories of

   _____, _____, and

   _____.

*The starred items refer to material covered in Exploring Further.
†Some questions pertain to the Prologue as well as to Chapter 1 of the text.

8. _____ is society's pool of knowledge regarding the industrial arts.

9. An economic system must determine the level and composition of society's

   _____.

10. Adam Smith was among the first to describe how a free, competitive economy can function, without central planning or government

    interference, to allocate _____ efficiently. He emphasized

    the virtues of the _____ that leads the private
    interests of firms and individuals toward socially desirable ends, and he was

    suspicious of firms sheltered from _____, since he believed

    there would be _____ effects on resource allocation.

11. Smith's optimism was in keeping with the intellectual climate of his time, the Age of Enlightenment, when people believed in rationality. Leave markets

    _____, said Smith, and beware of firms with too much

    _____ and of unnecessary government

    _____.

12. Value judgments are in the realm of _____ economics. They

    (can, cannot) _____ be tested by an appeal to facts. They

    (can, cannot) _____ be proven in the way that the laws of
    physics can be.

13. The forests of the United States are an important national resource. If these

    forests are used for lumber, they (can, cannot) _____ be used

    for recreation. There (is, is not) _____ enough forest
    land for both recreation and lumber. If we use a certain portion of the

    nation's forests for recreation, the _____ is the forgone lum-
    ber that could have been derived.

True-False

_____ 1. U.S. unemployment has been relatively high in the last few years. This suggests that the United States is operating inside its production possibilities curve.

_____ 2. Adam Smith emphasized the importance of increased specialization and division of labor.

_____ 3. When economists refer to goods as being scarce, they mean that these items are monopolized by a few people. If goods were distributed equitably, there would be no problem of scarcity.

_____ 4. When a society uses resources to produce one good, it must sacrifice alternatives that could have been made instead.

_____ 5. The problem of choosing which goods to produce is not likely to confront a firm, once it is established, but it does confront society.

_____ 6. Since it passes the tax laws, Congress is the only branch of the government concerned with economics.

_____ 7. All other things equal, economies that produce more capital tend to grow faster.

_____ 8. Some emerging market economies have suffered financial crises relating to banking, debt, and currency problems.

_____ 9. Avoiding excessive unemployment is not a task that can be assigned to a particular individual, family, or firm.

Multiple Choice

1. Adam Smith emphasized how the fundamental economic problems could be solved efficiently by

   a. command.
   b. tradition.
   c. the price system.
   d. monopoly.
   e. government agencies.

2. Economics can best be defined as the study of

   a. financial activities.
   b. interpersonal relationships.
   c. making a living.
   d. the allocation of scarce resources.
   e. a human being's reaction to his or her environment.

3. When we reduce the level of unemployment, the effect may be

   a. depression.
   b. inflation.
   c. decreased output.
   d. deflation.
   e. increased purchasing power of the dollar.

4. The problem of distributing society's output among its members must be resolved by

   a. planned economies.
   b. any society that survives.
   c. any society based largely on the price system.
   d. any society based largely on tradition.
   e. any society.

5. Which of the following is *not* included as capital?

   a. A new taxicab
   b. An old taxicab
   c. A school building
   d. A pencil used by an author
   e. A hot dog eaten by an author
       while writing a book

6. Susan Smith's father asks her to help her younger brother with his homework. She refuses until her father promises to pay her $5. She could obtain $6 by babysitting for the equivalent length of time. The opportunity cost of having Susan help her brother in this way is

   a. $5.
   b. $6.
   c. less than $5.
   d. more than $6.
   e. at least $8.

7. Holding constant the amount of capital and natural resources, the greater is a country's labor force, the greater

   a. the amount of equipment that each worker must use.
   b. its rate of investment.
   c. its inefficiency.
   d. its output of capital goods.
   e. none of the above.

Discussion and Extension Questions

1. Robinson Crusoe apparently spent a lot of his waking hours in what we would usually deem leisure activities. Does this not imply he had a severe unemployment problem? Why would you not be worried about his unemployment but you would be concerned about the unemployed in the United States?

2. "The best things in life *are* free, and hence outside the realm of economics: the air we breathe, a view of a sunset, libraries, and liberty. Many other things ought to be free as well, like medical care." Discuss.

3. How do families, as opposed to an entire economy like the United States or China, solve the four basic economic problems?

4. Someone said that economists study how people make choices and that sociologists study why people have no choices to make. What does that statement mean?

5. A lawyer charges what some would regard as an exorbitant sum for a simple matter like drawing up a will. How do economic principles in this chapter help you understand this?

6. What is the opportunity cost of (a) spending an evening at a movie? (b) a college education?

7. What characteristics do economic problems tend to have in common?

8. Is economics concerned solely with solving practical problems?

9. If resources are not fully employed, is it true that an economy must give up some of one good in order to get more of another good?

10. Adam Smith was suspicious of firms that are sheltered from competition. Can you think of some reasons for this suspicion? Is Microsoft sheltered from competition? If so, how? Is the typical U.S. wheat farmer sheltered from competition? Is so, how?

Problems

1. Suppose that the costs due to crime and the opportunity costs of resources used in law enforcement are as follows:

Proportion of criminals caught and convicted	Costs due to crime	Opportunity costs of resources used in law enforcement	Total costs
		(billions of dollars)	
0.4	60	10	70
0.5	50	—	68
0.6	40	30	—
0.7	30	50	80
0.8	—	80	100

   a. Fill in the three blanks.
   b. What proportion of criminals should society try to catch and convict? Why?
   c. Suppose the costs due to crime were to increase by $5 billion at each possible level of law enforcement. In other words, suppose that each of the figures in the second column of the table (*Costs due to crime*) were to increase by $5 billion. Would this affect the optimal proportion of criminals that society should try to catch and convict? Why or why not?

2. Suppose that the average cost per mile of operating your car (including insurance and taxes) is 18 cents. If you are contemplating taking a 200-mile trip, are you correct in assuming that your out-of-pocket costs for the trip will be 18 cents per mile? Why or why not?

3. If the opportunity cost of producing an extra million tons of steel exceeds the value of the extra million tons of steel, should society produce the extra million tons of steel? Why or why not?

4. What do you regard as the answer to the inflation problem that has plagued the United States? Since you are just beginning the study of economics, we do not expect you to have a well-thought-out answer, but you probably have some opinions on this subject. When you have formulated your answer to this question, ask yourself the following questions:

a. What theories (if any) do I employ? (And what is a theory?)
b. On what facts does my answer rest? Where did these facts come from, and how do I know they are correct?
c. What value judgments do I make? To what extent would other interested parties share these value judgments?
d. Is my answer politically feasible? Would Congress and other parts of the political system approve it?

5. Indicate whether each of the following resources is land, capital, or labor: oil deposits in Saudi Arabia _____, Thomas Edison's work on the lightbulb _____, the Empire State Building in New York City _____, the copies of this textbook on the shelves of your college bookstore _____, and Big Sur _____.

6. Peter Jones stumbles accidentally on to a large cache of rifles buried in his backyard. He donates them to the local police department. The police commissioner, in a speech lauding Jones for his altruism, says that Jones has given an important resource (namely, the guns) to the city government, thus making them a free resource. From the point of view of economics, is this use of terms correct? Why or why not?

7. During the past 50 years, the U.S. economy has increased its automobile production by an enormous amount. At the same time, it has increased its production of most other types of goods and services. Does this mean that the opportunity cost of the increased automobile production was negative? Why or why not?

8. In late 1993, about 6 percent of the labor force was unemployed; how can anyone say that labor is scarce?

9. Mary Mineo, a graduate student, has one 8-hour day per week that she can devote to earning extra money. She can write stories for the local newspaper, or she can babysit, or she can divide her time between the two jobs. (For example, she can spend 3 hours writing stories and 5 hours babysitting.) If she babysits, she gets $4 per hour. If she spends her day writing stories, it takes her 1 hour to write the first story, 2 hours to write the second story, and 5 hours to write the third story because she runs out of ideas and becomes less productive as time goes on. Assume that she must write an integer number of stories a day.

a. If she receives $15 per story, should she do any babysitting if she wants to maximize her income during the day?
b. If she receives $25 per story, should she do any babysitting if she wants to maximize her income during the day?
c. What is the lowest price per story that enables her to do no babysitting and still maximize her income?

d. If she spends the first 5 hours of the day babysitting, what is the opportunity cost to her of spending the remaining 3 hours babysitting?
e. If she spends the first 7 hours of the day babysitting, what is the opportunity cost to her of spending the remaining hour babysitting?

*10. Suppose that a society's production possibilities curve is as follows:

	Output (per year)	
Possibility	Food (millions of tons)	Tractors (millions)
A	0	30
B	4	28
C	8	24
D	12	20
E	16	14
F	20	8
G	24	0

a. Is it possible for this society to produce 30 million tons of food per year?
b. Can it produce 30 million tractors per year?
c. Suppose this society produces 20 million tons of food and 6 million tractors per year. Is it operating on the production possibilities curve? If not, what factors might account for this?
d. Plot the production possibilities curve in the graph.

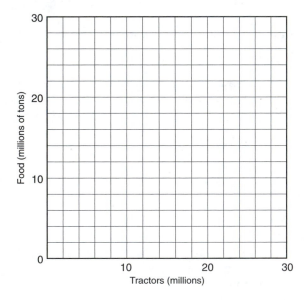

e. What is the cost to society if food output is increased from 12 to 16 million tons per year? If this increase occurs, what effect do you think it will have on this society's production possibilities curve next year?

f. Suppose this society is governed by a dictator who feels that a tractor is worth infinitely more than a ton of food. What point on the production possibilities curve (of those presented in the preceding table) would the dictator choose? What problems would arise if he chose this point?

*11. Suppose that a government faces a choice among various levels of defense, represented by the production of missiles, and food, represented by the production of corn. The following figures indicate the various combinations of missiles and corn that the country can produce:

Possibility	Missiles (number per year)	Corn (millions of bushels per year)
A	0	11
B	2	10
C	4	8
D	6	6
E	8	3
F	10	0

a. Plot the relevant production possibilities curve in the graph.

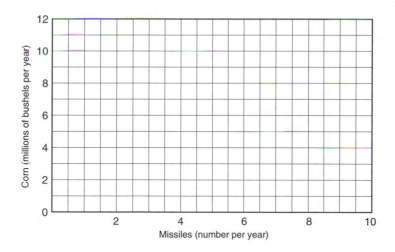

b. Can this country produce more than 12 million bushels of corn per year? Can it produce more than 10 million bushels per year? Can it produce more than 11 missiles per year? Can it produce more than nine missiles per year?

c. Suppose the government of this country decides that, in the interests of national security, it must produce four missiles per year. What is the maximum number of bushels of corn it can produce?

*The starred item pertains to material covered in Exploring Further.

    d.   Measured in terms of corn, what is the cost of producing four missiles per year rather than two missiles per year?

    e.   Suppose that this country develops and obtains new technology that enables it to produce 50 percent more corn at each level of missile production shown in the table. Will the new production possibilities curve be closer to or farther from the origin than the one graphed in part a?

    f.   Under the conditions described in part e, what is the cost of producing four missiles per year rather than two missiles per year?

ANSWERS

Completion Questions

1. higher, wages   2. unemployment   3. prices, inflation   4. 31 million, 11 percent   5. choice, best   6. forecast, uncertainty   7. land, labor, capital
8. Technology   9. output   10. resources, invisible hand, competition, undesirable
11. alone, economic power, intervention   12. normative, cannot, cannot   13. cannot, is not, opportunity cost

True-False

1. True   2. True   3. False   4. True   5. False   6. False   7. True   8. True
9. True

Multiple Choice

1. c   2. d   3. b   4. e   5. e   6. b   7. e

Problems

1. a.   The blank in the second row is 18, the blank in the third row is 70, and the blank in the fifth row is 20.
    b.   50 percent, because this minimizes the total costs to society.
    c.   No, because the minimum total costs to society would still be achieved when 50 percent are caught and convicted.

2. No, because some of the costs are not out-of-pocket costs. You pay a fixed amount for insurance and (some) taxes, regardless of how many miles you drive. Therefore, you do not increase these costs by making the trip.

3. No, because the forgone output of other goods is more valuable than the extra steel.

5. Land, labor, capital, capital, land.

6. No, because rifles are not free. They have a positive price in the market place, even though Jones happened to donate them.

7. No. During the past 50 years, the amount of resources and the available technology in the U.S. economy have changed greatly, allowing increased production of automobiles and other goods. But, if we had chosen to produce fewer automobiles, we surely could have produced more of other things. Hence, the opportunity cost was positive.

8. It is not possible to get all of the labor one wants for the asking. The price of labor is positive.

9. a. She has four alternatives. (1) She can devote 8 hours to babysitting; this will bring in $32. (2) She can devote 1 hour to writing and 7 hours to babysitting; this will bring in $43. (3) She can devote 3 hours to writing and 5 hours to babysitting; this will bring in $50. (4) She can devote 8 hours to writing; this will bring in $45. Therefore, she should do some babysitting.

   b. The opportunity cost of writing the third story is $20, since this is what she could earn in 5 hours of babysitting. Since she gets $25 for this story, she is better off writing the story than devoting 5 hours to babysitting.

   c. $20.

   d. The amount that she could earn by writing two stories.

   e. The amount that she could earn by writing one story.

10. a. No.

    b. Yes.

    c. No. Inefficiency or unemployment of resources might account for this.

    d.

    e. Tractor output must be reduced from 20 million to 14 million. The production possibilities curve will not shift as far outward next year if this increase in food output occurs, because less tractors will be available then.

    f. 30 million tractors and no food. Mass starvation would be likely to result if such a (foolish) policy were adopted.

11. a.

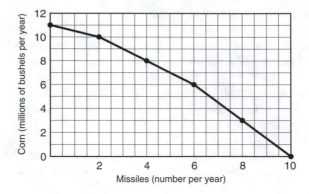

b. No. Yes. No. Yes.
c. 8 million bushels.
d. 2 million bushels of corn.
e. Farther from the origin.
f. 3 million bushels of corn.

CHAPTER 2

Markets and Prices

Chapter Profile

Consumers and firms are the basic units composing the private sector of the economy. A market is a group of firms and individuals in touch with each other to buy some commodity or service. When a market for a homogeneous product contains so many buyers and sellers that none of them can influence the price, economists call it a *perfectly competitive market.*

There are two sides to every market: the demand side and the supply side. The demand side can be represented by the market demand curve, which almost always slopes downward to the right and whose location depends on consumer tastes, the number and income of consumers, and the prices of other commodities.

The supply side of the market can be represented by the market supply curve, which generally slopes upward to the right and whose location depends on technology and resource prices.

The equilibrium price and equilibrium quantity of a commodity are given by the intersection of the market demand and market supply curves. If conditions remain reasonably stable for a time, the actual price and quantity should move close to the equilibrium price and quantity.

To determine which goods and services society produces, the price system sets up incentives for firms to produce what consumers want. To the extent that they produce what consumers want and are willing to pay for, firms reap profits; to the extent that they do not, they experience losses.

The price system sets up strong incentives for firms to produce goods at minimum cost. These incentives take the form of profits for firms that minimize costs and losses for firms that operate with relatively high costs. To determine who gets what, the price system results in people receiving an income that depends on the quantity of resources they own and the prices that these resources command.

The price system establishes incentives for activities that result in increases in a society's per-capita income. For example, it influences the amount of new capital goods produced, as well as the amount society spends on educating its labor force and improving its technology.

There are circular flows of money and products in a capitalist economy. In product markets, firms provide products to consumers and receive money in return. In resource markets, consumers provide resources to firms and receive money in return.

The price system, despite its many virtues, suffers from serious limitations. There is no reason to believe that the distribution of income generated by the price system is equitable or optimal. Also, there is no way for the price system to handle public goods properly, and because of external economies or diseconomies, the price system may result in too little or too much of certain goods being produced.

Concepts for Review

consumer	market supply curve	public goods
firm	market	external economy
market demand curve	public sector	external diseconomy
product market	resource market	circular flow
equilibrium quantity	equilibrium price	perfectly competitive market
substitutes	complements	actual price
excess supply	excess demand	

Completion Questions

1. Since wheat can be substituted to some extent for corn as livestock feed, the quantity of wheat demanded depends on the price of corn as well as on the

   price of wheat. If the price of corn is high, (more, less) _____

   wheat is demanded since it is profitable to substitute _____

   for _____. If the price of corn is low, (more, less)

   _____ wheat is demanded since it is profitable to substitute

   _____ for _____.

2. Belgium is a small country; the United States is a huge country. Clearly, at a given price of wheat, the quantity demanded by U.S. consumers

   (exceeds, is less than) _____ the quantity demanded by Belgian consumers. Even if consumer tastes, income, and other factors are held constant, this would still be true simply because the United States has

   so many more _____ in the relevant market.

3. As technology progresses, it becomes possible to produce commodities more

   _____, so that firms often are willing to supply a given

   amount of a product at a (lower, higher) _____ price than formerly. Thus, technological change often causes the supply curve to shift to

   the (left, right) _____.

4. The supply curve for a commodity is affected by the prices of the

   _____ (labor, capital, and land) used to produce it. Decreases in the price of these inputs make it possible to produce

   commodities more _____. Firms may then be willing to

   supply a given amount of a product at a _____ price,

   causing the supply curve to shift to the (left, right) _____. On the other hand, increases in the price of inputs may cause it to shift to the (left, right) _____.

5. An equilibrium is a situation where there is no tendency for _____. In other words, it is a situation that can _____. Therefore, an equilibrium price is a price that can be _____.

6. When the actual price exceeds the equilibrium price, there will be (downward, upward) _____ pressure on the price. Similarly, when the actual price is less than the equilibrium price, there will be (downward, upward) _____ pressure on the price. There is always a tendency for the actual price to move (toward, away from) _____ the equilibrium price, but it should not be assumed that this movement is always _____. Sometimes it takes a _____ time for the actual price to get close to the equilibrium price. Sometimes the actual price _____ gets to the equilibrium price because, by the time it gets close, the equilibrium price changes.

7. In general, a shift to the right in the demand curve results in a(n) (decrease, increase) _____ in the equilibrium price, and a shift to the left in the demand curve results in a(n) (decrease, increase) _____ in the equilibrium price. This conclusion depends on the assumption that the supply curve slopes upward to the (left, right) _____, but this assumption is generally true.

8. In general, a shift to the right in the supply curve results in a(n) (decrease, increase) _____ in the equilibrium price, and a shift to the left in the supply curve results in a(n) (decrease, increase) _____ in the equilibrium price. Of course, this conclusion depends on the assumption that the demand curve slopes downward to the (left, right) _____, but this assumption is generally true.

9. The demand curve for a product shows how much of that product consumers want at various _____. If consumers do not want much of a product at a certain price, its demand curve indicates that fact by being positioned close to the _____ axis at that price. In other words, the demand curve shows that, at this price for the product, the amount consumers buy is _____.

True-False

_____ 1. When the price of a good is below equilibrium, there is excess demand equal to the horizontal distance between the supply and demand curves.

_____ 2. A decrease in price causes consumers to shift the demand curve to the right.

_____ 3. No equilibrium price or equilibrium quantity exists if a good's demand curve is a horizontal line and its supply curve is a vertical line.

_____ 4. As long as the actual price exceeds the equilibrium price, there ordinarily is downward pressure on the price.

_____ 5. A shift to the left in the demand curve results in an increase in the equilibrium price.

_____ 6. The flow of money income from firms to consumers is exactly equal to the flow of expenditure from consumers to firms so long as consumers spend all their income.

_____ 7. The price system results in each person receiving an income that depends on the quantity of resources he or she owns and the prices they command.

_____ 8. The market supply curve depends on technology and the income of consumers.

_____ 9. One prerequisite for a perfectly competitive market is that the product sold by various producers be homogeneous.

_____ 10. A product's demand curve is an important determinant of how much firms produce of the product, since it indicates the amount of the product demanded at each price.

_____ 11. For the individual product, the question of who gets what is solved by the equality of the quantity demanded and quantity supplied.

_____ 12. The amount society invests in educating, training, and upgrading its labor resources is determined entirely outside the price system.

_____ 13. Since a shift in demand for apples leads to a change in their supply, it is impossible to say anything about what happens to either the equilibrium price or the quantity sold.

_____ 14. Markets for individual commodities must always be in equilibrium since the amount actually sold is always equal to the amount actually bought.

_____ 15. A decrease in supply raises the equilibrium price and lowers the equilibrium sales.

Multiple Choice

1. A decrease in the price of a good together with an increase in the quantity sold would result from

   a. an increase in supply.
   b. a decrease in supply.
   c. an increase in demand.

   d. a decrease in demand.
   e. both a decrease in demand and a decrease in supply.

2. If the supply of fishing licenses increases,

   a. the quantity of fishing poles demanded probably decreases.
   b. the supply of fishing poles probably decreases.
   c. the price of fishing licenses probably increases.
   d. the demand for fishing poles probably increases.
   e. none of the above.

3. Between 1974 and 1979, per-capita coffee consumption fell in the United States while the price per pound of coffee more than doubled. One possible explanation is

   a. that the supply of coffee decreased during this period.
   b. that the demand for coffee increased during this period.
   c. that both the demand and supply of coffee increased.
   d. that coffee's supply curve is a vertical line.
   e. none of the above.

4. If the government were to announce that it would no longer allow private parties to buy uranium oxide (so the government would be the sole buyer) and it would buy all uranium oxide at $20 per pound, which of the following diagrams would represent the demand curve for uranium oxide in the United States?

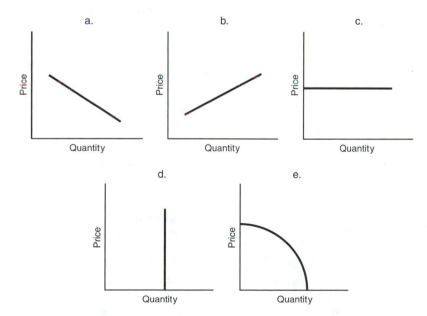

5. If people addicted to drug X must buy some given quantity of it (but not more than that quantity) and will pay whatever price is necessary (and if nonaddicts do not buy drug X), which of the diagrams in the previous question represents the demand curve for drug X?

6. Which of the following does *not* affect the demand curve for fishing poles?

    a. Pollution of local streams and rivers
    b. An increase in the price of fishing licenses
    c. An increase in the population
    d. An increase in the price of fish
    e. An increase in the price of a fishing pole

7. If the quantity supplied of gasoline exceeds the quantity demanded when gasoline is $1.10 a gallon, and the quantity demanded exceeds the quantity supplied at $1.00 a gallon, the equilibrium price of gasoline is

    a. $1.00.
    b. $1.10.
    c. below $1.00.
    d. above $1.10.
    e. between $1.00 and $1.10.

8. The equilibrium price of a commodity is given by

    a. the actual price minus the input costs.
    b. the intersection of market demand and supply curves.
    c. the first point at which market demand exceeds market supply.
    d. the actual price.
    e. none of the above.

9. The position of the supply curve is *not* directly affected by

    a. the state of technology.
    b. the prices of resources used.
    c. the number of consumers.
    d. all of the above.
    e. none of the above.

10. The price system

    a. sets up incentives for firms to produce what consumers want.
    b. determines each person's income through the price of his or her resources.
    c. may result in an unequal distribution of society's output.
    d. all of the above.
    e. none of the above.

11. The amount of new capital goods produced, the amount that society invests in education and training, and the rate of technological change are all influenced in the United States by

    a. the price system.
    b. government action.
    c. neither a nor b.
    d. both a and b.

12. A perfectly competitive market does *not* require

    a. a homogeneous product.
    b. so many buyers and sellers that none can influence price.
    c. a constant price.
    d. both a and b.
    e. any of the above.

Discussion and Extension Questions

1. "What do you give a woman who already has an abundance of gold? Diamonds of course," according to David Savidan of TAG Heuer. The watchmaker is using Olympic track star Marion Jones to highlight a new luxury sports watch. Use a supply and demand model to analyze.

2. "The supply curve influences the demand curve, since the more produced of a commodity, the more people want of it (or the more producers convince them they want)." Discuss and evaluate.

3. Late in 2003, a cow infected with bovine spongiform encephalopathy (BSE or "mad cow") was discovered in the United States. How do you think this affected the market for beef? The market for chicken?

4. When we placed controls on gasoline prices in 1973–74, there still remained the problem of rationing a scarce good. How did we do it? Would you regard the mechanism we used as better or worse than alternative methods of rationing? Why?

5. The discussion about an equilibrium point in the text focused on the equilibrium price and situations where the actual price was either above or below that equilibrium price. To see if you understand the argument, explain the adjustment mechanism in terms of equilibrium quantity. Begin with a quantity that is less than the equilibrium quantity; what pressures exist to move toward an equilibrium? When the price is too low for equilibrium we say that, at the prevailing price, the quantity people want to buy exceeds the amount suppliers want to sell. What is the counterpart if the quantity is too low for equilibrium?

6. Which factors influence the position of the market demand curve for corn? Which factors influence the position of the market supply curve for corn? What happens to the equilibrium price of corn if the market demand curve shifts to the right? What happens if it shifts to the left?

7. What happens to the equilibrium price of corn if the market supply curve shifts to the right? What happens if it shifts to the left?

8. Why and how did the government change the Food Stamp Program? How might our changing attitudes toward welfare and food stamps be related to a strong economy?

9. The United States largely funds basic education through taxes. This is partly because education is viewed as a case of external economy. Would you agree? Explain.

Problems

1. Suppose that the market demand curve for corn is as follows:

Price of corn (dollars per bushel)	Quantity of corn demanded (millions of bushels per year)
0.50	100
1	80
2	60
3	40
4	30
5	20

a. How much corn would be demanded if the price were $0.50? Plot the demand curve in the following graph:

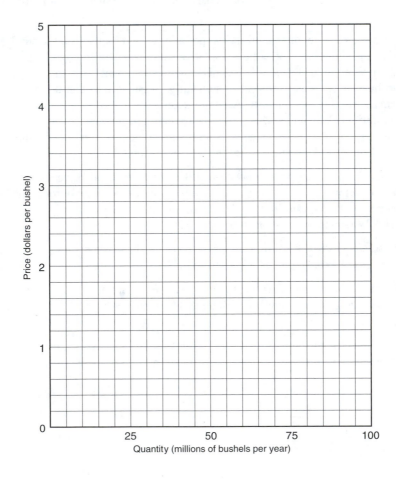

b. Suppose that the market supply curve for corn is as follows:

Price of corn (dollars per bushel)	Quantity of corn supplied (millions of bushels per year)
0.50	10
1	30
2	60
3	70
4	80
5	90

How much corn would be supplied if the price were $0.50? $2? Plot the supply curve.

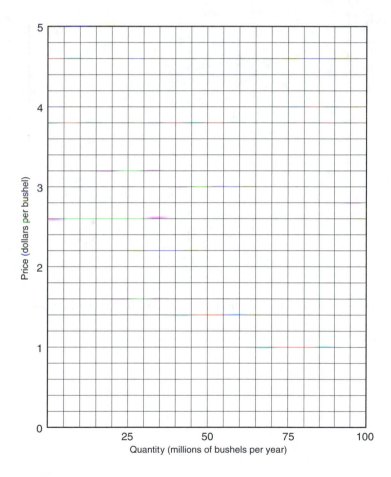

c. Using the preceding data, what is the equilibrium price for corn? Plot the demand and supply curves, and relate these curves to the equilibrium price.

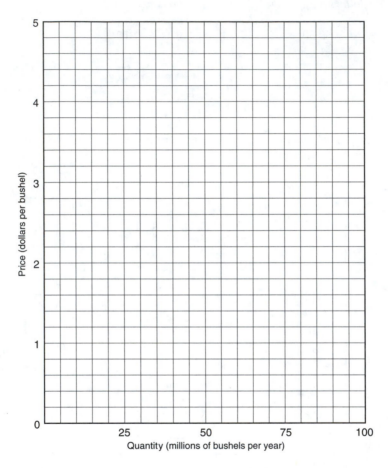

2. Suppose that the quantity of wheat supplied at various prices is as follows:

Quantity of wheat supplied (millions of bushels)	Price of wheat (dollars per bushel)
1,000	1
1,500	2
2,000	3
2,500	4

a. Plot the supply curve for wheat in the following graph. How much will be produced if the price is $3.50 per bushel (and the supply curve is linear)?

b. Suppose that, because of a technological change—a new, drought-resistant type of grain—farmers are willing to supply 20 percent more wheat at each price. Plot the new supply curve.

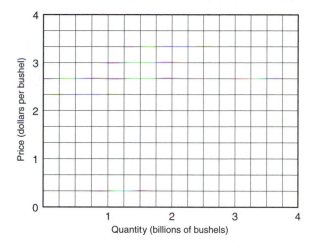

c. Suppose that the demand curve for wheat is as follows:

Quantity of wheat demanded (millions of bushels)	Price of wheat (dollars per bushel)
3,000	1
2,500	2
2,000	3
1,500	4

Plot this demand curve in the graphs in parts a and b.

d. Under these new circumstances, is the equilibrium price higher or lower than under the old circumstances, assuming that the demand curve remains constant?

e. Suppose the demand curve in the new circumstances is unknown, but the supply curve is as indicated in part b. If the equilibrium price under the new circumstances is $3 per bushel, at what point along the horizontal axis does the demand curve intersect the supply curve?

3. Suppose that the demand curve for tickets to the Metropolitan Opera for a performance of *Carmen* is as follows:

Price of a ticket (dollars)	Quantity demanded
56	3,000
60	2,800
64	2,600
68	2,400
72	2,200
76	2,000
80	1,800

a. If the Metropolitan Opera House has 2,400 seats, what is the equilibrium price of a ticket for this performance?

b. What is the shape of the supply curve for tickets?

c. If the Metropolitan Opera House sets the price of a ticket at $72, will the house be full?

d. Is there a shortage or a surplus of tickets? How big will it be?

e. In a free market, would the price of a ticket rise or fall?

4. The demand curve for fishing poles is $P = 50 - 10Q$, where P is the price of a fishing pole (in dollars) and Q is the quantity demanded per year (in millions).

a. If the government orders the producers of fishing poles to produce 1 million fishing poles per year, what is the equilibrium price of a fishing pole?

b. If the current price of a fishing pole is $60, would you expect the price to rise or fall once the government order occurs?

c. Suppose that, after it issues this order, the government sets a ceiling of $30 on the price of a fishing pole. Will a surplus or shortage result? How big will it be?

*5. If both supply and demand in a competitive market increase, one can predict the direction of change of output but not of price. If supply increases but demand decreases, one cannot, without further knowledge, be certain about the direction of either the price or the quantity change. Do you agree with this statement? Explain.

*The starred item pertains to material covered in Exploring Further.

*6. Use a diagram to show that a rise in the price of margarine could be a response to a rise in the price of butter.

*7. According to *Business Week,* all major chocolate makers shared a basic problem some time ago. Production costs were going up, sales were going down, and the price of a standard candy bar rose from 30¢ to 40¢. Depict this situation graphically and explain why a successful attempt to make candy appealing to more customers would cause only a further rise in price.

8. How do you reconcile the hypothesis that "the quantity demanded varies inversely with price" (law of demand), with the statement that "a rise in demand leads to a rise in price, other things equal"?

*9. It is impossible for the price of a commodity to fall at the same time the demand for the commodity rises. Comment, using supply and demand curves.

10. Distinguish between a change in supply and a change in the quantity supplied.

*11 "When it is said that there are shortages in some market, we know that that market is out of equilibrium. Take natural gas for instance. In the late 1970s, there were shortages. Some people argued that these were due to the government price controls while others claimed that they were due to cold winters combined with the stockpiling of natural gas because firms and individuals feared a shortage might develop. The first group of people worried that releasing the controls would lead to very high prices, while the second group concluded that the shortage would disappear as soon as it warmed up and people became less worried." Explain each side's argument using diagrammatic analysis.

Answers

Completion Questions

1. more, wheat, corn, less, corn, wheat   2. exceeds, consumers   3. cheaply, lower, right   4. resources, cheaply, lower, right, left   5. change, persist, maintained
6. downward, upward, toward, rapid, long, never   7. increase, decrease, right
8. decrease, increase, right   9. prices, vertical, small

*The starred items pertain to material covered in Exploring Further.

True-False

1. True 2. False 3. False 4. True 5. False 6. True 7. True 8. False
9. True 10. True 11. True 12. False 13. False 14. False 15. True

Multiple Choice

1. a 2. d 3. a 4. c 5. d 6. e 7. e 8. b 9. c 10. d 11. d
12. c

Problems

1. a. 100 million bushels.

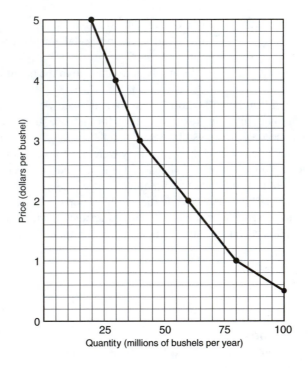

b. 10 million bushels. 60 million bushels.

c. $2 a bushel.

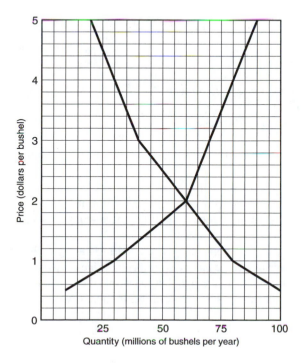

2. a.   2,250 million bushels.

  b.

  c.   The demands are as plotted in parts a and b.
  d.   Lower.
  e.   At 2,400 million bushels of wheat.
3. a. $68
  b.   A vertical line at 2,400 seats.
  c.   No.
  d.   A surplus of 200 tickets.
  e.   Fall.
4. a.   Since $50 - 10(1) = 40$, the equilibrium price of a fishing pole is $40.
  b.   Fall.
  c.   Since $Q = 5 - 0.1P$, the quantity demanded equals $5 - 0.1(30) =$
       2 million fishing poles when the price is at its ceiling of $30. Since the
       quantity supplied equals 1 million, there will be a shortage of 1 million
       fishing poles per year.
5. If the demand and supply curves both shift to the right, the equilibrium
    quantity must increase but the equilibrium price may rise or fall. If the
    supply curve shifts to the right but the demand curve shifts to the left, the
    equilibrium price falls but the equilibrium quantity may rise or fall.

The preceding left-hand panel shows a case where supply falls (from Q_0 to Q_1); the right-hand panel shows a case where it rises (from Q_0 to Q_2).

6. Butter and margarine are substitutes. An increase in the price of butter might shift the demand curve for margarine to the right, as shown next, and result in an increase (from P to P') in the price of margarine.

Quantity of margarine

7. These facts seem to suggest that the supply curve for candy bars shifted to the left, as shown here:

Quantity of candy bars

If candy is made appealing to more customers, this means that the demand curve shifts to the right, which causes a further rise in price.

8. The first hypothesis states that the demand curve slopes downward and to the right. The second hypothesis states that a shift of the demand curve to the right results in an increase in the equilibrium price. There is no contradiction between them.

9. If the supply of the commodity rises at the same time that its demand rises, the price may fall, as shown here:

10. A change in supply is a shift in the supply curve, while a change in the quantity supplied is a movement along the supply curve.

11. The first group felt that the price P_c was set below the equilibrium price by government controls, as shown here:

If the controls are released, the price will rise to P_e.

The second group felt that the demand curve had shifted to the right and the price had not increased, so there was a shortage of $Q_D - Q_S$, as shown here:

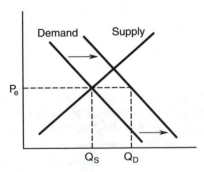

If the demand curve shifts back to its original position when the weather warms up and people become less worried, the shortage will disappear.

CHAPTER 3

National Income and Product

Chapter Profile

A key indicator of the health of any country's economy is the gross domestic product (GDP), which measures the total value of the final goods and services the country produces in a particular period. This is the level of final goods and services produced times the prices at which they sold. Remember the circular flow model: Money flows into the business sector as goods and services are sold; money flows out of the business sector as firms distribute that money. Counting either stream of money flow gives us the value the business sector produced.

Since GDP is affected by the price level, it must be "deflated" or adjusted for changes in the price level, at which point it is called real GDP, or GDP in constant dollars. The government has made a major adjustment in how this is calculated. Prior to 1995, the government evaluated the real GDP of every year using only the prices of the base year (the fixed-weighted method). This causes problems when prices change relative to each other, which over time they do. Since 1995, the government calculates the real GDP of any two years twice, using the prices of each year and then averages the two results (the chain-weighted method).

GDP is not an ideal measure of total economic output let alone a satisfactory measure of economic well-being, even given the problems with our price adjustment. In addition to missing some output, GDP does not reflect a country's population (although it is possible to include this by dividing the population into GDP to find GDP per person, or per capita). GDP does not include quality of life issues such as leisure or a clean environment and does not accurately reflect changes in the quality of goods produced. Finally, GDP does not reflect the distribution of goods or their social value. As long as the degree of error is relatively consistent from year to year, the overall pattern of GDP growth remains valid, but if the error changes, our GDP growth estimates are inaccurate.

One approach to GDP is the expenditures approach, which regards GDP as the sum of all expenditures involved in taking the total output of final goods and services off the market. To determine GDP in this way, one must add up all the spending on final goods and services. Economists distinguish among four broad categories of spending: personal consumption expenditures, gross private domestic investment, government purchases, and net exports. GDP equals the sum of these four items.

Another approach to GDP is the income approach, which regards GDP as the sum of incomes derived from the production of this year's output (plus depreciation and indirect business taxes). To determine GDP in this way, one must add up all the income stemming from the production of this year's total output (plus depreciation and indirect business taxes). Economists identify five broad categories of income: compensation of employees, rents, interest, proprietors' income, and corporate profits. The GDP equals the sum of these five items (plus depreciation and indirect business taxes).

Concepts for Review

gross domestic product
National Income and
   Product Accounts
final goods and services
intermediate good
transfer payments
base year
current dollars
constant dollars
real GDP
price index
fixed-weighted method

deflating
value added
expenditure approach
   to GDP
personal consumption
   expenditure
gross private domestic
   investment
government purchases
net exports
chain-weighted method

income approach to
   GDP
compensation of
   employees
rents
interest
proprietors' income
corporate profits
depreciation
indirect business
   taxes

Completion Questions

1. The four parts of the total amount spent on final goods and services are

    _____, _____, _____,

    and _____.

2. The value in money terms of the total output of final goods and services in the

    economy during a certain period of time is called the _____.

3. Bread purchased by a consumer is a(n) (final, intermediate) _____
    good, but flour to be used in manufacturing bread is a(n) (final,

    intermediate) _____ good. Clearly, we would be double
    counting if we counted both the bread and the flour used to make the bread

    as _____. To avoid this, we include only the value of

    (final, intermediate) _____ goods and services in gross
    domestic product.

4. Government transfer payments are payments made by the government to

    individuals who (do, do not) _____ contribute to production in

    exchange for them. Since these payments are not for _____, it

    would be (correct, incorrect) _____
    to include them in GDP.

5. Private transfer payments are gifts or other transfers of wealth from one

   _____ or _____ to another. These are not

   payments for _____, so they are not included in GDP.

6. Expressed in (current, constant) _____ dollars, gross
   domestic product is affected by changes in the price level. Expressed in

   (current, constant) _____ dollars, gross domestic product is
   not affected by the price level because the prices of all goods are

   maintained at their _____ level. In recent years, inflation has
   caused gross domestic product expressed in (current, constant)

   _____ dollars to increase more rapidly than gross domestic

   product in (current, constant) _____ dollars.

7. An important function of a price index is to convert values expressed in (current,

   constant) _____ dollars into values expressed in (current,

   constant) _____ dollars. This conversion, known

   as _____, can be achieved simply by dividing values

   expressed in (current, constant) _____ dollars by the price
   index.

8. The contribution of a firm or industry to the final output is measured by the

   concept of _____. Wheat and the _____
   of flour mills and bakers are part of the value added in the process of making
   bread. The GDP figures indicate that the U.S. economy is turning more

   toward producing _____, rather than _____.

9. Gross domestic product equals the income paid out (or owed) as

   _____, _____, _____,

   _____, and _____, plus two other items,

   indirect business taxes and depreciation. Indirect business taxes are

   _____ taxes, _____ taxes, and other
   taxes that firms consider as part of their costs. In other words, gross domestic

   product exactly equals the total _____ on output.

10. If consumers regard a pound of butter as 10 times as valuable as a pencil and if an economy's 2003 and 2004 outputs were as shown next, the economy's total output (as measured by its value to consumers) was

(greater, less) _____ in 2004 than in 2003. Specifically, it

(increased, decreased) _____ by _____

percent. In national income accounting, a good's _____ is used to measure the value consumers attach to it.

	Output	
	2003	2004
Pencils (millions)	200	220
Butter (millions of pounds)	30	29

11. Suppose that $100 worth of apples is used (together with $100 worth of labor by cider producers) to make $200 worth of apple cider and $200 worth of apple cider (together with $100 worth of labor by drink producers) is used to make $300 worth of a potent apple drink that is marketed at New England colleges on football weekends. If $600 worth of the apple drink is sold, the value added by

the apple producers equals _____, the value added by the

cider producers equals _____, and the value added by the

apple drink producers equals _____. The total value added by these three groups of firms is (greater than, equal to, less than)

_____ the value of the apple drink sold to consumers.

12. Over a five-year period, GDP in current dollars rose from $4 trillion to $6 trillion. If, during the same period, the price index rose from 1.0 to 1.2, then GDP in

constant dollars is _____ percent greater than before. If the price index does not take proper account of quality improvements in goods during this period, the rise in the price level is probably (greater, less)

_____ than 20 percent and the rise in real GDP is probably

(greater, less) _____ than originally estimated.

13. An economy consists of only two firms, Macy's and Bloomingdale's. During 2004, Macy's reduces its inventories by $2 million, while Bloomingdale's increases its inventories by $3 million. At the beginning of 2000, each firm had inventories of $10 million. If there were no other gross private domestic investment in 2004, domestic gross private investment during that year

equaled _____.

True-False

_____ 1. Corporate profits, as defined in the national income accounts, do not include retained earnings.

_____ 2. It is possible that the value to society from government goods and services is greater than the value put into GDP for the government goods and services.

_____ 3. During 2001, the Acme Washing Machine Company produces $10 million worth of washing machines but sells only $9 million of them. The remaining $1 million worth of washing machines is included in GDP in 2002 when they are sold.

_____ 4. Gross domestic product does not include intermediate goods.

_____ 5. When expressed in current dollars, the gross domestic product is not affected by changes in the price level.

_____ 6. Expenditures by General Motors on paper, typewriters, and fuel oil are all included in consumption expenditure.

_____ 7. The smallest part of the total amount spent on final goods and services in the United States is net exports of goods and services.

_____ 8. Gross domestic product has one drawback as a measure that must be faced; it does not take into account the fact that plant and equipment wear out with use.

_____ 9. If a new version of a drug is put on the market at the same price as the old version and the output and cost of the new drug are the same as the old drug, GDP will not increase, even though the new drug is twice as effective as the old one.

_____ 10. Consumption includes your expenditures on meals and clothing, and your parents' expenditures on the family car or on an electric washer and dryer.

_____ 11. The capital consumption allowance in the national income accounts includes the wear and tear on an automobile owned by a college professor who drives it to and from work.

_____ 12. In recent years, the net effect of the foreign sector, as represented by net exports, has been to decrease U.S. GDP.

_____ 13. If the Malone family buys a 15-year-old house from Mr. D. Teece, a (hypothetical) real estate speculator, this purchase would be included in gross private domestic investment.

_____ 14. Net exports include goods but not services.

_____ 15. If a retired naval officer builds himself a bookshelf, this is included in the gross domestic product.

_____ 16. If the president of General Motors drives her car to her office, this is included in the gross domestic product.

Multiple Choice

1. Which of the following would *not* be included in gross private domestic investment?

   a. An increase in McDonald's inventory of hamburger rolls
   b. Expenditures on a new Broadway theater
   c. The purchase of a new taxi by Yellow Cab Company
   d. The purchase of a new washing machine by the Jones family
   e. The purchase of a new washing machine by the Acme Laundry

2. Which of the following would *not* be included in government purchases of goods and services?

   a. The Defense Department's expenditure of $1 billion on a new missile
   b. The National Science Foundation's expenditure of $1 billion for basic research
   c. The Department of Health, Education, and Welfare's expenditure of $1 billion on welfare
   d. Iowa's expenditure of $1 billion on the construction of schools
   e. All of the above

3. Which of the following is *not* an indirect business tax?

   a. Pennsylvania's general sales tax
   b. New York's cigarette tax
   c. U.S. corporate income tax
   d. Pennsylvania corporation income tax
   e. Both c and d

4. Which of the following transactions would be included in the gross domestic product?

   a. Bill White buys a secondhand bicycle for $70.
   b. Bill Green gives his bicycle to his cousin.
   c. John Black buys a new bicycle for $150.
   d. Jerry Brown buys two shares of stock in a bicycle firm.
   e. Mort Gray steals John Black's new bicycle.

5. In the national income accounts, indirect business taxes include

   a. government transfer payments.
   b. private transfer payments.
   c. all personal taxes.
   d. excise taxes.
   e. personal income taxes.

6. If a set of goods and services costs $5,000 in constant dollars (1960 prices) and $7,000 in current dollars, by about how much has their price changed between 1960 and now?

   a. 20 percent
   b. 40 percent
   c. 50 percent

   d. 70 percent
   e. 80 percent

7. GDP takes no account of

   a. exports.
   b. services produced.
   c. the social costs of environmental pollution.

   d. all of the above.
   e. a and b.

8. It is customary for gross domestic product to be expressed in terms of

   a. current dollars.
   b. constant dollars.
   c. price index.

   d. all of the above.
   e. a or b.

9. Marantz produces a hi-fi receiver in 2004 which is sold to a retailer in December 2004. It is sold to a consumer in 2005. This receiver is included in

   a. consumption expenditure in 2005.
   b. investment in 2005.
   c. disinvestment (a decline in inventory) in 2005.
   d. all of the above.
   e. none of the above.

10. Mrs. Harris spends the morning cleaning her house and cooking lunch. This is not included in the GDP because it is

   a. already included in the value of her husband's output.
   b. a nonmarket transaction.
   c. valued at cost.
   d. unproductive of any economic output.
   e. none of the above.

Discussion and Extension Questions

1. "Value added is a poor measure of an industry's contribution to GDP because it does not take any account of the environmental pollution caused by the industry. Also, it is based entirely on market prices." Discuss and evaluate.

2. What difficulties would you encounter in trying to compare levels of economic welfare across countries (say, for example, the United States versus Great Britain, India, Sweden, Mexico, and China) using gross domestic product as your yardstick?

3. "Gross domestic product is a sexist measure because it discriminates against women, many of whom work in the home." Comment and evaluate.

4. Does the gross domestic product include the value of all goods and services produced? If not, which ones does it include?

5. How are government services valued in computing GDP? Why is the sale of secondhand goods excluded from GDP?

6. "If you don't subtract depreciation in the calculation of total national output, you are making a mistake similar to double counting intermediate goods." In what ways are the two mistakes similar? In what ways are they different?

7. If each taxpayer hired his or her neighbor to fill out his or her tax return, would this affect the gross domestic output? If so, how? Would you favor including in GDP the value of time spent by citizens filling out tax returns? Why or why not?

8. "Aid to the poor is not included in government purchases of goods and services; consequently, it is not included in GDP. Yet such aid is of enormous benefit to the population and the improvement in the income distribution should be regarded as an output of the economic system." Comment in detail.

9. In the 1970s and 1980s more women enter the labor force; this was accompanied by a rise in sales of fast foods, convenience foods, cleaning services, and daycare. What might this mean for our estimates of GDP growth during this time?

Problems

1. a. Gopherland is a country where the price level has been rising at a rate of 5 percent per year. Gross domestic product in current dollars was 10 percent higher in 2004 than in 2003 and 3 percent higher in 2003 than in 2002. In terms of constant dollars, how much greater was Gopherland's GDP in 2004 than in 2002?

   b. Gopherland's largest firm, the Gopherland Iron Company, sold $3 million worth of iron in 2004. It purchased $1.2 million worth of goods and services from other firms, paid $0.5 million in interest, and paid $0.3 million in excise and property taxes. Since its depreciation allowance was $0.3 million, its profit was $0.7 million. How much was its value added in 2004?

   c. In 2002, Gopherland's exports equaled its imports, and its gross private domestic investment equaled its government expenditures. Its personal consumption expenditure was double its government expenditure and equaled $400 million. What was its GDP in 2002?

2. Suppose we could add up all of the money transactions in the United States during this year. Would this total amount equal, exceed, or be less than this year's GDP? Why?

3. The nation of Erewhon reports that its capital consumption allowance in 2001 is negative. What would this mean? Is it possible or not?

Answers

Completion Questions

1. consumption expenditure, investment, government purchases of goods and services, net exports   2. gross domestic product   3. final, intermediate, output, final   4. do not, production, incorrect   5. person, private organization, production   6. current, constant, base-year, current, constant   7. current, constant, deflating, current   8. value added, services, services, goods   9. wages, rent, interest, proprietor's income, corporate profit, sales, excise, claims   10. greater, increased, 2, price   11. $200, $200, $200, equal to   12. 25, less, greater   13. $1 million

True-False

1. False   2. True   3. False   4. True   5. False   6. False   7. True   8. True   9. True   10. True   11. False   12. True   13. False   14. False   15. False   16. False

Multiple-Choice

1. d   2. c   3. e   4. c   5. d   6. b   7. c   8. e   9. d   10. b

Problems

1. a. Gross domestic product in current dollars in 2004 equals $1.10 \times 1.03 \times$ gross domestic product in current dollars in 2002. The price level in 2004 is 10 percent higher than in 2002. Hence, in terms of 2002 dollars, GDP in 2004 is $(1.10/1.10) \times 1.03 \times$ GDP in 2002. In other words, it is 3 percent higher than in 2002.
   b. $1.8 million.
   c. $800 million.
2. It would exceed GDP, because transactions involving intermediate goods and secondhand goods, as well as purely financial transactions, would be included in this total but excluded from GDP.
3. This would mean that a negative amount of plant and equipment wore out, which clearly is unrealistic.

CHAPTER 4

Business Fluctuations and Unemployment

Chapter Profile

National output tends to rise and approach its potential (that is, its full-employment) level for a while, then falter and fall below this level, then rise to approach it once more, and so on. These ups and downs are called *business fluctuations,* or *business cycles.* Each cycle can be divided into four phases: trough, expansion, peak, recession. These cycles are very irregular and highly variable in length and amplitude. Unemployment tends to be higher at the trough than at the peak; inflation tends to be higher at the peak than at the trough.

Until the 1930s, most economists were convinced that the price system, left to its own devices, would ensure the maintenance of full employment. They thought it unlikely that total spending would be too small to purchase the full-employment level of output and argued that prices would be cut to keep goods selling and wages would be cut to keep workers employed. A notable exception was Karl Marx, who felt that the capitalistic system would suffer from worse and worse unemployment, leading to the system's eventual collapse.

John Maynard Keynes, in the 1930s, developed a theory to explain how the capitalist economic system remained mired in the Great Depression, with its tragically high levels of unemployment. Contrary to the classical economists, he concluded that there was no automatic mechanism in a capitalistic system to generate and maintain full employment—or, at least, generate it quickly enough to be relied on in practice.

The aggregate demand curve shows the level of real national output that demanded at each price level. One reason why it slopes downward and to the right is that increases in the price level push up interest rates and increases in interest rates reduce real national output.

The short-run aggregate supply curve shows the level of real national output supplied at each price level if the prices of all inputs are fixed. Since increases in the price level tend to raise the profitability of firms' increasing output, the short-run aggregate supply curve tends to slope upward to the right.

The equilibrium level of real national output and the equilibrium price level are given by the intersection of the aggregate demand and supply curves. Changes in equilibrium occur when aggregate demand or aggregate supply shifts; this can create unemployment or inflation.

Unemployment is of various types: frictional, structural, and cyclical. The overall unemployment rate conceals considerable differences among types of people. The Bureau of Labor Statistics publishes monthly data concerning unemployment rates for various segments of the population. High levels of unemployment impose great costs on society.

In the long run, when input prices can adjust fully to eliminate the unemployment or shortage of inputs (like labor), the aggregate supply curve is vertical. Real national output is at its potential level.

Concepts for Review

business cycle	frictional unemployment
trough	structural unemployment
expansion	cyclical unemployment
peak	potential GDP
recession	full employment
depression	short-run aggregate supply curve
prosperity	Say's law
aggregate demand curve	*long-run aggregate supply curve
horizontal range	vertical range
positively sloped range	

Completion Questions

1. When there is substantial unemployment, the short-run aggregate supply curve may be (vertical, downward sloping, close to horizontal)

   _____. There (is, is not) _____ so much upward pressure on prices as output increases because there are plenty of unemployed workers and other resources.

2. An increase in the price level (increases, decreases) _____

   interest rates; this (reduces, increases) _____ total output.

   Thus, the aggregate demand curve slopes _____.

3. When an economy's resources are fully employed, its short-run aggregate supply curve tends to be (horizontal, upward sloping, vertical)

   _____. This is because further increases in the price level

   result in (considerable, no) _____ extra output.

4. A rightward shift of the aggregate demand curve increases total output but not the price level if the economy is situated at the (horizontal,

   positively sloped, vertical) _____ range of the short-run aggregate supply curve. It increases the price level but not total output if the economy is situated at the (horizontal, positively sloped, vertical)

   _____ range of the short-run aggregate supply curve. It increases both the price level and total output if the economy is situated at

   the (horizontal, positively sloped, vertical) _____ range of the short-run aggregate supply curve.

*The starred items pertain to material covered in Exploring Further.

5. When the unemployment rate has been very high and the government has wanted to reduce unemployment, it frequently has used its fiscal and monetary policies to shift the aggregate demand curve to the (right, left)

    _____. If inflation is a serious problem and the government wants to keep a tight lid on the price level, it often uses its fiscal and monetary policies to shift the aggregate demand curve to the (right, left)

    _____.

6. If the short-run aggregate supply curve shifts to the right, the result is likely to be

    (increased, decreased) _____ total output and a (higher,

    lower) _____ price level. If the short-run aggregate supply

    curve shifts to the left, the result is likely to be (increased,

    decreased) _____ total output and a (higher, lower)

    _____ price level.

7. A decrease in the price level (reduces, increases) _____
    the real value of the currency and government bonds held by the public. This

    results in a(n) (increase, decrease) _____ in consumption
    expenditures. A decrease in the price level (increases, decreases)

    _____ the average money cost of a transaction,

    (increasing, decreasing) _____ the demand for money,

    which will (increase, decrease) _____ the interest rate.

    Therefore, the aggregate demand curve slopes _____ and to

    the _____.

8. The _____ is the point where national output is lowest relative

    to its potential level. The _____ is the point where
    national output is highest relative to its potential level.

9. During the Great Depression, the aggregate demand curve shifted to the (left,

    right) _____. During World War II, the aggregate demand

    curve shifted to the (left, right) _____.

10. During the 1970s, the short-run aggregate supply curve shifted to the (left, right)

    _____ because of the actions of Arab and other oil-producing

    countries which (increased, decreased) _____
    the price of oil substantially.

11. If a peak occurs in March 2006, we can be sure that an expansion (will, will not)

    _____ begin in March 2006. If a recession ends in January

2007, we can be sure that a trough (will, will not) _____
occur in January 2007. If a peak occurs in April 2007, we (can, cannot)

_____ be sure that April 2007 is a time of prosperity.

12. Between 1929 and 1933, real GDP fell by almost _____.
Two factors that contributed to this debacle were the contraction of

_____ and the reduction in the _____

supply. Unemployment rates were excessive until _____.

True-False

_____ 1. The aggregate demand curve assumes that the money supply is fixed.

_____ 2. In a typical year, the production of soft drinks tends to be over 20 percent higher in July or August than in January or February. This is an example of the business cycle.

_____ 3. Regardless of the shape of the short-run aggregate supply curve, a shift of the aggregate demand curve upward and to the right results in inflation.

_____ 4. If the short-run aggregate supply curve is very steep, expansionary policies result in considerable inflation but a relatively small increase in real output.

_____ 5. Inflation generally is eliminated by a rightward shift of the aggregate demand curve.

_____ 6. The aggregate demand curve slopes downward and to the right for the same reasons that a demand curve for an individual commodity slopes downward and to the right.

_____ 7. If the money supply is fixed, increases in the price level reduce interest rates.

_____ 8. Frictional unemployment occurs when the unemployed lack the skills to fill new jobs.

_____ 9. In the horizontal range of the short-run aggregate supply curve, it is assumed that there is little or no downward pressure on prices as output decreases because of the rigidity of wages and of prices.

_____ 10. The vertical range of the short-run aggregate supply curve is a simplification because it is generally possible to get a bit more output from any economic system.

_____ 11. In the horizontal range of the short-run aggregate supply curve, a rightward shift of the aggregate demand curve has no effect on output.

_____ 12. When the economy is at its potential GDP, cyclical unemployment is zero.

_____ 13. In the 1990s, the U.S. economy experienced the longest expansion in its history.

_____ 14. During any decade, the number of troughs must equal the number of peaks.

Multiple Choice

1. During the typical business cycle, there is more variation in the output of

   a. consumer goods than in the output of capital goods.
   b. agriculture than in nonfarm output.
   c. breakfast cereals than in the output of machine tools.
   d. all of the above.
   e. none of the above.

2. An upward shift of the aggregate demand curve *cannot* result in

   a. an increase in both the price level and real output.
   b. an increase in the price level without an increase in real output.
   c. an increase in real output without an increase in the price level.
   d. an increase in the price level and a decrease in real output.
   e. any of the above.

3. Suppose that the aggregate demand curve is $P = 120 - Q$, where P is the price level and Q is the real output (in billions of dollars). If the short-run aggregate supply curve (which is a horizontal line) shifts upward from $P = 105$ to $P = 110$, the real output will

   a. fall from $10 billion to $5 billion.
   b. increase from $5 billion to $10 billion.
   c. fall from $15 billion to $10 billion.
   d. increase from $10 billion to $15 billion.
   e. none of the above.

4. Suppose that the short-run aggregate supply curve is $P = 20Q$, where P is the price level and Q is the real output (in billions of dollars). If the aggregate demand curve shifts from $P = 105 - Q$ to $P = 115.5 - Q$, the price level will increase from

   a. 100 to 105.
   b. 105 to 115.5.
   c. 100 to 110.
   d. 100 to 115.5.
   e. none of the above.

5. A leftward shift of the aggregate demand curve has the same effect as a rightward shift of the aggregate demand curve if the economy is in

   a. the horizontal range of the short-run aggregate supply curve.
   b. the vertical range of the short-run aggregate supply curve.
   c. the positively sloped range of the short-run aggregate supply curve.
   d. a depression.
   e. none of the above.

6. If the price level rises and output falls, this could be due to

    a. a rightward shift of the aggregate demand curve.
    b. a leftward shift of the aggregate demand curve.
    c. a rightward shift of the short-run aggregate supply curve.
    d. a leftward shift of the short-run aggregate supply curve.
    e. none of the above.

7. If the price level rises and output rises, this could be due to

    a. a rightward shift of the aggregate demand curve.
    b. a leftward shift of the aggregate demand curve.
    c. a rightward shift of the short-run aggregate supply curve.
    d. a leftward shift of the short-run aggregate supply curve.
    e. none of the above.

Discussion and Extension Questions

1. In the late 1990s, many economists felt the U.S. economy was in danger of overheating—entering an inflationary period. What measures might one look at to see if this were true? What could be happening with aggregate supply and demand to cause this?

2. What measures would you look at to see whether a recession was beginning? Explain in detail why you think each would be a good indicator. Also comment on the limitations of each one.

3. During the business cycle, would you expect that ice cream purchases would vary as much as expenditures on machine tools? Would you expect that shoe sales would vary as much as the sales of bulldozers? Would you expect that cosmetics purchases would vary as much as expenditures on computers?

4. In country X, output and employment rise but the price level remains unchanged. Using aggregate demand and supply curves, explain how this combination of events could occur. Can you be sure that it is due solely to a shift in one of these curves? If so, can you tell whether the aggregate demand or the aggregate supply curve shifted?

5. Booms in the nineteenth century were associated with events like railroad building and the California gold rush. Why do you think these events were associated with boom periods? Suppose that a vast new space program was begun. Do you think that it would promote a boom? Why or why not?

6. President George W. Bush encouraged the passage of a tax cut on dividends (the share of corporate profit distributed to stockholders). A number of politicians supporting the bill claimed that this would increase investment and GDP growth.

If true, explain how the policy would work using the aggregate supply and demand model. Do you believe that this policy will be effective at increasing investment? At increasing GDP? Defend your position.

Problems

1. The aggregate demand curve for economy A follows:

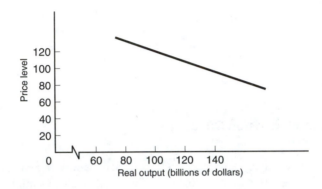

   a. If the short-run aggregate supply curve is a vertical line at real output = $140 billion, what is the price level?
   b. If the short-run aggregate supply curve is a horizontal line at price level = 120, what is the real output?
   c. If the equation for the short-run aggregate supply curve is $P = -40 + Q$, where P is the price level and Q is the real output (in billions of dollars), what are the price level and real output?

2. The aggregate demand curve and the short-run aggregate supply curve for economy B follow. As you can see, the aggregate demand curve shifts downward and to the left.

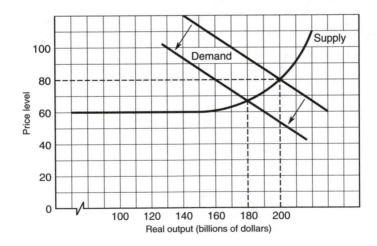

a. What is the effect of the shift of the aggregate demand curve on the price level? Specifically, what is the price level before and after the shift?
b. What is the effect of the shift of the aggregate demand curve on the real output? Specifically, what is the real output before and after the shift?
c. If economy B is devastated by an earthquake that reduces its productive capacity by 50 percent, how will the aggregate supply curve be affected?

3. Aggregate supply is $P = -20 + 2Q$, while aggregate demand is $P = 1000 - 8Q$, where Q is the real output in billions of dollars and P is the price level.

a. Find the equilibrium level of output and prices.
b. If aggregate supply shifts from $-40 + 2Q$, what is the new equilibrium level of output and prices?
c. Was this a shift of aggregate supply to the left or right?

4. In nation D, the aggregate demand curve is $P = 5,000 - 5Q$, where P is the price level and Q is the total real output in billions of dollars. The short-run aggregate supply curve (in the relevant range) is $P = 0.5Q$.

a. What is the equilibrium value of the total real output?
b. What is the equilibrium value of the price level?

Answers

Completion Questions
1. close to horizontal, is not   2. increases, reduces, downward and to the right
3. vertical, no   4. horizontal, vertical, positively sloped   5. right, left
6. increased, lower, decreased, higher   7. increases, increase, decreases, decreasing, decrease, downward, right   8. trough, peak   9. left, right
10. left, increased   11. will not, will, cannot   12. one-third, investment, money, World War II

True-False
1. True   2. False   3. False   4. True   5. False   6. False   7. False
8. False   9. True   10. True   11. False   12. True   13. True   14. False

Multiple Choice
1. e   2. d   3. c   4. c   5. e   6. d   7. a

Problems

1. a. 100.
   b. $100 billion.
   c. The price level is 100 and the real output is $140 billion.
2. a. The price level falls from 80 to about 68.
   b. Real output falls from $200 billion to $180 billion.
   c. It shifts upward and to the left.
3. a. To find eqilibrium set the aggregate demand equation equal to the aggregate supply equation and solve for Q. Then, substitute Q back into one of the equations and solve for P:

$$1000 - 8Q = -20 + 2Q \qquad 1000 - 8Q = P$$
$$1020 = 10Q \qquad 1000 - 8(102) = P$$
$$102 = Q \qquad 1000 - 816 = P$$
$$184 = P$$

   b. Do the same with the new aggregate supply equation:

$$1000 - 8Q = -40 + 2Q \qquad 1000 - 8Q = P$$
$$1040 = 10Q \qquad 1000 - 8(104) = P$$
$$104 = Q \qquad 1000 - 832 = P$$
$$168 = P$$

   c. Aggregate supply shifts to the right.
4. a. $P = 5,000 - 5Q = 0.5Q$. Therefore, $Q = 5,000/5.5 = 909$.
   b. $P = 0.5Q = 5,000/11 = 454.5$.

CHAPTER 5

The Determination of National Output
and the Keynesian Multiplier

Chapter Profile

The consumption function (the relation between personal consumption expenditure and disposable income) is at the heart of the Keynesian theory of the determination of national output. Many studies have examined the consumption function, some based on cross-section data, some based on time-series data. From the consumption function, one can determine the marginal propensity to consume, which is the proportion of an extra dollar of income that is spent on consumption, as well as the saving function (the relationship between total saving and disposable income) and the marginal propensity to save (the proportion of an extra dollar of income that is saved).

The level of gross private domestic investment is determined by the expected rate of return from capital and the interest rate. The expected rate of return from capital is the perceived rate of return that businesses expect to obtain if new buildings are put up, new equipment is added, or inventories are increased. The interest rate is the cost of borrowing money. The level of investment is directly related to the expected rate of return from capital and inversely related to the interest rate.

The equilibrium level of gross domestic product is at the point where intended spending on final goods and services equals GDP. If intended spending exceeds GDP, GDP tends to increase. If intended spending falls short of GDP, GDP tends to fall.

If GDP is below its equilibrium level, the total amount spent on goods and services exceeds the total amount produced, so firms' inventories are reduced. Firms step up their output rates, thus increasing GDP. If GDP is above its equilibrium value, the total amount spent on goods and services fall short of the total amount produced, so firms' inventories rise. Firms cut their output rates, thus reducing GDP.

Investment expenditure tends to vary from year to year by greater percentages than consumption expenditure. This is due in part to the irregularity of innovation, the durability of capital goods, and the differences from year to year in the extent to which existing productive capacity is utilized.

A $1 billion change in intended investment results in a change in equilibrium GDP of 1/MPS billions of dollars, where MPS is the marginal propensity to save. In other words, the multiplier equals 1/MPS. The multiplier can be interpreted in terms of—and derived from—the successive stages of the spending process.

Holding disposable income constant, personal consumption expenditure is likely to depend on the amount of wealth in the hands of the public, the ease and cheapness with which consumers can borrow money, the expectations of the public, the amount of durable goods on hand, the income distribution, and the size of the population. Changes in these factors are likely to cause shifts in the consumption function. A shift in the consumption function also has an amplified effect on GDP, a $1 billion shift in the consumption function results in a change of $1/MPS billion in GDP.

Concepts for Review

disposable income
consumption function
marginal propensity to consume
average propensity to consume
*shifts in the consumption function
expected rate of return
interest rate
autonomous spending

45-degree line
saving function
income-expenditure analysis
multiplier
marginal propensity to save
capacity utilization
induced spending

Completion Questions

1. The level of investment is influenced heavily by the _____ of

   business executives. If business executives believe that their _____
   are about to drop, they are unlikely to invest much in additional capital

   goods. On the other hand, if they believe that their _____
   are about to increase greatly, they may be led to invest heavily in

   _____.

2. The relation between consumption expenditure and disposable income is called

   the _____.

3. If the consumption function is

$$C = 400 + 0.7D,$$

   where D is disposable income, the average propensity to consume (increases,

   decreases) _____ as income rises. When $D = 1,000$, the average

   propensity to save is (positive, negative) _____. The marginal

   propensity to consume equals _____.

*The starred items pertain to material covered in Exploring Further.

4. In general, a (more, less) _____ rapid rate of technological change is likely to result in more investment. Also, as a firm's sales go (up, down) _____, its need for plant, equipment, and inventory goes up. And the more (optimistic, pessimistic) _____ business expectations are, the greater the amount of investment.

5. If the consumption expenditure is proportional to the disposable income, the average propensity to consume is (greater than, less than, equal to) _____ the marginal propensity to consume, and the average propensity to save is (greater than, less than, equal to) _____ the marginal propensity to save.

6. The average propensity to consume and the average propensity to save must always equal _____. The marginal propensity to save is the _____ divided by the _____. The marginal propensity to save can also be expressed as _____ so that the multiplier can also be written as _____.

7. The equilibrium value of GDP will be at the point on the horizontal axis where the _____ line intersects the _____ line. If GDP is below this point, intended spending (exceeds, is less than) _____ GDP. If GDP is above this point, intended spending (exceeds, is less than) _____ GDP.

True-False

_____ 1. If the marginal propensity to consume is 0.8 and disposable income is $200 billion, personal consumption expenditure equals $160 billion.

_____ 2. If the average propensity to consume is 0.9 and disposable income is $100 billion, personal consumption expenditure equals $90 billion.

_____ 3. The marginal propensity to save plus the marginal propensity to consume equals the average propensity to save plus the average propensity to consume.

_____ 4. The proportion of total income consumed must always equal the marginal propensity to consume.

_____ 5. The marginal propensity to save is equal to the slope of the consumption function.

_____ 6. The marginal propensity to consume does not, in general, equal the average propensity to consume.

_____ 7. The level of investment is influenced by the level of sales and the stock of capital goods needed to produce the output to be sold.

_____ 8. Since the cost of an investment is bound to increase with the increase in the rate of interest, all other things equal, a given investment is less profitable when the interest rate is high than when it is low.

_____ 9. Investment expenditures are not influenced by the cost of capital goods.

_____ 10. Prices are held constant in the income-expenditures model.

Multiple Choice

1. The marginal propensity to save increases as disposable income rises. Consequently, the difference between the marginal propensity to consume and the marginal propensity to save

   a.　decreases as disposable income rises.
   b.　increases as disposable income rises.
   c.　increases and then decreases as disposable income rises.
   d.　decreases and then increases as disposable income rises.
   e.　remains constant as disposable income rises.

2. Which of the following relationships is a direct one?

   a.　The relationship between consumption expenditure and disposable income
   b.　The relationship between saving and disposable income
   c.　The relationship between saving and the rate of interest
   d.　The relationship between consumption expenditure and population
   e.　All of the above

3. Which of the following relationships is *not* an inverse one?

   a.　The relationship between the rate of interest and investment
   b.　The relationship between the average propensity to consume and disposable income
   c.　The relationship between the average propensity to save and disposable income
   d.　The relationship between the percent of the existing capital stock utilized and investment
   e.　Both c and d

4. The level of investment is influenced by

   a.　the interest rate.
   b.　the optimism or pessimism of expectations.
   c.　the rate of technological change.
   d.　the level of output relative to the capacity of existing plant and equipment.
   e.　all of the above.

5. At any particular level of disposable income, the marginal propensity to save plus the marginal propensity to consume must equal

a. 0.
b. 1.
c. 100.

d. 1,000.
e. 10,000.

6. Intended investment increases by $1,000 in an economy where the marginal propensity to save is 0.2. The amount of extra spending in the *first* stage of the spending and respending process is

a. $200.
b. $400.
c. $600.

d. $800.
e. $1,000.

7. Continuing question 6, the amount of extra spending in the *second* stage of the spending and respending process is

a. $200.
b. $400.
c. $600.

d. $800.
e. $1,000.

8. Continuing question 6, the amount of extra spending in *all* stages of the spending and respending process is

a. $1,000.
b. $2,000.
c. $3,000.

d. $4,000.
e. $5,000.

Discussion and Extension Questions

1. "The consumption function is a deficient concept because many of the items people consume are provided by the government (for example, police protection and public education) and the amount people spend on these items is not included in the economist's concept of consumption expenditure." Discuss and evaluate.

2. John Roberts is a wealthy dentist whose income in 2004 is $40,000 because he took most of the year off to vacation in Florida. His younger brother, Bill, is a high-school teacher who made $40,000 in 2004 as a result of full-time employment. Do you think that the consumption expenditures of these two brothers are the same in 2004? Why or why not?

3. Discuss the importance of nonincome factors on consumption expenditure. Include in your discussion facts concerning the stock market boom of the last 10 years.

4. As it stands, can the simple model described in this chapter be used to forecast GDP? Why or why not?

5. "Because of habit and inertia, the level of personal consumption expenditure in one year depends on its level in the previous year, as well as on disposable income." Do you agree? Why or why not?

Problems

1. In the nation of Chaos on the Styx, there is the following relationship between consumption expenditure and disposable income:

Consumption expenditure (billions of dollars)	Disposable income (billions of dollars)
120	100
200	200
270	300
330	400
380	500
420	600

a. Plot the consumption function for this nation in the following chart:

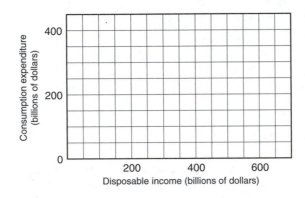

b. What is the marginal propensity to consume when disposable income is between $100 billion and $200 billion? When disposable income is between $300 billion and $400 billion? When disposable income is between $500 billion and $600 billion?

c. If the nation of Chaos on the Styx consumes $5 billion more at each level of disposable income than shown in the table, is this a shift in the consumption function or a movement along the consumption function?

d. Using the data given, plot the saving function for Chaos-on-the-Styx.

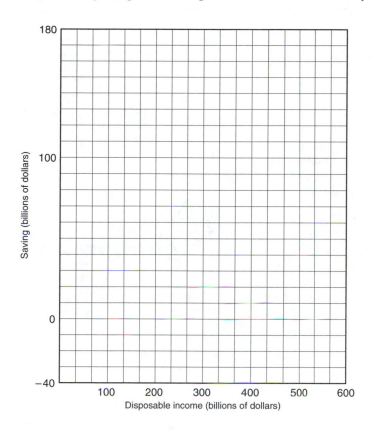

e. What is the marginal propensity to save when disposable income is between $100 billion and $200 billion? When disposable income is between $300 billion and $400 billion? When disposable income is between $500 billion and $600 billion?

f. If you combine your answers to parts b and e, what is the sum of the marginal propensity to consume and the marginal propensity to save under the three situations covered?

g. If, as described in part c, the nation consumes $5 billion more at each level of disposable income than shown in the table, draw the new consumption function (in the graph provided in part a) and the new saving function (in the graph provided in part d). If no change occurs in either function, write "no change" as your answer.

2. Suppose that the Bugsbane Music Box Company is considering investing in seven projects, identified as A to G. The expected rate of return from each project is given next.

Project	Expected rate of return (percent)
A	12
B	8
C	7
D	15
E	25
F	11
G	9

a. If the firm can borrow money at 10 percent interest, which projects are clearly unprofitable?

b. Suppose that the interest rate increases to 13 percent. Which projects are unprofitable now?

3. Suppose that $1 of income is transferred from a person whose marginal propensity to consume is 0.9 to someone whose marginal propensity to consume is 0.8. What is the effect on total consumption expenditure? On saving?

4. Country X's consumption function is such that personal consumption expenditure equals $90 billion if disposable income equals $100 billion. The marginal propensity to save equals 1/3.

a. Fill in the value of personal consumption expenditure and the average propensity to consume corresponding to each of the following values of disposable income:

Disposable income (billions of dollars)	Personal consumption expenditure (billions of dollars)	Average propensity to consume
150	———	———
200	———	———
250	———	———
300	———	———

b. In 2005, Country X's economists believe that the consumption function described in part a is no longer valid. In that year, disposable income is $200 billion and personal consumption expenditure is $175 billion. Is there evidence of a shift in the consumption function?

c. Can we tell what the new marginal propensity to consume is? If so, how? If not, why not?

5. Suppose that each of the following events occurs in 2007. Taken by itself, would each increase the amount that firms want to invest?

   a. A major invention occurs which makes it possible to convert coal into gasoline cheaply.
   b. A major recession occurs.
   c. One-fifth of California's capital stock is obliterated because of an earthquake.
   d. Interest rates fall by about 2 percentage points.
   e. Because of decreases in productivity, costs rise rapidly in the construction industry.

6. Suppose that each of the following events occurs in 2007. Taken by itself, would each shift the consumption function upward, downward, or have no effect?

   a. The liquid assets held by consumers increase by $50 billion.
   b. The *Wall Street Journal* and other newspapers print stories indicating that there may be a recession developing.
   c. Disposable income goes up by $30 billion.
   d. A substantial increase in population occurs.
   e. Convincing evidence is found that the world will soon come to an end.

7. Assume that Muppetland has no government expenditures, the economy is closed (no exports or imports), and there are no taxes or government transfer payments or undistributed corporate profits. In 2007, suppose that firms want to invest $200 billion and the consumption function is as follows:

Disposable income (billions of dollars)	Consumption expenditure (billions of dollars)
900	750
1,000	800
1,100	850
1,200	900
1,300	950
1,400	1,000

a. Plot the consumption function here:

b. Plot the $C + I$ line here, together with the 45-degree line:

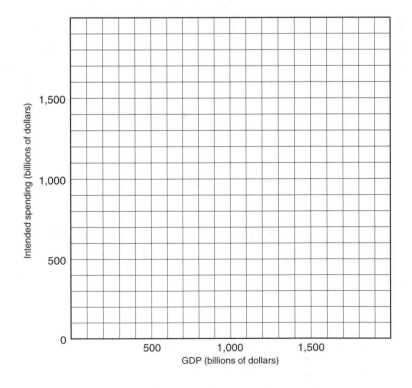

c. Will the GDP be at its equilibrium level if it equals $900 billion? Why or why not?

d. Will the GDP be at its equilibrium level if it equals $1,100 billion? Why or why not?

e. Will the GDP be at its equilibrium level if it equals $1,000 billion? Why or why not?

f. If the GDP is $1,000 billion, what is the value of the multiplier?

g. If intended investment increases by $1 billion, by how much does the equilibrium GDP increase?

h. If the consumption function shifts upward by $1 billion, by how much does the equilibrium GDP increase?

Answers

Completion Questions

1. expectations, sales, sales, capital goods   2. consumption function
3. decreases, negative , 0.7   4. more, up, optimistic   5. equal to, equal to
6. 1, change in savings, change in disposable income, $1 - MPC$, $1/(1 - MPC)$.
7. $C + I$, 45-degree, exceeds, is less than

True-False

1. False   2. True   3. True   4. False   5. False   6. True   7. True   8. True
9. False   10. True

Multiple Choice

1. a   2. e   3. e   4. e   5. b   6. e   7. d   8. e

Problems

1. a.

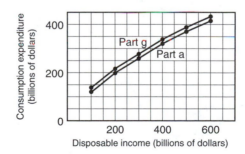

b. 0.8, 0.6, 0.4.

c. A shift in the consumption function, because consumption expenditure is higher at each level of disposable income.

d.

e. 0.2, 0.4, 0.6.

f. 1 in each case.

g. Given in answers to parts a and d.

2. a. Projects B, C, and G.

b. Projects A, B, C, F, and G.

3. Consumption expenditure falls by $0.10. Saving increases by $0.10.

4. a.
123¹/₃	0.82
156²/₃	0.78
190	0.76
223¹/₃	0.74

b. Yes.

c. No, because we know only one point on the new consumption function.

5. a. Yes.

b. No.

c. Yes.

d. Yes.

e. No.

6. a. Upward.

b. Downward.

c. No effect.

d. Upward.

e. Upward.

7. a.

b.

c. No. Intended spending exceeds the GDP, and there is an unintentional decline in inventories.

d. No. The GDP exceeds intended spending, and there is an unintentional increase in inventories.

e. Yes. The GDP equals intended spending.

f. 2.

g. $2 billion.

h. $2 billion.

CHAPTER 6

Fiscal Policy and National Output

Chapter Profile

The equilibrium level of GDP is where the intended spending on GDP equals GDP. If net exports are zero, the intended spending equals the intended levels of consumption, investment, and government purchases. A $1 billion change in government purchases causes the same change in equilibrium GDP as a $1 billion change in intended investment or a $1 billion shift in the relation between consumption expenditures and GDP. In any of these cases, there is a multiplier effect.

An increase in the tax rate shifts the relationship between consumption expenditure and GDP downward, reducing the equilibrium value of GDP. A decrease in the tax rate shifts the relationship upward, increasing the equilibrium value of GDP.

Policy makers receive a lot of help in stabilizing the economy from our automatic stabilizers: automatic changes in tax revenues, unemployment compensation and welfare payments, corporate dividends, family saving, and farm aid that occur with the ups and downs of the economy. However, the automatic stabilizers can only cut down on variations in unemployment and inflation, not eliminate them.

Discretionary programs are often used to supplement the effects of these automatic stabilizers. Such discretionary actions include changing government expenditure on public works and other programs, changing welfare payments and other such transfers, and changing tax rates. An important problem with some of these tools of fiscal policy is the lag in time before they can be brought into play.

In the past 60 years, government spending has increased considerably both in absolute terms and as a percentage of total output. (It is now about one-third of our total output.) To a large extent, this increase has been due to our greater military responsibilities, as well as to the fact that, as their incomes have risen, our citizens have demanded more schools, highways, and other goods and services provided by government. Also, government transfer payments have grown substantially.

To get the money to cover most of these expenditures, governments collect taxes from individuals and firms. At the federal level, the most important form of taxation is the personal income tax; at the local level, the property tax is very important; and at the state level, sales (and excise) taxes are the biggest money raisers.

If a recession is imminent or considerable resources are unemployed (recessionary gap), governments frequently use fiscal policy to push the aggregate demand curve to the right, increasing production and jobs. If a substantial increase in the price level (inflationary gap) appears likely, governments frequently use fiscal policy to shift the aggregate demand curve to the left, decreasing the price level from what it otherwise would have been.

*If net exports are not zero, intended spending equals the intended levels of consumption, investment, government purchases, and net exports. If net exports are

*The starred item pertains to material covered in Exploring Further.

positive ($X > M_I$), then the foreign sector has increased intended spending and thus equilibrium GDP. If net exports are negative ($X < M_I$), then the foreign sector has decreased intended spending and thus equilibrium GDP.

Concepts for Review

government purchases

$C + I + G$ line

Council of Economic Advisers

automatic stabilizers

recessionary gap

tax cut of 1964

Employment Act of 1946

discretionary fiscal policy

government transfer payments

$C + I + G + (X - M_I)$ line

inflationary gap

Completion Questions

1. If the marginal propensity to consume is 0.75, an extra $1 billion in government expenditure increases equilibrium GDP by _____ billion. A reduction of $5 billion in government expenditure reduces equilibrium GDP by _____ billion.

2. Two major economic targets the government should aim at are _____ and _____. If there is full employment but unacceptable inflation, the government might (increase, reduce) _____ spending. Structural features of our economy that tend to iron out business fluctuations and push in the direction of full employment at stable prices are called _____.

3. The slope of the relationship between consumption and GDP (increases, decreases) _____ as the tax rate decreases. This means that the marginal propensity to consume out of GDP (increases, decreases) _____ as the tax rate decreases. Consequently, the multiplier— the amount by which GDP changes if intended investment changes (or the consumption function shifts, or government expenditures change)—(increases, decreases) _____ as the tax rate goes down and (increases, decreases) _____ as the tax rate goes up. In other words, as the tax rate increases, GDP becomes (more, less) _____ sensitive to changes in investment, government spending, and the consumption function.

4. The amount of income tax collected by the federal government goes (down, up) _____ with increases in GDP and goes (down, up) _____ with decreases in GDP. Moreover, because the income

tax is progressive, the average tax rate goes (down, up) _____

with increases in GDP, and goes (down, up) _____ with
decreases in GDP.

5. When GDP falls off and unemployment increases, tax collections (fall, rise)

    _____, so _____ falls less than GDP,

    thus _____ falls less, which tends to (cut, increase)

    _____ the fall in GDP. When GDP rises too quickly and
    the economy begins to suffer from serious inflation, tax collections (fall,

    rise)_____, which tends to (cut, increase) _____
    the increase in GDP.

6. When GDP falls off and unemployment increases, the tax collections that finance

    unemployment compensation go (down, up) _____ because of

    (increased, lower) _____ employment. At the
    same time, the amount paid out to unemployed workers goes (down, up)

    _____. But, when GDP rises too quickly and inflation besets
    the economy, the tax collections to finance unemployment

    compensation go (up, down) _____, while the amount paid

    out goes (up, down) _____ because there is much (less,

    more)_____ unemployment.

7. Because corporations generally maintain their dividends even though their
   sales fall off and also limit the increase in dividend payments even when their
   sales rise, their dividend policies tend to (stabilize, destabilize)

    _____ the economy. To the extent that consumers tend to

    be (fast, slow) _____ to raise or lower their spending in
    response to increases or decreases in their income, this too tends to

    (stabilize, destabilize) _____ the economy.

8. When there is high unemployment, the government may (cut, increase)

    _____ tax rates (as it did in 2003). If inflation is the problem,

    the government may (cut, increase) _____ taxes
    (as it did in 1968).

True-False

_____   1. Walter Heller played an important role in getting the tax cut of 1964
               enacted.

_____   2. The Council of Economic Advisers has served Congress since its cre-
               ation in 1976.

_____ 3. If the marginal propensity to save is 0.2 and taxes are imposed so consumers must pay $1 billion to the government at each level of GDP, consumption expenditure at each level of GDP is $200 million less than before the imposition of the taxes.

_____ 4. If the marginal propensity to save is 0.2 and both taxes and government expenditures on goods and services are increased by $1 billion, the equilibrium level of GDP increases by $5 billion.

_____ 5. Government discretionary programs like varying tax rates and welfare payments are not the same as the automatic stabilizers.

_____ 6. Fiscal policy often takes a long time to enact; this reduces its effectiveness at economic stabilization.

Multiple Choice

1. Suppose that the amount of consumption expenditure at each level of disposable income (both in billions of dollars) is as follows:

Consumption expenditure	Disposable income
300	500
315	520
330	540
345	560

If taxes are zero, investment equals $60 billion, and government expenditures on goods and services equal $150 billion, the equilibrium value of GDP is

a. $500 billion.
b. $520 billion.
c. $540 billion.
d. $560 billion.
e. none of the above.

2. Suppose the amount of consumption expenditure at each level of disposable income is as shown in question 1. If taxes equal $100 billion at each level of GDP, investment equals $100 billion, and government expenditure on goods and services equals $200 billion, the equilibrium value of GDP is

a. between $520 billion and $540 billion.
b. $520 billion.
c. $540 billion.
d. $560 billion.
e. none of the above.

3. If there is high unemployment, Keynes would say that the government should *not*

a. reduce taxes.
b. decrease government expenditures.
c. enact tax credits.
d. change depreciation.
e. do any of the above.

4. Which of the following is *not* considered an automatic stabilizer?

    a.   Changes in tax revenues that occur with economic activity
    b.   Unemployment compensation
    c.   Farm aid programs
    d.   Government expenditure for public works
    e.   Corporate dividend policies

5. To supplement the effects of automatic stabilizers, discretionary programs are used; these include

    a.   redistricting.
    b.   changing tax rates.
    c.   increasing congressional vacations.
    d.   family saving.
    e.   all of the above.

Discussion and Extension Questions

1. "The whole purpose of automatic stabilizers is to reduce the value of the multiplier." Discuss.

2. A member of the Federal Reserve Board once said, "If we attempted a more stimulative program, business would spend less." Explain what he meant and indicate its significance for public policy. Do you agree? Why or why not?

3. "Fiscal policy is a political subterfuge whereby the government spends and taxes more and more until the economy is socialized." Comment and evaluate.

4. "If defense spending were cut, we would have mass unemployment. Regardless of the worthiness of defense spending, it is required to prevent a massive, long-term depression." Comment and evaluate, using a production possibilities curve.

5. "Fiscal policy is of no importance because temporary changes in income due to government spending and tax changes do not alter people's spending much. For example, the tax increase of 1968 did not curb inflationary pressures because it was viewed as temporary." Comment and evaluate.

6. If the economy is suffering from an undesirably high rate of unemployment, what measures can the government take to improve the situation? How quickly can these measures be adopted? If the economy is suffering from an undesirably high rate of inflation, what measures can the government take to improve the situation? How quickly can these measures be adopted?

7. What are the automatic stabilizers for the U.S. economy? What are the major tools of discretionary fiscal policy? How do they differ? Why are both considered important?

Problems

1. Suppose that the consumption function in Gopherland is as follows:

Disposable income (billions of dollars)	Consumption expenditure (billions of dollars)
900	750
1,000	800
1,100	850
1,200	900
1,300	950
1,400	1,000

a. Suppose that intended investment is $200 billion and government expenditure is $100 billion. Plot the $C + I + G$ curve and the 45-degree line in the graph. (Full-employment GDP equals $1,400 billion.)

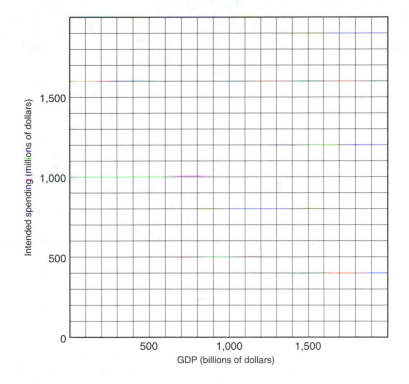

b. What is the equilibrium value of GDP?
c. What sorts of measures can be taken by the government to promote noninflationary full employment?
d. What would be the effect on the equilibrium level of GDP of a $1 billion increase in government expenditure?

e. What would be the effect on the equilibrium level of GDP of a $1 billion decrease in government expenditure?

f. Plot the relationship between consumption expenditure and GDP if taxes equal 10 percent of GDP. Suppose that intended investment is $200 billion and government expenditure is $100 billion. Plot the $C + I + G$ line and the 45-degree line in the graph. What is the equilibrium level of GDP?

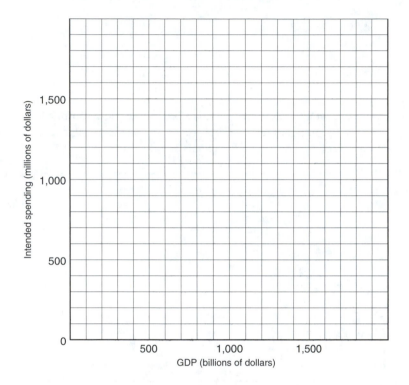

g. Holding other factors constant, what effect does an increase in the tax rate have on the equilibrium level of GDP?

h. Holding other factors constant, what effect does a decrease in the tax rate have on the equilibrium level of GDP?

2. a. In the country of Badger, the consumption function is as follows:

Disposable income (millions of dollars)	Consumption expenditure (millions of dollars)
900	700
1,000	750
1,100	800
1,200	850
1,300	900

Suppose that intended investment is $100 million. What is the equilibrium level of GDP if government expenditures are $200 million (and taxes are zero)?

   b. Suppose that Badger increases its government expenditures by $10 million. What is the effect on its equilibrium GDP? Does GDP increase or decrease? By how much?

   c. Suppose that the government of Badger imposes a personal income tax that takes $16^2/3$ percent of everyone's pretax income. What now is the relationship between GDP and consumption expenditure (both in millions of dollars)? Fill in the blanks in the following table:

GDP	Consumption expenditure
————	700
————	750
————	800
————	850
————	900

   d. What is the equilibrium value of Badger's GDP if intended investment is $100 million and government expenditure is $350 million?

e. Plot the consumption function in Badger in this graph.

f. Plot below the relationship between consumption expenditure and GDP after Badger imposes the personal income tax:

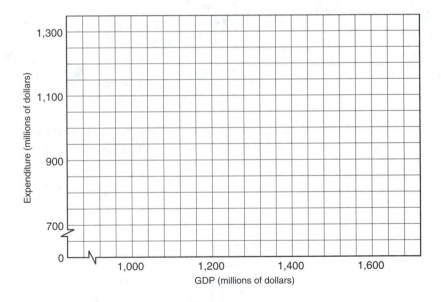

g. In the graph in part f, plot the $C + I + G$ line for Badger under the conditions described in part d. Where does this line intersect the 45-degree line? What is the significance of this intersection point?

h. Suppose that $1,100 billion is the full-employment GDP. What sorts of measures can the government of Badger take to produce noninflationary full employment?

3. Suppose that the following set of equations defines a model of our basic economy:

$$C_d = 200 + 0.8Y_d$$
$$\text{GDP} = Y_d$$
$$I_d = 160,$$

where C_d equals intended consumption expenditure, I_d equals intended investment, and Y_d equals disposable income. We now add a government sector to this model. In particular, let both government spending (on goods and services) and taxes equal $500 million.

a. Represent this economy in the grid that follows:

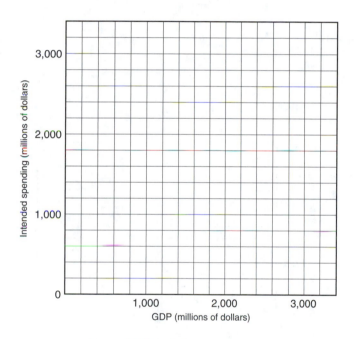

b. Determine equilibrium GDP and show it in the diagram of part a.
c. What is the multiplier for this economy? Demonstrate that your result is correct.
d. Government spending increases to $700 million, while everything else remains constant. What happens to equilibrium GDP?

Answers

Completion Questions
1. $4, $20   2. full employment, a stable price level, reduce, automatic stabilizers
3. increases, increases, increases, decreases, less   4. up, down, up, down   5. fall,
disposable income, consumption, cut, rise, cut   6. down, lower, up, up, down, less
7. stabilize, slow, stabilize   8. cut, increase

True-False
1. True   2. False   3. False   4. False   5. True   6. True

Multiple Choice
1. c   2. e   3. b   4. d   5. b

Problems
1. a.

b. $1,200 billion.
c. The government could increase its expenditures by $100 billion, or it
    could encourage private investment or consumption.
d. It would increase equilibrium GDP by $2 billion.
e. It would reduce equilibrium GDP by $2 billion.

f.

$1,091 billion.
  g. It reduces the equilibrium value of GDP.
  h. It increases the equilibrium value of GDP.
2. a. $1,100 million.
    b. Equilibrium GDP increases by $20 million.
    c.   *GDP*
          (millions of dollars)
          _____
                    1,080
                    1,200
                    1,320
                    1,440
                    1,560
    d. $1,200 million.
    e.

f.

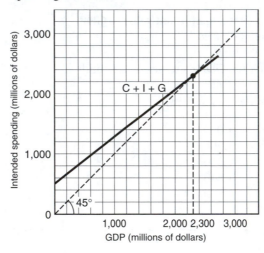

g. The $C + I + G$ line is shown in the graph. $1,200 million. This is the equilibrium value of GDP.

h. The government can increase taxes, decrease its spending, or discourage private spending on investment.

3. a.

b. $2,300 million. See part a.
c. 5. A $1 increase in investment increases GDP by $5.
d. It increases by $1,000 million.

CHAPTER 7

Inflation

Chapter Profile

Inflation is a general upward movement of prices. Runaway inflation occurs when the price level increases very rapidly, as in Germany after World War I. Creeping inflation occurs when the price level rises a few percent per year, as in the United States during the 1950s and 1960s. The consumer price index, published monthly by the Bureau of Labor Statistics, is a key measure of the rate of inflation.

High rates of inflation produce considerable redistribution of income and wealth. People with relatively fixed incomes, such as the elderly, tend to take a beating from inflation. Unanticipated inflation hurts lenders and benefits borrowers, since it results in the depreciation of money: The money repaid has less value than the money borrowed. Inflation can also have a devastating effect on savers, especially when the inflation rate is greater than the interest rate. In this case, money loses value faster than it accumulates interest. The penalties (and rewards) resulting from inflation are meted out arbitrarily, with no regard for society's values or goals. Substantial rates of inflation may also reduce efficiency and total output in part by diverting resources from productive investment (creating capacity, output, and jobs) to speculative investment on commodities such as gold and in part by creating an environment of uncertainty.

Demand-side inflation can be viewed as a rightward shift of the aggregate demand curve along the upward-sloping or vertical portion of the short-run aggregate supply curve. It results in an inverse relationship between unemployment and inflation, as demonstrated by the Phillips curve.

The Phillips curve shows the relationship between the rate of increase of the price level and the level of unemployment. If the Phillips curve remains fixed, it poses an awkward dilemma for policy makers. If they reduce unemployment, inflation increases; if they reduce inflation, unemployment increases. During 1955–69, there was a fairly close relationship between the inflation rate and the unemployment rate.

Supply-side inflation can be viewed as the leftward shift of the aggregate supply curve caused by a general increase in production cost or a disruption of productive ability. Supply-side inflation reduces both production and jobs as well as increases the price level. During the 1970s and early 1980s, this was caused by large increases in oil prices by OPEC. The effects of this oil shock were so great the Phillips curve significantly shifted upward and to the right. High unemployment and high inflation occurred simultaneously. During the late 1980s and early 1990s, the Phillips curve in the United States shifted to the left and downward, resulting in simultaneously low unemployment and inflation. The combination of unemployment and inflation (sometimes called the *misery index*) fell to the lowest levels in a generation until the recession of 2001.

Concepts for Review

inflation   creeping inflation
runaway inflation   consumer price index
demand-side inflation   money income
Phillips curve   real income
supply-side inflation   NAIRU (natural rate of unemployment)
anticipated inflation   unanticipated inflation
tax surcharge of 1968

Completion Questions

1. Unanticipated inflation hurts _____ and benefits

   _____, since it results in the depreciation of money.

2. The most widely quoted measure of inflation in the United States is the

   _____.

3. Runaway inflation is likely to result in (increased, reduced)

   _____ national output.

4. The consumer price index equaled 144.5 in 1993 and 184 in 2003 (base period

   1982–84). The price level rose by about _____ percent during
   this decade. One limitation of the CPI is that it does not include the prices of
   _____ or _____. A more inclusive

   index is the _____ deflator.

5. If the Murphy family's money income increases by 10 percent per year,
   and its real income increases by 8 percent per year, the price level must

   be rising by _____ percent per year. If the price level
   continues to rise at this rate and you invest in a bond yielding 6 percent

   interest per year, you will receive _____ percent interest in
   real terms.

6. If lenders foresee an inflation rate of 10 percent per year, they are unlikely
   to lend money at 10 percent or less because it would mean they would

   receive an interest rate of _____ percent or less in real terms.
   If lenders anticipate increased inflation, they will tend to (increase,

   decrease) _____ interest rates.

True-False

_____ 1. If deflation occurs at 5 percent per year, a family living on a fixed dollar
            income would experience an increase in its real income of about 5
            percent per year.

_____ 2. Deflation is a general *downward* movement of the price level. An unanticipated deflation tends to redistribute income from borrowers to lenders.

_____ 3. Inflation tends to cut everyone's income.

_____ 4. All changes in output, employment, and the price level are due to the business cycle.

_____ 5. When actual GDP equals potential GDP, a large increase in total spending results in inflation, since little or no increase in real output can occur.

_____ 6. By the late 1990s, the NAIRU appeared lower than it had been in years due to a surge in productivity.

_____ 7. Since the Phillips curve slopes downward, unemployment and inflation always move in the opposite direction.

_____ 8. During periods of rapid inflation, firms find it difficult to plan ahead and invest efficiently, because they are very uncertain about what future prices will be. The result is inefficiency and waste. Thus, both inflation and unemployment result in social waste.

Multiple Choice

1. Inflation tends to benefit

   a. the older generation.
   b. lenders who anticipate the rate of inflation correctly.
   c. lenders who underestimate the rate of inflation.
   d. borrowers who obtain money from lenders who anticipate the rate of inflation correctly.
   e. none of the above.

2. Increases in spending tend to be inflationary when

   a. there is full employment.
   b. actual GDP equals potential GDP.
   c. the labor force increases in quantity or quality.
   d. all of the above.
   e. a and b.

3. During a period of accelerating inflation, interest rates tend to

   a. fall because the value of money falls.
   b. fall because the unemployment rate tends to fall.
   c. rise because the value of money falls.
   d. rise because the unemployment rate tends to fall.
   e. be unaffected.

4. During a deflation, you would be wise to invest in

a. land.
b. diamonds.
c. a or b.
d. gold.
e. government bonds.

5. During inflation, government receipts tend to

a. rise because the country's taxpayers move into higher tax brackets where the average tax rate is higher.
b. fall because Congress reduces tax rates to offset inflation.
c. rise because more receipts are needed to pay the higher interest costs on the national debt due to inflation.
d. remain constant.
e. none of the above.

6. In the short run, creeping inflation is likely to

a. reduce national output sharply.
b. be directly related to the level of unemployment.
c. wipe out the savings of people on fixed incomes.
d. hurt lenders and benefit borrowers.
e. all of the above.

7. There are only two goods, X and Y. Consumers spend half of their income on X and half on Y. Between 2000 and 2001, the price of X rose by 5 percent, and the price of Y rose by 15 percent. If the consumer price index equals 100 in 2000, what does it equal in 2001?

a. 100
b. 105
c. 110
d. 115
e. None of the above

8. In the previous question, suppose that consumers spend more than half of their income on X. Under these circumstances, what would the consumer price index be in 2001?

a. 105
b. 110
c. Between 105 and 110
d. Between 110 and 115
e. 115

Discussion and Extension Questions

1. Prior to his election in 1976, President Carter was quoted by the *New York Times* as saying, "I'd put my emphasis on employment and take my chances on inflation." Using the concepts developed in this chapter, explain in your own words what he meant. Do you think that President Reagan's attitude was the same as Carter's? What about President George W. Bush?

2. Suppose that the unemployed refuse to work unless they receive unrealistically high wages. For example, a high school dropout worth no more than $2 per hour may insist on receiving $6 per hour. If so, isn't it inflationary and foolish to try to achieve full employment?

3. In 2002, the Federal Reserve Bank of San Francisco stated that "the standard Phillips curve model consistently overpredicted inflation during the 1990s when the unemployment rate was dropping to a 30-year low." Does this represent a breakdown of the model? Why or why not?

4. "Unless some people benefited from inflation, the nation would not tolerate it." Do you agree? Why or why not?

5. In his 1979 *Economic Report*, President Carter said, "A large part of the worsening of inflation last year . . . stemmed from poor productivity." By *poor productivity,* he meant that output per hour of labor did not increase as fast as in previous years. Why would this affect the rate of inflation?

Problems

1. In Israel, the annual inflation rate was about 50 percent in 1978, and nearly 100 percent during the summer of 1979, according to William C. Freund of the New York Stock Exchange. In the *New York Times* on June 24, 1979, Freund concluded that, "The solution lies in marshalling the necessary political courage and consensus. . . . It is political fortitude, above all else, which is needed now— to cut back on excess claims against resources, to promote production and pro-ductivity, and to relieve intense demand pressures." Indicate how this advice is related to the discussion presented in this chapter. What specific measures would you suggest to accomplish these results?

2. Commenting on the previously cited inflation in Israel, the *Jerusalem Post* observed that "75 percent of Israeli families live in flats they own. Most of these were bought with government assistance and low interest mortgages. The payments on these mortgages are peanuts in light of our current inflation spiral. Someone who received a loan of 200,000 Israeli pounds at the beginning of the year—even at 32 percent interest—will have earned about 65,000 Israeli pounds by the end of it, clear and nontaxable. This sum is possibly more than his annual wages, so why complain?" Does this prove that inflation is of no consequence? Why or why not? Explain in detail.

3. Mr. Rich has $1 million in cash, bank accounts, and savings and loan accounts. They are his only assets.

   a. If the inflation rate is 8 percent, how much must Mr. Rich save per year to maintain the real value of his assets?
   b. If all Mr. Rich's income is taxable, what is the minimum amount he must make per year if he wants to maintain the real value of his assets? (He must pay 70 percent of his income in taxes.)

4. Suppose that there are only three commodities, X, Y, and Z. The price per pound of each commodity in 2003 follows, together with the number of pounds of each commodity consumed in 2003:

	2003	
Commodity	Price per pound (dollars)	Number of pounds consumed (millions)
X	1	5
Y	2	8
Z	3	12

   a. What is the total amount spent on these commodities in 2003?
   b. The price per pound of each commodity in 2004, together with the number of pounds of each commodity consumed in 2004, follows:

	2004	
Commodity	Price per pound (dollars)	Number of pounds consumed (millions)
X	1.08	6
Y	2.15	8
Z	3.30	13

   What is the total amount spent on these commodities in 2004?
   c. If we divide the answer to part b by the answer to part a, do we get a proper price index? Why or why not?

   d. If we average the 2004 prices of the three commodities, we get

$$\frac{\$1.08 + \$2.15 + \$3.30}{3} = \frac{\$6.53}{3} = \$2.177.$$

If we average the 2003 prices of the three commodities, we get

$$\frac{\$1 + \$2 + \$3}{3} = \frac{\$6}{3} = \$2.$$

One way to obtain a price index is to divide $2.177 by $2.00 and multiply the result by 100. If we do this, we get 108.8. Why do statisticians regard an index number of this sort as being too crude for most purposes?

    e.   Another way to calculate a price index is by calculating how much the amounts of these commodities consumed in 2003 would have cost in 2004 and dividing this cost by how much they actually cost in 2003. (The result should be multiplied by 100.) Compute this price index, using the preceding data. What advantages do you think this price index has over the one computed in part d?

5. a.   Suppose that the Phillips curve in France in 2004 was as shown on the following graph. What rate of increase of the price level would be associated with a 5 percent unemployment rate? What unemployment would be associated with a 6 percent rate of increase of the price level?

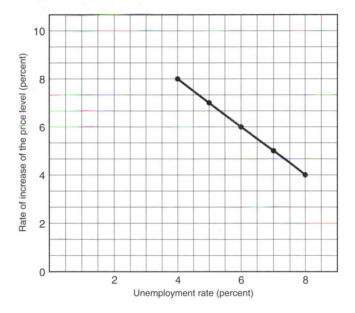

b.   The Phillips curve in part a pertained to 2004. Suppose that the Phillips curve in France in 2005 is as follows:

Unemployment rate (percent)	Rate of increase of the price level (percent)
2	6
4	5
6	4
8	3

Plot the 2005 Phillips curve in this graph:

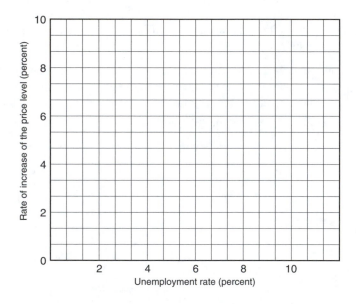

c.   Compare this Phillips curve to the one in part a. Summarize what occurred.

6. The Phillips curve in economy D shifts upward and to the right.

a.   Economy D's leading liberal legislator says that this shift means an increase in unemployment. Is she right?

b.   Economy D's leading conservative legislator says that this shift means an increase in inflation. Is he right? Why or why not?

c.   Economy D's prime minister says that, despite this shift, her administration will reduce both unemployment and inflation. Is she right? Why or why not?

Answers

Completion Questions
1. lenders, borrowers   2. consumer price index   3. reduced   4. 27.3, industrial machinery, raw materials, GDP   5. 2, 4   6. zero, increase

True-False
1. True   2. True   3. False   4. False   5. True   6. True   7. False   8. True

Multiple Choice
1. e   2. e   3. c   4. e   5. a   6. d   7. c   8. c

Problems
1. Total spending is so great that the price level is being pushed up at a very rapid rate. The government might reduce its own expenditures or increase taxes.
2. No, even though some people may have protected themselves, many others are hurt by the resulting redistribution of income. Also, an inflation of this sort is likely to affect the efficiency of the economy.
3. a. About $80,000.
   b. $266,667, since he must make at least $80,000 after taxes. If all his income is subject to a tax of 70 percent, he must make $80,000/0.3, or $266,667, before taxes.
4. a. $57 million.
   b. $66.58 million.
   c. No, because the amount consumed of each commodity is not held constant.
   d. Because the price of each commodity is not weighted by the amount of the commodity consumed. Also, the result depends on the units to which the prices pertain. For example, if the price of commodity Y pertains to an ounce, not a pound, the result differs.
   e. ($62.20 million/$57 million) $\times$ 100 = 109.1. This index does not have the limitations cited in part d.

5. a. 7 percent, 6 percent.
   b.

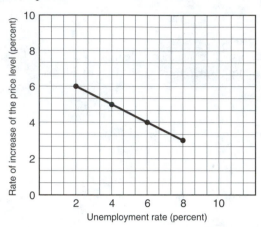

   c. The Phillips curve shifted to the left and downward, indicating that this economy can now sustain a lower combination of unemployment and inflation than before.
6. a. Not necessarily. If the country is willing to tolerate more inflation, it may be able to avoid an increase in unemployment.
   b. Not necessarily. If the country is willing to tolerate more unemployment, it may be able to avoid an increase in inflation.
   c. No, not unless the curve can be shifted downward and to the left.

CASE 1

Does the Consumer Price Index Overstate Increases in the Cost of Living?

COUNCIL OF ECONOMIC ADVISERS[1]

Many researchers have argued that the consumer price index (CPI) overstates increases in the cost of living. Much of this research comes from the Bureau of Labor Statistics (BLS), which produces the CPI. This research has identified several possible sources of bias; the degree of consensus on the importance of each varies.

Substitution Bias

The CPI prices a fixed market basket of commodities. Shares of these commodities in the basket are based on spending patterns observed in a base period. But consumers do not buy the same basket of goods from year to year. When the prices of some goods rise more quickly than those of other goods, consumers often substitute away from those that have become relatively expensive and toward others that have become relatively cheap. Increases in the CPI measure how much additional income a typical consumer would need to buy the base-period market basket at the new prices. In contrast, a true cost-of-living index would measure how much more income a consumer needs to maintain the same level of economic well-being, taking into account the ability to substitute among goods. By ignoring substitution, the CPI overstates increases in the cost of living.

Substitution bias takes place at two levels, given the way the CPI is constructed. At the "upper" level, substitution occurs among the basic categories that make up the CPI's market basket—for example, when consumers switch from apples to oranges (2 of the 207 categories). But these 207 categories are themselves made up of numerous individual items. For example, the apples category consists of a sample of Delicious, Granny Smith, Macintosh, and other varieties. Thus a second, "lower" level of substitution takes place within categories when the price of, say, Delicious apples rises and consumers shift to other varieties. . . .

[1]*Economic Report of the President* (Washington, D.C.: U.S. Government Printing Office, 1997), pp. 67–72.

Quality Adjustment

Measuring inflation properly requires distinguishing between changes in the underlying price and changes in quality. The BLS measures quality changes when it can. Some are easy to measure, for example when bakers double the size of their chocolate chip cookies. Others are more difficult but straightforward; for example, optional automobile equipment that later becomes standard, such as air bags or antilock brakes, can be quality-adjusted by its price when it was sold as an option. Quality adjustments generally have a significant effect on price increases as measured by the CPI. For example, the BLS estimates that in 1995 quality adjustment reduced the increase in the CPI by 2 percentage points compared with what it would have been based on listed prices.

The BLS does not adjust for other, more difficult problems because the agency cannot make direct quality adjustments in the absence of quantifiable data. For example, televisions are less likely to need repair than they were a decade ago, and some surgical procedures are more likely to be successful today than in the past. But repair rates for televisions and success rates for surgery cannot be computed until years after the purchase. Several studies on quality adjustment are available; most suggest that BLS methods fail to capture a wide range of quality changes. However, these studies focus on a relatively few categories of the CPI—possibly those where the quality bias is presumed largest—making it difficult to assess the magnitude of the overall quality bias in the CPI.

New Products

New products, such as air conditioners in the 1950s or videocassette recorders in the 1980s, usually decline sharply in price during the first years they are available for sale. But these products are not usually included in the CPI basket until years after their introduction, and so the CPI never records their initial price declines.

Outlet Substitution

Over time, consumers may change their shopping patterns, shifting from high-priced to low-priced outlets, where the quality of service is often lower. Current methods assume that all of the difference in price between high- and low-priced outlets reflects differences in the quality of service. To the extent this assumption is not appropriate, current methods overlook one source of price decline.

To sum up, recent research has identified several possible sources of bias in the CPI. A commission appointed by the Senate Finance Committee recently reported on these sources of bias. The magnitudes of some of these biases are based on hard estimates around which there is broad agreement. On the magnitudes of other biases, however, consensus has yet to emerge.

Implications of CPI Bias for Other Economic Statistics

The CPI is used as an input for calculating many other economic statistics, and therefore the potential biases in its measurement have consequences beyond our view of inflation. The accuracy of many economic measures is critically dependent on how well we measure price changes. . . . Most of the biases in the CPI result in an overdeflation, of GDP, biasing real output growth downward. . . . Productivity is also calculated from real GDP, so overestimates of CPI inflation would lead us to underestimate productivity growth. The accuracy of many other statistics, such as real median household income and real earnings, that are directly converted from nominal values by the CPI would also be affected.

Although removing CPI bias would change some of the details of our views of productivity and income trends, it would not radically alter our views on such fundamental issues as the productivity slowdown that began around 1973 or the increase in income inequality over the past two decades. Although bias in the CPI would mean that real growth and productivity have been higher recently than official measures indicate, that bias would also apply to longer term measures of growth and productivity. To explain away the decrease in productivity growth, the CPI would have to be not merely biased but *increasingly* biased over time. It is certainly plausible that the increased share of the service sector in the economy has made it harder to measure quality, with the consequence that the approximately 2-percentage-point estimate of the slowdown in productivity overestimates the true reduction. Yet it would require an implausibly large increase in CPI bias to explain away the entire slowdown as an artifact of mismeasurement.

Similarly, CPI bias might be depressing measures of real wages, but that does not change the fact that real wages today are growing more slowly than in the 1950s and 1960s. Also, the increase in income inequality . . . is one widely discussed phenomenon that is completely unaffected by CPI measurement. . . .

Discussion Questions

1. Explain how the consumer price index ignores the ability of consumers to substitute among goods.

2. Why does the proper measurement of inflation require distinguishing between changes in the underlying price of a good and changes in quality?

3. Would the removal of errors in the consumer price index show that there was no productivity slowdown after 1973?

4. Would the removal of these errors show that there has been no increase in income inequality in the past 25 years?

CHAPTER 8

Money and the Banking System

Chapter Profile

Money performs several basic functions. It serves as a medium of exchange, a standard of value, and a store of value. The money supply, narrowly defined, is composed of coins, currency, demand deposits, and other checkable deposits. Economists include demand (and other checkable) deposits as part of the money supply because you can pay for goods and services about as easily by check as with cash. In addition to this narrow definition of money, broader definitions include savings and time deposits (also money market mutual fund balances and money market deposit accounts). It is not easy to draw a line between money and nonmoney, since many assets have some of the characteristics of money.

Commercial banks have two primary functions. First, they hold demand (and other checkable) deposits and permit checks to be drawn on them. Second, they lend money to firms and individuals. Most of our money supply is not coin and paper currency but demand (and other checkable) deposits. This money is created by banks.

Whereas the earliest banks held reserves equal to deposits, modern banks practice fractional-reserve banking. That is, their reserves equal only a fraction of their deposits. The Federal Reserve System requires every commercial bank (and other thrift institutions with checkable deposits) to hold a certain percentage of its deposits as reserves. The major purpose of these legal reserve requirements is to control the money supply.

Banks have become much safer than 60 or 100 years ago, in part because of better management and regulation as well as the government's stated willingness to insure and stand behind their deposits. However, bank failures still occur, and bank regulation is not as stringent as it might be. The United States experienced serious failures in the S & L industry in the 1980s; Japan suffered a much larger banking crisis a little later. Poor government policies worsened both.

*The banking system as a whole can increase its demand deposits by an amount equal to its excess reserves divided by the legally required ratio of reserves to deposits. Thus, if excess reserves in the banking system equal a certain amount, the banking system as a whole can increase demand deposits by the amount of the excess reserves divided by the legally required ratio of reserves to deposits.

*If there is a deficiency in reserves in the banking system, the system as a whole must decrease demand deposits by the amount of this deficiency divided by the legally

*The starred items pertain to material covered in Exploring Further.

required ratio of reserves to deposits. Demand deposits are decreased by banks' selling securities or refusing to renew loans, just as demand deposits are increased by banks' making loans and investments.

Concepts for Review

money
coins
currency
demand deposits
fractional-reserve banking
FDIC

M1
M2
legal reserve requirements
excess reserves
Federal Reserve System

Completion Questions

1. Bank A has no excess reserves. Its balance sheet follows. (All figures are in millions of dollars.)

Assets		Liabilities and net worth	
Reserves	20	Demand deposits	100
Loans and securities	_____	Net worth	30

Its loans and securities equal _____. The reserve requirement is

_____ percent.

2. Bank B has excess reserves of $3 million. Its balance sheet follows. (All figures are in millions of dollars.)

Assets		Liabilities and net worth	
Reserves	_____	Demand deposits	90
Loans and securities	_____	Net worth	10

If the reserve requirement is 20 percent, bank B's reserves equal

_____, and its loans and securities equal _____.

3. _____ is when banks hold reserves that are much less than the amount they owe their depositors.

4. When William Malone pays $8 for a haircut, this is an example of the use of money as a _____. When Mary Malone keeps $400 in her checking account, this is an example of the use of money as a(n)

_____. When John Malone announces that he receives $6 an hour as a lifeguard, this is an example of the use of money as a(n)

_____.

5. A commercial bank can lend the amount by which its reserves are in excess of the _____.

6. The higher is the required ratio of reserves to deposits, the (larger, smaller) _____ is the amount by which the banking system can increase the money supply on the basis of a given amount of excess reserves.

*7. If there is a $10,000 decrease in reserves (and the required ratio of reserves to deposits is 1/6), the entire banking system reduces demand deposits by _____ if there are no excess reserves.

8. The _____ can influence the money supply by influencing the amount of reserves and the legal reserve requirements.

9. Banks tend to hold large excess reserves when _____ or _____.

10. The _____ insures the accounts of depositors in practically all banks so that, even if a bank fails, the depositor will get his or her money back up to _____, as of 2000.

*11. When excess _____ are made available to the banking system, the system as a whole can increase _____ by an amount equal to the amount of excess reserves multiplied by the _____ of the required ratio of reserves to deposits. For instance, if the banking system has excess reserves of $50,000 and the required ratio of reserves to deposits is 1/8, to determine how much the banking system can increase demand deposits, we must divide _____ by _____. The increase in demand deposits is _____.

*12. The narrow definition of money is known as _____; it includes _____, _____, and _____.

*13. To obtain the total decrease in demand deposits resulting from a deficiency in reserves, divide the deficiency by the _____.

14. A bank creates money by lending or investing its _____ reserves. If banks had to keep reserves equal to their deposits, they (could, could not) _____ create money.

*The starred items pertain to material covered in Exploring Further.

True-False

_____ 1. If bank X's loans and securities are higher than bank Y's, bank X's legally required reserves must be higher than bank Y's.

_____ 2. If the reserve requirement is 20 percent, this means that a bank belonging to the Federal Reserve System must maintain legal reserves equal to 20 percent of its assets.

_____ 3. If Marcia Jones pays back a $1,000 loan from her cousin, this results in a $1,000 decline in the money supply.

_____ 4. If Marcia Jones pays back a $1,000 loan from the First National Bank, the supply of money is reduced by $1,000 when she pays by check or cash.

_____ 5. The Fed sets reserve requirements just barely above the level needed to keep banks safe under ordinary business conditions.

_____ 6. A bank may have less than 20 percent of its total demand deposits in cash reserves.

_____ 7. The most important reason for legal reserve requirements is to keep banks from failing.

_____ *8. To obtain the total increase in demand deposits that can result from a certain amount of excess reserves, divide the amount of excess reserves by the legally required ratio of reserves to deposits.

_____ 9. Commercial banks invest in local, state, and federal government bonds.

_____ 10. Many banks experience an increase in reserves at about the same time.

_____ 11. The safety of a bank depends entirely on the level of its legal reserves.

_____ 12. One noteworthy characteristic of any bank's balance sheet is that a very large percentage of its liabilities must be paid on demand.

_____ 13. The earliest banks held reserves equal to the amount they owed depositors and were simply places where people stored their gold.

_____ *14. The effect on the level of demand deposits of a $10,000 shortfall in reserves is larger than the creation of $10,000 in excess reserves.

_____ 15. The U.S. S & L crisis as well as the Japanese banking crisis was caused in part by bad loans on overvalued assets and by rising interest rates.

*The starred items pertain to material covered in Exploring Further.

Multiple Choice

1. The Third National Bank has demand deposits of $1 million, and the legal reserve requirement is 15 percent. If its excess reserves are equal to its legal reserves, its total reserves are

   a. $100,000.
   b. $150,000.
   c. $300,000.
   d. not obtainable from the information given.
   e. none of the above.

2. The Fourth National Bank has demand deposits of $20 million and excess reserves of $1 million. Then, the legal reserve requirement is raised by 5 percentage points, after which the bank no longer has any excess reserves. The new legal reserve requirement is

   a. 10 percent.
   b. 15 percent.
   c. 20 percent.
   d. not obtainable from the information given.
   e. none of the above.

3. Bank X has excess reserves of $2,000. Then, Shirley Morrison deposits $1,000 in cash in bank X, which sends this amount to the Federal Reserve bank. If the legal reserve requirement is 20 percent, bank X's excess reserves now are

   a. $2,000.
   b. $2,200.
   c. $2,800.
   d. $3,000.
   e. none of the above.

4. In the previous question, bank X's total reserves increase by the following amount because of Ms. Morrison's deposit and bank X's deposit at the Fed:

   a. $200.
   b. $800.
   c. $1,000.
   d. not obtainable from the information given.
   e. none of the above.

5. Which of the following five is the best measure of the money supply?

   a. The U.S. gold reserves
   b. Coins and currency in circulation
   c. U.S. bank reserves
   d. The GDP of the United States
   e. M1

6. M2 includes all the following *except*

   a. currency.
   b. savings accounts.
   c. money market accounts.
   d. credit cards.
   e. time accounts under $100,000.

7. An increase in legal reserve requirements is likely to have the least effect on the quantity of demand deposits if banks have

   a. no excess reserves.
   b. excess reserves of $1,000.
   c. excess reserves of $10,000.
   d. excess reserves of $10 million.
   e. excess reserves of $1 billion.

8. If a commercial bank receives a deposit of $15,000 and it maintains the legally required reserves (which are 20 percent of deposits), it can lend against this deposit

 a. $2,500.   d. $15,000.
 b. $5,000.   e. all of the above.
 c. $12,000.

9. A bank can increase its reserves by

 a. selling securities.
 b. creating currency.
 c. decreasing employee vacations.
 d. all of the above.
 e. none of the above.

10. The major purpose of legal reserve requirements is to

 a. control interest rates.
 b. control the money supply.
 c. avoid simultaneous contraction.
 d. satisfy demands in case there is a run on the bank.
 e. none of the above.

11. The safety of a bank depends on

 a. the level of its reserves.
 b. the wisdom of its loans and investments.
 c. the amount of its assets that can readily be turned into cash.
 d. all of the above.
 e. none of the above.

Discussion and Extension Questions

1. Stephen Neal, former chair of the House Banking Committee, contends "the Federal Reserve has played politics in the past." He cites the big increase in money growth during the 1972 election year, calling it "destructive." Why would the Fed want to increase the money supply in an election year? Does the Fed agree with this contention? What do you think?

2. Secondary reserves are securities held by banks that have a ready market and can be sold easily and quickly. Suppose your local banker says that the secondary reserves held by the bank consist of real estate and stock in a South African mining company. Would you be concerned? Why or why not?

3. "Commercial banks should have to pay high interest rates on money left in checking accounts. It is inefficient, unjust, and anticompetitive for them not to do so." Comment and evaluate.

4. So long as there is no panic and the bank makes sound loans and investments, could most banks get along with less reserves than they hold at present? Why do commercial banks hold as much in the way of reserves as they do?

5. Why does the Federal Reserve impose legal reserve requirements? Are the banks safer than they were 50 or 100 years ago? Why or why not?

6. Suppose that someone receives $10,000 in newly printed currency and deposits it in his bank.

   a. Can this bank create $50,000 of additional new money, if the legal reserve requirement is 16²/3 percent?
   b. Can this bank create $8,333 in new money? If so, how?
   c. Can the banking system as a whole create $50,000 of additional new money?

*7. a. Suppose that the legally required ratio of reserves to deposits is 20 percent. If there are no excess reserves and the total reserves of the banking system are reduced by $5 billion, what is the effect on demand deposits?

   b. If the legal reserve requirement is 20 percent, what effect do currency withdrawals or excess reserves have on the amount of demand deposits that the banks can support?

Problems

1. Suppose that the balance sheet (in millions of dollars) of Crooked Arrow National Bank is currently as follows:

Assets		*Liabilities and net worth*	
Reserves	0.5	Demand deposits	2.5
Loans and securities	3.0	Net worth	1.0

The bank is legally required to hold reserves equal to at least 20 percent of its demand deposits.

*The starred item pertains to material covered in Exploring Further.

a. Suppose the depositors withdraw $100,000. Indicate the amounts of the individual items on the bank's balance sheet after this withdrawal.

Assets (millions of dollars)		Liabilities and net worth (millions of dollars)	
Reserves	_____	Demand deposits	_____
Loans and securities	_____	Net worth	_____

b. Will the bank have the required legal reserves after the withdrawal? If not, what courses of action are open to it?

2. Suppose that depositors deposited $100,000 of new money in the Crooked Arrow National Bank, rather than withdrew $100,000.

a. What effect does this have on the bank's reserves? By how much can the bank increase its loans?

b. Suppose that Crooked Arrow National Bank lends out the maximum amount it can under these circumstances. It lends this amount to Joan Brown, who uses it to buy a piece of equipment from the Ace Machine Tool Company, which deposits it in the First National Bank. Show the effect of this transaction together with the $100,000 deposit on the balance sheet of the Crooked Arrow National Bank by filling in the blanks.

Crooked Arrow National Bank

Change in reserves	_____
Change in demand deposits	_____
Change in loans and securities	_____
Change in net worth	_____

c. Show the effect of the transaction in part b on the balance sheet of the First National Bank by filling in the blanks.

First National Bank

Change in reserves	_____
Change in demand deposits	_____
Change in loans and securities	_____
Change in net worth	_____

d. Can the First National Bank increase its loans? If so, by how much?

e. Suppose that the First National Bank lends the maximum amount (according to part d) to William Cooper, who buys land from Jane Jones, who deposits the amount to her account at the Second National Bank. Show the effect of this transaction together with Brown's deposit on the balance sheet of the First National Bank by filling in the blanks.

First National Bank

Change in reserves	_____
Change in demand deposits	_____
Change in loans and securities	_____
Change in net worth	_____

f. Show the effect of the transaction in part e on the balance sheet of the Second National Bank by filling in the blanks.

Second National Bank

Change in reserves	_____
Change in demand deposits	_____
Change in loans and securities	_____
Change in net worth	_____

g. Can the Second National Bank increase its loans? If so, by how much?

h. How much bank money can the banking system as a whole support on the basis of $100,000 of new reserves?

3. a. Suppose that the Federal Reserve reduces the reserve requirement from 20 to 15 percent while the bank's balance sheet is as shown in problem 1. After the reduction, does the bank have excess reserves? If so, how much?

b. Suppose that the Federal Reserve increases the reserve requirement from 20 to 25 percent while the bank's balance sheet is as shown in problem 1. After the increase, is the bank be short of the legally required reserves? If so, by how much?

4. Bank C lends $5,000 to a depositor, Mary Monroe, by crediting her checking account balance with a $5,000 deposit.

a. What is the effect of this transaction on the bank's assets?

b. What is the effect of this transaction on the nation's money supply (defined as M1)? What is its effect on M2?

c. If Mary Monroe transfers the $5,000 from her checking account to her savings account at the bank, what is the effect on M1? What is the effect on M2?

*5. Suppose that commercial bank reserves are $50 billion, the legal reserve requirement is 20 percent, and currency (and coins) in the hands of the public is $10 billion.

   a.   If there are no excess reserves, what does M1 equal?

   b.   If commercial bank reserves fall to $49 billion while currency in the hands of the public increases to $11 billion, what is M1 if the other assumptions remain valid?

   c.   Suppose the reserve requirement increases to 25 percent (but the other assumptions in part b remain valid). What is M1?

6. Bank G has the following balance sheet:

Assets (millions of dollars)		Liabilities and net worth (millions of dollars)	
Reserves	30	Demand deposits	80
Loans and securities	70	Net worth	20

   a.   Suppose the legal reserve requirement is 15 percent. Indicate what bank G's balance sheet will look like if it makes all the new loans it can (and if all the money it lends is checked out to depositors at other banks).

Assets (millions of dollars)		Liabilities and net worth (millions of dollars)	
Reserves	_____	Demand deposits	_____
Loans and securities	_____	Net worth	_____

   b.   Suppose the legal reserve requirement is 20 percent. Indicate what bank G's balance sheet will look like if it makes all the new loans it can make (and if all the money it lends is checked out to depositors at other banks).

Assets (millions of dollars)		Liabilities and net worth (millions of dollars)	
Reserves	_____	Demand deposits	_____
Loans and securities	_____	Net worth	_____

*The starred item pertains to material covered in Exploring Further.

*7. The consolidated balance sheet for all commercial banks in the economy is as follows:

Assets (billions of dollars)		Liabilities and net worth (billions of dollars)	
Reserves	23	Demand deposits	99
Loans and securities	86	Net worth	10

Suppose the public deposits $1 billion in currency in the banks and the banks send the $1 billion to the Federal Reserve.

a. Suppose the legal reserve requirement is 15 percent. Indicate what the consolidated balance sheet for all commercial banks will look like if the banking system makes all the new loans it can.

Assets (billions of dollars)		Liabilities and net worth (billions of dollars)	
Reserves	_____	Demand deposits	_____
Loans and securities	_____	Net worth	_____

b. Suppose the legal reserve requirement is 20 percent. Indicate what the consolidated balance sheet for all commercial banks will look like if the banking system makes all the new loans it can.

Assets (billions of dollars)		Liabilities and net worth (billions of dollars)	
Reserves	_____	Demand deposits	_____
Loans and securities	_____	Net worth	_____

*The starred item pertains to material covered in Exploring Further.

Answers

Completion Questions

1. $110 million, 20   2. $21 million, $79 million   3. Fractional-reserve banking
4. medium of exchange, store of value, standard of value   5. legally required
reserves   6. smaller   7. $60,000   8. Federal Reserve System   9. loans seem to
be very risky, interest rates are very low   10. FDIC, $100,000   11. reserves,
demand deposits, reciprocal, $50,000, 1/8, $400,000   12. M1, coins, currency,
demand deposits   13. the legally required reserve ratio   14. excess, could not

True-False

1. False   2. False   3. False   4. True   5. False   6. True   7. False
8. True   9. True   10. True   11. False   12. True   13. True   14. False
15. True

Multiple Choice

1. c   2. d   3. c   4. c   5. e   6. d   7. e   8. c   9. a   10. b   11. d

Problems

1. a.

| *Assets* | | *Liabilities and net worth* | |
(millions of dollars)		*(millions of dollars)*	
Reserves	0.4	Demand deposits	2.4
Loans and securities	3.0	Net worth	1.0

   b. No. It can refuse to renew loans or sell securities.

2. a. Reserves will increase by $100,000. The bank can increase its loans by
$80,000.

   b.

Crooked Arrow National Bank

Change in reserves	+$20,000
Change in demand deposits	+$100,000
Change in loans and securities	+$80,000
Change in net worth	None

   c.

First National Bank

Change in reserves	+$80,000
Change in demand deposits	+$80,000
Change in loans and securities	None
Change in net worth	None

d. Yes. $64,000.

e.
First National Bank

Change in reserves	+$16,000
Change in demand deposits	+$80,000
Change in loans and securities	+$64,000
Change in net worth	None

f.
Second National Bank

Change in reserves	+$64,000
Change in demand deposits	+$64,000
Change in loans and securities	None
Change in net worth	None

g. Yes. $51,200.
h. $500,000.
3. a. Yes. $125,000.
   b. Yes. $125,000.
4. a. They increase by $5,000.
   b. Both M1 and M2 rise by $5,000.
   c. M1 decreases by $5,000, but there is no effect on M2.
5. a. $260 billion.
   b. $256 billion.
   c. $207 billion.

6.   *(billions of dollars)*

a.	Reserves	12	Demand deposits	80
	Loans and securities	88	Net worth	20
b.	Reserves	16	Demand deposits	80
	Loans and securities	84	Net worth	20

7.   *(billions of dollars)*

a.	Reserves	24	Demand deposits	160
	Loans and securities	146	Net worth	10
b.	Reserves	24	Demand deposits	120
	Loans and securities	106	Net worth	10

CHAPTER 9

The Federal Reserve and
Monetary Policy

Chapter Profile

The Federal Reserve System is responsible for regulating and controlling the money supply. Established in 1913, the Federal Reserve System is composed of the commercial banks, 12 regional Federal Reserve Banks, and the Federal Reserve Board, which coordinates the activities of the system. The Federal Reserve is the central bank of the United States and has great discretionary power over monetary policy.

Monetary policy is concerned with the money supply and interest rates. Its purpose is to attain and maintain full employment without excessive inflation. When a recession seems imminent, the monetary authorities are likely to increase the money supply and reduce interest rates. On the other hand, when the economy is in danger of overheating and inflation threatens, the monetary authorities are likely to rein in the money supply and push up interest rates.

Monetary policy and fiscal policy are influenced by Congress, the Treasury, and other segments of the government and the public at large. The chief responsibility for the formulation of monetary policy lies with the Federal Reserve Board and the Federal Open Market Committee (FOMC). To a very large extent, monetary policy operates by changing the quantity of bank reserves.

The most important tool of monetary policy is open market operations, which involve buying and selling government securities in the open market by the Federal Reserve. When the Fed buys government securities, this increases bank reserves. When the Fed sells government securities, this reduces bank reserves.

The Fed can also tighten or ease money by increasing or decreasing the discount rate or the legal reserve requirements. An increase in either rate reduces the money supply, while a decrease in either increases the money supply.

Concepts for Review

monetary policy
Federal Reserve Board
Federal Open Market Committee
discount rate

central banks
Federal Reserve Banks
legal reserve requirements
open market operations

Completion Questions

1. If the monetary authorities think that a recession is developing, they tend to (increase, decrease) _____ the excess reserves of the banks.

2. When a serious inflation seems imminent, the monetary authorities are most likely to (increase, decrease) _____ the rate of growth of the money supply and (increase, decrease) _____ interest rates.

3. Increases in the legal reserve requirement are likely to (increase, reduce) _____ the amount of demand deposits the banking system can support.

4. The _____ is composed of the Federal Reserve Board plus the presidents of five Federal Reserve Banks.

5. Loans to commercial banks are _____ on the consolidated balance sheet of the Federal Reserve Banks.

6. When the economy is at appreciably less than full employment, many economists believe that increases in the money supply tend to (increase, decrease) _____ real GDP, and decreases in the money supply tend to (increase, decrease) _____ real GDP with relatively little effect on the _____ level.

7. As full employment is approached, increases in the money supply tend to affect the _____ level, as well as real _____. And once full employment is reached, increases in the money supply result primarily in (increases, decreases) _____ in the price level, since real output cannot (increase, decrease) _____ appreciably.

8. If the banking system has $1 billion in _____, it can support $6.25 billion in demand deposits when the legal reserve requirement is 16 percent. It can support only $5 billion in demand deposits when the legal reserve requirement is 20 percent. Thus, increases in the legal reserve requirements tend to (increase, decrease) _____ the amount of demand deposits the banking system can support.

9. If the banking system has $1 billion in reserves and $8 billion in demand deposits, there are no _____ when the legal reserve requirement is 12.5 percent. If the Federal Reserve lowers the legal reserve requirement to 10 percent, the amount of legally required reserves is _____ million. The banks then have _____

million in excess reserves, which means that they can (increase, decrease)

_____ the amount of their demand deposits.

True-False

_____ 1. The discount rate is the rate of interest that the state governments pay member banks on their reserves kept with the Fed.

_____ 2. The excess reserves of the commercial banks are increased by $1/r$ dollars (where r is the legal reserve requirement) for every dollar of government securities the Fed buys from the public.

_____ 3. A reduction in the discount rate has a direct effect on member bank reserves; it increases them in much the same way that open market purchases of government securities by the Fed increases them.

_____ 4. Banks are expected to borrow from the Federal Reserve for only short periods.

_____ 5. The policies of the Federal Reserve are always dictated by the Treasury's financing needs.

_____ 6. Open market operations are the most important techniques used by the Fed to control the money supply.

_____ 7. Although the Federal Reserve is responsible to Congress, Congress has established no clear guidelines for its behavior. Therefore, the Federal Reserve has had wide discretionary powers over monetary policy.

_____ 8. The commercial banks that are members of the Federal Reserve System can borrow from the Federal Reserve when their reserves are low (if the Fed is willing).

_____ 9. Changes in the discount rate have an effect on people's expectations.

_____ 10. There is often a long lag between an action by the Fed and its effect on the economy.

_____ 11. When the Fed buys government securities, bank reserves decrease.

_____ 12. Often the Fed is criticized for paying too little attention to the long lags between its actions and their effects on the economy.

_____ 13. In 2001 and 2002, the Fed repeatedly increased interest rates in fear of inflation.

_____ 14. The Fed reacted to the 1929 and 1987 stock market drops with very similar policies.

Multiple Choice

1. If the Federal Reserve sells $50 million of U.S. government securities, this will result in

   a. an increase of $50 million in member bank reserves.
   b. a decrease of $50 million in member bank reserves.
   c. an increase of more than $50 million in member bank reserves.
   d. a decrease of more than $50 million in member bank reserves.
   e. leaving member bank reserves unaffected.

2. If the Federal Reserve increases the legal reserve requirement from 15 to 20 percent and this reduces excess reserves by $5 billion, total demand deposits in the economy must equal

   a. $50 billion.   d. $150 billion.
   b. $75 billion.   e. none of the above.
   c. $100 billion.

3. If the legal reserve requirement is 20 percent and commercial banks borrow $1 billion from the Federal Reserve, then immediately

   a. their reserves fall by $1 billion.
   b. their reserves fall by $5 billion.
   c. their reserves increase by $1 billion.
   d. their reserves increase by $5 billion.
   e. none of the above.

4. If the public wants to hold $1 in currency for every $3 in demand deposits and the legal reserve requirement is 0.1, an increase of $1 million in the money supply (M1) results in an increase in the amount of currency in the hands of the public of

   a. $100,000.   d. $400,000.
   b. $250,000.   e. none of the above.
   c. $333,333.

   (Assume that demand deposits are the only checkable deposits.)

5. If total demand deposits equal $2 billion, bank reserves equal $500 million, and excess reserves equal $100 million, the legal reserve requirement is

   a. 15 percent.   d. 25 percent.
   b. $16^2/3$ percent.   e. 30 percent.
   c. 20 percent.

6. The most important method used by the Federal Reserve Board to influence bank reserves is

   a. changing legal reserve requirements.
   b. issuing new government securities.
   c. open market operations.
   d. changing the discount rate.
   e. congressional testimony.

7. The major effect of an increase in the discount rate is

   a.   on people's expectations.   d.   an increase in the prices
   b.   easier money.   of stocks and bonds.
   c.   an increase in reserves.   e.   increasing bank loans.

8. The Federal Reserve cannot

   a.   provide facilities for check collection.
   b.   lend money to banks.
   c.   change the discount rate.
   d.   regulate mortgage terms and installment contracts.
   e.   do any of the above.

9. If banks have little or no excess reserves and the legal reserve requirement is
   raised, they may

   a.   sell securities.   d.   all of the above.
   b.   refuse to renew loans.   e.   none of the above.
   c.   reduce their demand deposits.

10. The discount rate

   a.   can be increased or decreased by the Fed.
   b.   usually is changed only once or twice a decade.
   c.   encourages borrowing if it is increased.
   d.   determines how much the Fed can borrow from the banks.
   e.   all of the above.

Discussion and Extension Questions

1. During World War II and up until 1951, the Federal Reserve agreed with the U.S.
   Treasury to keep the interest rates on Treasury bonds low and stable so as to keep
   the Treasury's borrowing costs as low as possible.

   a.   Explain how the Federal Reserve might accomplish this goal.
   b.   Do you think that such an agreement might limit the Federal Reserve's
        ability to counteract undesirable swings in aggregate demand? Explain
        your response.

2. Governor Meyer of the Federal Reserve Board said in an October 2000 speech
   that, "The motivation for granting independence to central banks is to insulate
   the conduct of monetary policy from political interference, especially interference motivated by the pressures of elections to deliver short-term gains
   irrespective of longer-term costs. . . . Even a limited degree of independence,
   taken literally, could be viewed as inconsistent with democratic ideals and, in
   addition, might leave the central bank without appropriate incentives to carry
   out its responsibilities. Therefore, independence has to be balanced with
   accountability." Comment on this quote.

3. According to Thomas Dernburg and Duncan McDougall, "The initiative in conducting open market operations is firmly in the hands of the Fed. In contrast, the effect of a change in the discount rate depends on the unpredictable response of commercial banks." Comment and evaluate.

4. Suppose that the Fed buys $1 million of government securities from Bethlehem Steel. What is the effect on the quantity of bank reserves? Suppose it sells $1 million of government securities to Bethlehem Steel. What is the effect on the quantity of bank reserves?

5. What is the effect on the amount of demand deposits of increases in the legal reserve requirements? Use a numerical example in your response.

6. What is the effect of changes in the discount rate? What variables has the Fed looked at to determine whether to change the discount rate?

7. Use a newspaper or the Internet (www.federalreserve.gov/fomc/#calendars) to find the next meeting of the FOMC. What are the current economic conditions of concern to the Fed? What statistics is it probably watching to measure the health of the U.S. economy? Does the Fed currently have a tight money, loose money, or neutral bias? Try to predict what the Fed will do and see how accurate your prediction was.

Problems

1. Suppose that the Crooked Arrow National Bank has the following balance sheet (in millions of dollars):

Assets		Liabilities and net worth	
Reserves	0.5	Demand deposits	2.5
Loans and securities	3.0	Net worth	1.0

   a. If the legal reserve requirement is 20 percent, does the bank have any excess reserves? If so, how much?

   b. Suppose that the Fed lowers the reserve requirement, with the result that the bank has excess reserves of $25,000. What is the new legal reserve requirement?

   c. Suppose that the Fed lowers the reserve requirement, with the result that the bank has excess reserves of $100,000. What is the new legal reserve requirement?

2. Suppose that on May 1, 2005, the Federal Reserve sells $100 million of U.S. government securities to the public, which pays for them by check.

    a.   Show below the effect of this sale on the balance sheets of the Federal Reserve and the commercial banks:

Federal Reserve

Assets		Liabilities	
Government securities	_____	Member bank reserves	_____

Commercial banks (balance sheet for all banks combined)

Assets		Liabilities	
Reserves	_____	Demand deposits	_____

    b.   Does this transaction have any effect on the balance sheets of the members of the public who bought the bonds? If so, what is the effect?

    c.   If the commercial banks had no excess reserves before the sale of these bonds, do they have any excess reserves after the sale? Do they have less than the legally required reserves after the sale?

    d.   Suppose the Fed bought, rather than sold, $100 million of U.S. government securities and these securities were bought from the general public. Would this transaction result in an increase or decrease in member bank reserves? By how much would reserves increase or decrease? Is this the sort of result that the Fed would have desired during the period in 1981 when it was trying hard to fight inflation?

3. Suppose that the banking system has no excess reserves, total reserves are $50 billion, and total demand deposits are $200 billion. Suppose that the following graph shows the net (of repayments) amount that the banking system borrows from the Federal Reserve if the discount rate equals the levels shown there.

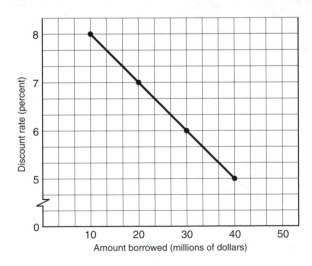

a. How much will the banking system borrow if the discount rate is 7 percent? 5 percent? What is the legal reserve requirement?
b. If the Fed wants to increase the money supply by $40 million, what discount rate should it set? (Assume that banks maintain no excess reserves.)
c. If the Fed wants to have the same effect on bank reserves as if it bought $20 million worth of government securities in the open market, what discount rate should it set?

4. From the following figures, construct the consolidated balance sheet of the 12 Federal Reserve Banks. (All figures are in billions of dollars.)

Gold certificates	10	Reserves of banks	30
Other liabilities and net worth	5	Other assets	10
Securities	100	Treasury deposits	5
Outstanding Federal Reserve Notes	90	Loans to commercial banks	10

5. Given the consolidated balance sheet in problem 4, what effect does each of the following transactions (taken by itself) have on this balance sheet?

a. The Federal Reserve sells $100 million in securities to the public (which pays by check).
b. The Federal Reserve lowers the discount rate; this results in banks borrowing $50 million from the Fed.
c. The U.S. government buys $1 billion worth of aerospace equipment, which is paid for by checks on the Treasury's deposits at the Fed.

6. Given that each of the transactions described in problem 5 occurs (separately), what is the effect in each case on the potential money supply if the legal reserve requirement is 20 percent?

7. Suppose that the Federal Reserve purchases $100 million of U.S. government securities from *commercial banks.*

a. What will be the effect on the balance sheet of the Federal Reserve Banks?
b. What will be the effect on the balance sheet of the commercial banks?
c. What is the effect on the potential money supply if the legal reserve requirement is 20 percent?

8. Suppose that the Federal Reserve sells $100 million of U.S. government securities to *commercial banks.*

a. What will be the effect on the balance sheet of the Federal Reserve banks?
b. What will be the effect on the balance sheet of the commercial banks?
c. What is the effect on the potential money supply if the legal reserve requirement is 25 percent?

9. The public wants to hold $1 in currency for every $3 in demand deposits. The legal reserve requirement is 20 percent and commercial banks hold no excess reserves. There are no checkable deposits other than demand deposits.

    a. If the Federal Reserve wants to reduce the quantity of money by $2 billion, how much of a decrease must occur in demand deposits?

    b. To obtain this decrease in demand deposits, by how much must bank reserves decline?

    c. To reduce bank reserves by this amount, how many billions of dollars worth of government securities should the Federal Reserve sell? (Be careful. Because of the $2 billion decrease in the quantity of money, the public wants to hold $0.5 billion less in currency.)

10. The public wants to hold $1 in currency for every $3 in demand deposits. The legal reserve requirement is 25 percent and commercial banks hold no excess reserves. There are no checkable deposits other than demand deposits.

    a. If the Federal Reserve wants to increase the quantity of money by $6 billion, how much of an increase must occur in demand deposits?

    b. To obtain this increase in demand deposits, by how much must bank reserves increase?

    c. To increase bank reserves by this amount, how many billions of dollars worth of government securities should the Federal Reserve buy?

Answers

Completion Questions
1. increase   2. decrease, increase   3. reduce   4. Federal Open Market Committee   5. assets   6. increase, decrease, price   7. price, output, increases, increase   8. total reserves, decrease   9. excess reserves, $800, $200, increase

True-False
1. False   2. False   3. False   4. True   5. False   6. True   7. True   8. True   9. True   10. True   11. False   12. True   13. False   14. False

Multiple Choice
1. b   2. c   3. c   4. b   5. c   6. c   7. a   8. d   9. d   10. a

Problems
1. a. No. Its reserves are just equal to the legally required amount.
      b. 19 percent.
      c. 16 percent.

2. a.

Federal Reserve *(millions of dollars)*

Assets		Liabilities	
Government securities	−100	Member bank reserves	−100

Commercial banks *(millions of dollars)*

Assets		Liabilities	
Reserves	−100	Demand deposits	−100

    b. Yes. The public has $100 million more in U.S. government securities and $100 million less in demand deposits.

    c. No. Yes.

    d. An increase. $100 million. No.

3. a. $20 million. $40 million. 25 percent.

    b. 8 percent.

    c. 7 percent.

4.

Assets		Liabilities and net worth	
Gold certificates	10	Outstanding Federal	
Securities	100	Reserve Notes	90
Loans to commercial		Reserves of banks	30
banks	10	Treasury deposits	5
Other assets	10	Other liabilities and	
	130	net worth	5
			130

5. a. Securities, − $100 million; Reserves of banks, − $100 million

    b. Loans to commercial banks, + $50 million; Reserves of banks, + $50 million

    c. Treasury deposits, − $1 billion; Reserves of banks, + $1 billion

6. a. It decreases by $500 million.

    b. It increases by $250 million.

    c. It increases by $5 billion.

7. a. Securities, + $100 million; Reserves of banks, + $100 million

    b. Securities, − $100 million; Reserves, + $100 million

    c. It increases by $500 million.

8. a. Securities, − $100 million; Reserves of banks, − $100 million

    b. Securities, + $100 million; Reserves, − $100 million

    c. It decreases by $400 million.

9. a. $1.5 billion.

    b. $300 million.

    c. $0.8 billion (0.3 to banks plus 0.5 to public).

10. a. $4.5 billion.

    b. $1.125 billion.

    c. $2.625 billion (1.125 from banks and 1.5 from public).

CHAPTER 10

Supply Shocks and Inflation

Chapter Profile

The Phillips curve shows the relationship between the rate of increase of the price level and the level of unemployment. If the Phillips curve remains fixed, it poses an awkward dilemma for policy makers. If they reduce unemployment, inflation increases; if they reduce inflation, unemployment increases. During 1955–69, there was a fairly close relationship between the inflation rate and the unemployment rate. Then, something unforeseen by most economists occurred. The inflation and unemployment rates subsequently did not conform at all closely to the relationship that prevailed in the 1960s. Both the unemployment rate and the inflation rate tended to be much higher than in the 1960s; and in the 1990s, both unemployment and inflation fell back to the low levels of the 1960s. In fact, by the end of the 1990s, disinflation (falling inflation) and deflation (negative inflation) were major concerns. Historically, these are associated with falling aggregate demand and, therefore, falling sales, profits, jobs, and incomes. In the 1990s, however, this was the result of rising aggregate supply creating simultaneously low inflation and unemployment.

A supply shock can disrupt the relationship between unemployment and inflation shown by the Phillips curve. Major changes in the availability of important resources such as oil, in crop yields, or even in the cost of labor caused by expectations of inflation can alter the ability of the economy to support production and jobs without significant inflation. Such a shift in aggregate supply can cause both unemployment and inflation to rise or fall together instead of moving against each other.

The accelerationists, led by Milton Friedman, believe that the downward-sloping Phillips curve is only a short-run relationship. In the long run, they believe that it is vertical. In their view, expansionary policies that result in inflation will reduce unemployment only temporarily, with the result that the government, if it sets out to reduce unemployment to below its natural level, must permit higher and higher rates of inflation.

To reduce the inflation rate (at a given unemployment rate), governments have tried price and wage controls. Although a few economists favor such controls during peacetime, most do not agree. Such controls are likely to distort the allocation of resources, be difficult to administer, and run counter to our desire for economic freedom.

Many countries have experimented with various kinds of incomes policies. An incomes policy contains targets for prices and wages for the economy as a whole, more detailed guides for price and wage decisions in particular industries, and some mechanisms to get firms and unions to follow these guides. The Kennedy-Johnson guidelines were one form of incomes policy. Although guidelines of this sort have a short-term effect on the price level, how much effect they have in the long run is hard to say.

A variety of types of tax-based incomes policies have been proposed in recent years. Such policies use the tax system or subsidies to induce firms to hold down prices and workers to hold down wages.

Although it is very unlikely that a catastrophe like the Great Depression will recur, our recent experience indicates that we have a long way to go before we understand the workings of the economy well enough to achieve continuous full employment without inflation. Also, even if the advice of its economists were always correct, there is no assurance that the government would always pursue policies leading toward economic stabilization.

Concepts for Review

supply-side inflation
wage-price spiral
wage and price controls
stagflation
Phillips curve
expectations

incomes policies
accelerationists
supply shock
deflation
long-run Phillips curve

Completion Questions

1. One basic cause of supply-side inflation is the market power of

   _____ and _____.

2. The more inflation people expect, the further _____ and

   _____ from the origin the short-run Phillips curve is likely
   to be.

3. The ability of labor to increase its wage is likely to depend to a considerable

   extent on the _____.

4. The _____ shows the relationship between the rate of
   increase of the price level and the level of unemployment.

5. _____ have an overall target, detailed guides for wage and
   price decisions, and a mechanism to get firms and unions to observe the guides.

6. The wage-price spiral sometimes is at the core of _____.

7. Expectations of decreased inflation tend to push the Phillips curve (upward,

   downward) _____.

8. The government would like to shift the Phillips curve (upward, downward)

   _____.

9. Friedman and Phelps claimed that the traditional downward-sloping Phillips

   curve shows a (short-run, long-run) _____ relationship and

   that, in the (short run, long run) _____, the Phillips curve is

   _____.

True-False

_____ 1. The Phillips curve is likely to be different in different countries and shift over time in the same country.

_____ 2. The wage-price spiral is the basis for demand-side inflation.

_____ 3. In the face of supply-side inflation, most economists advocate government controls of wages and prices.

_____ 4. Both an incomes policy and price and wage controls use persuasion to induce firms and unions to follow their guides voluntarily.

_____ 5. Guidelines are not effective when there are strong inflationary pressures due to improper monetary and fiscal policies.

_____ 6. No existing economic model can provide policy makers with reliable quantitative estimates of the way the money supply, government expenditures, or tax rates should be altered to provide full employment with stable prices.

_____ 7. Judging from the experience of the past 50 years, we seem to have learned how to avoid very serious depressions, but we have not yet learned how to attain full employment with stable prices.

_____ 8. Until we can better estimate the quantitative effects of policy changes of various magnitudes, it is unreasonable to expect that monetary and fiscal policies can be used with precision to achieve our national goals.

_____ 9. The low inflation of the late 1990s and early 2000s has been linked to falling productivity.

_____ 10. During World War II, and some other wartime emergencies, the government imposed controls on wages and prices.

_____ 11. Some economists feel that reliance on guidelines is dangerous because it focuses attention on symptoms rather than causes of inflation.

_____ 12. Low unemployment and inflation at the same time is known as _stagflation._

Multiple Choice

1. The position of the Phillips curve is likely to be influenced least by

   a. education of workers.
   b. increased mobility of workers.
   c. reduced discrimination.
   d. intellectual property rights.
   e. people's expectations about inflation.

2. By the late 1990s,

   a. the Phillips curve shifted to the left.
   b. inflation was between 4 and 5 percent.

   c.   unemployment rates fell to almost 5 percent.
   d.   all of the above.
   e.   none of the above.

3. The least effective approach to reducing supply-side inflation is

   a.   to reduce the market power of unions and firms.
   b.   government controls of prices and wages.
   c.   an incomes policy.
   d.   cutting taxes.
   e.   increasing global competition.

4. Under the Kennedy-Johnson wage-price guidelines, the government pressured unions and businesses to control their wages and prices. This policy

   a.   was successful because of strong economic demand.
   b.   started breaking down when wage guidelines did not keep up with inflation.
   c.   worked primarily at a time of falling inflation.
   d.   fell apart during the oil crisis of the late 1970s.
   e.   was successful because of extremely high unemployment.

5. Most economists oppose wage and price controls because they

   a.   result in a distortion of the allocation of resources.
   b.   are expensive to administer.
   c.   impair economic freedom.
   d.   all of the above.
   e.   none of the above.

6. The wage rate in industry A increases from $6.40 to $7.20 per hour, and labor productivity in industry A increases from 80 to 90. Unit labor cost

   a.   increases by $12\frac{1}{2}$ percent.
   b.   increases by about 27 percent.
   c.   decreases by about $12\frac{1}{2}$ percent.
   d.   decreases by about 27 percent.
   e.   none of the above.

7. Economists like Milton Friedman claim

   a.   the trade-off between unemployment and inflation is permanent.
   b.   people's expectations do not affect the Phillips curve.
   c.   in the long run, the Phillips curve is vertical.
   d.   all of the above.
   e.   none of the above.

Discussion and Extension Questions

1. During 1994, many economists, including Alan Greenspan, felt that inflationary forces were building; others disagreed. Briefly try to explain why this disagreement occurred. Pretend you must give your presentation to two separate

groups: a meeting of economists and a local civic organization interested in contemporary problems.

2. Does it make any difference if the government, to finance a budget deficit, borrows from the Fed rather than the general public?

3. What is the nature of supply-side inflation? What factors can cause shifts in the Phillips curve? What does the Phillips curve look like in the long run?

4. What are the disadvantages of adopting price and wage controls? What are the three elements of an incomes policy? Can guidelines save the day if monetary and fiscal policies generate strong inflationary pressures?

5. Discuss the role of lags in stabilization policy. Economists often distinguish between expenditure lags (lags before money is spent) and policy lags (lags due to policy makers). Do you think that there are differences between fiscal and monetary policy in the length of these lags? If so, what are these differences? What role do these lags play in causing our current difficulties in stabilizing the economy?

6. Some economists believe that there no longer is a trade-off between inflation and unemployment. Do you agree with them? Why or why not?

Problems

1. Labor productivity is increasing at an annual rate of 2 percent in economy C.

   a. If the wage level is increasing at an annual rate of 3 percent, are unit labor costs increasing or decreasing, and at what rate are they increasing or decreasing?

   b. Suppose that the wage level in the economy increases at a rate such that unit labor costs remain stable. At what rate is the wage level increasing?

   c. If the wage level in economy C's steel industry increases at the rate indicated in part b, at what rate do unit labor costs rise in the steel industry if labor productivity in steel is increasing at 1 percent per year?

   d. If the steel industry's price level increases at the same rate as its unit labor costs, at what rate does it rise under the circumstances in part c?

   e. Wage and price guidelines are established in economy C. Wages are allowed to increase at a rate equal to the rate of increase of labor productivity in the economy as a whole. Prices are allowed to increase at a rate equal to the rate of increase of unit labor costs. Do prices increase in all industries? If not, in which industries do prices increase?

2. The following table applies to a firm in economy D, which has an incomes policy stating that wage rates should rise by 8 percent per year. Assume that the firm and the union adhere to this policy.

Year	Wage rate per hour	Hours of labor	Wage bill	Total output	Price of product	Profits and nonwage costs
1998	$8.00	200	_____	1,500	$2	_____
1999	_____	_____	$1,728	1,650	$2	_____
2000	_____	200	_____	1,800	$2	_____

a. Fill in the blanks in the table.
b. What is the rate of increase of labor productivity between 1998 and 1999? Between 1999 and 2000?
c. What is the rate of increase of unit wage costs between 1998 and 1999? Between 1999 and 2000?
d. What is the rate of increase of unit profits and nonwage costs between 1998 and 1999? Between 1999 and 2000?
e. What changes occur in the proportion of total revenue going to labor?

Answers

Completion Questions
1. unions, firms   2. upward, out   3. unemployment rate   4. Phillips curve
5. Incomes policies   6. supply-side inflation   7. downward   8. downward
9. short-run, long run, vertical

True-False
1. True   2. False   3. False   4. False   5. True   6. True   7. True   8. True
9. False   10. True   11. True   12. False

Multiple Choice
1. d   2. a   3. d   4. b   5. d   6. e   7. c

Problems
1. a. They are increasing at 1 percent per year.
    b. 2 percent per year.
    c. 1 percent per year.
    d. 1 percent per year.
    e. No. They increase only in industries where the rate of increase of labor productivity is lower than in the economy as a whole.

2. a.

1998	$8.00	200	$1,600	1,500	$2	$1,400
1999	$8.64	200	$1,728	1,650	$2	$1,572
2000	$9.33	200	$1,866	1,800	$2	$1,734

    b. 10 percent. 9 percent.

    c. 2 percent decline. 1 percent decline.

    d. 2 percent increase. 1 percent increase.

    e. It is 53 percent in 1998, 52 percent in 1999, and somewhat less than 52 percent in 2000.

CHAPTER 11

Productivity, Growth, and Technology Policy

Chapter Profile

Compared with that of other major industrial countries, the United States' rate of growth of per-capita output generally was quite impressive over the past century, because of rapid technological change, increases in education and training, investment in plant and equipment, plentiful natural resources, and our social and entrepreneurial climate.

However, during the latter 1960s and the 1970s, the United States experienced a notable slowdown in its rate of increase of output per hour of labor. Among the factors often cited as being responsible for the slowdown were (1) the increase in the proportion of youths and women in the labor force, (2) the reduction in the rate of growth of the capital-labor ratio, (3) increased government regulation, and (4) the reduction in the proportion of GDP devoted to research and development. By the late 1990s, U.S. productivity growth rebounded as some of these factors were diminished or reversed. While some economists suspected this was a temporary phenomenon largely isolated in high-tech industries, more recent data suggest otherwise.

According to many observers, the productivity slowdown had been due in part to a decline in the rate of innovation in the United States. Tax credits for R & D, federal R & D grants and contracts, and expanded work by federal laboratories are among the measures proposed to help deal with whatever underinvestment in R & D exists. In 1981, an incremental R & D tax credit was enacted.

The United States' investment in plant and equipment (as a percentage of output) is considerably lower than that of some of its major international competitors, such as Germany and Japan. In 1981, Congress passed a tax bill that permitted accelerated depreciation of plant and equipment to encourage such investment. In the 1990s, the United States experienced a wave of investment that resulted in higher U.S. capital-labor growth than in most industrial countries. Whether this was due to government tax incentives, low interest rates, a strong economy, or the advances in computer technology is debated.

One of the strongest influences on the rate of innovation is the general economic climate. Measures that encourage economic growth, saving and investment, and price stability are quite likely to enhance our technological position. Indeed, improvements in our general economic climate may have more impact on the state of U.S. technology than many of the specific measures proposed to stimulate technological changes.

The Reagan administration pushed through Congress some very large tax cuts in 1981, the idea being to shift the aggregate supply curve to the right, as suggested by supply-side theory.

The Clinton administration advocated direct, purposeful investments in commercially relevant technologies. This was contrary to the views of its predecessor, the administration of George H. W. Bush, as well as the administration of George W. Bush, who has taken more supply-oriented tax cuts to Congress.

Concepts for Review

productivity	capital-labor ratio
research and development	Asian "miracle"
innovation	"new economy"
U.S. technological lead	supply-side economics
Laffer curve	

Completion Questions

1. During periods of recovery and prosperity, the U.S. economic growth rate was (high, low) _____; during depressions, it was (high, low) _____.

2. By 1840, the United States ranked fourth in per-capita income, behind _____, _____, and _____.

3. In the United States, the federal government is the source of about _____ of all R & D funds, which have been heavily concentrated on _____ and _____ technology.

4. The increase in the proportion of youths and women in the U.S. labor force may have been responsible for _____ to _____ percentage points of the difference between the average rate of productivity increase in 1947–66 and in 1966–73.

5. The reduction after 1973 in the rate of increase of the capital-labor ratio may have reduced the U.S. rate of productivity increase by up to _____ percentage points per year.

6. It is important to distinguish between a reduction in the rate of _____ in the United States and a reduction in the U.S. _____ over other countries.

7. The growth of output per hour in the United States (increased considerably, decreased considerably, was essentially constant) _____ during 1966–77 and (increased considerably, decreased considerably, was essentially constant) _____ during 1996–2003.

8. According to Laffer, U.S. tax rates were so _____ that the government took in _____ tax revenue.

9. An R & D _____ allows a firm to reduce its income tax liability by an amount equal to a certain percentage of its R & D expenditures.

10. A(n) _____ allows a firm to reduce its income tax liability by a certain percentage of the increase in its R & D expenditures.

True-False

_____ 1. The bulk of current R & D expenditures go for minor improvements rather than major advances.

_____ 2. The United States has grown more rapidly than any other industrialized country in the past 20 years.

_____ 3. The quality as well as the quantity of the population determines how much is produced.

_____ 4. As the baby boom generation ages and gains experience, productivity should rise.

_____ 5. In the early 2000s, productivity growth was consistently lower than the late 1970s and concentrated largely in high-tech industries.

_____ 6. The growth of Asian productivity is the highest in the world, due primarily to cultural factors.

_____ 7. During the late 1990s, real GDP per capita grew faster in the United States than other industrial countries.

_____ 8. Most economists believe the government should focus its R & D support on economically beleaguered industries.

_____ 9. Most economists believe the government should concentrate its technological efforts on what is essentially commercial development.

_____ 10. A sound coupling of technology and marketing is one characteristic that is most significant in distinguishing the relatively successful innovators from the relatively unsuccessful ones.

_____ 11. Rapid technological change always results in mass unemployment.

_____ 12. Measures that encourage investment are likely to encourage innovation as well.

_____ 13. Arthur Laffer claimed U.S. tax rates were on the left side of the Laffer curve.

_____ 14. A higher capital-labor ratio is generally associated with higher productivity.

Multiple Choice

1. If the United States is on the right of the Laffer curve, then a tax cut

   a. raises tax revenue.
   b. raises the national debt until the tax cut is reversed.
   c. requires lower government spending.
   d. lowers the level of taxable activity.
   e. lowers both nominal and real GDP.

2. The slowdown in U.S. productivity that occurred in the 1970s

   a. reduced the nation's rate of economic growth.
   b. helped increase the inflation rate.
   c. made some of our industries less globally competitive.
   d. all of the above.
   e. none of the above.

3. The pickup in U.S. productivity growth during the last few years has been due in part to

   a. increases in government regulations.
   b. new technology.
   c. increases in global competition.
   d. all of the above.
   e. b and c but not a.

4. The rate of return to society from investments in R & D is likely to exceed the rate of return from these investments to the firm or individual financing the R & D, because

   a. many of the benefits from the research accrue to firms and individuals other than the ones financing the R & D.
   b. R & D yields external economies.
   c. the risks to society from R & D are less than the risks to the firms carrying out the R & D.
   d. all of the above.
   e. none of the above.

5. From 1950 to 1964, the country with the highest growth rate, among the following five, was

   a. United States.   d. Japan.
   b. West Germany.   e. France
   c. Canada.

6. The least important factor in determining the rate of economic growth in the United States is

   a. increases in capital.   d. technological change.
   b. investment in education.   e. better worker health and training.
   c. the size of the national debt.

7. Which of the following tends to reduce the economic growth rate?

    a. Increased immobility of resources
    b. Growth of monopolies that prevent efficient allocation of resources
    c. Increased unemployment
    d. All of the above
    e. None of the above

8. Increases in the rate of technological change result in increases in aggregate unemployment

    a. always and necessarily.
    b. when total spending rises too slowly.
    c. when total spending rises rapidly and resources are already fully employed.
    d. all of the above.
    e. none of the above.

Discussion and Extension Questions

1. Writing in the *New York Times*, Edwin Dale pointed out that a communiqué of the Organization for Economic Cooperation and Development said that, "the steady economic growth needed to restore full employment and satisfy rising economic and social aspirations will not prove sustainable unless all member countries make further progress toward eradicating inflation." Using the concepts developed in this and previous chapters, explain in your own words what this passage means, and indicate whether you agree and why or why not.

2. "Economic growth is an archaic social objective. We have plenty of goods and services. Why should we strive for more?" Comment and evaluate.

3. Is the United States' technological lead relatively new or has it existed for a century or more? Is it true that independent inventors play practically no role at all today in the process of technological change? Discuss.

4. In February 2004, Alan Greenspan testified before Congress about the economy saying, "To date, the expansion of employment has significantly lagged increases in output. . . . New hires and recalls . . . are far below what historical experience indicates. To a surprising degree, firms seem able to continue identifying and implementing new efficiencies . . . and thus have found it possible so far to meet increasing orders without stepping up hiring." Comment on and discuss the implications of this trend.

5. Must increases in the rate of technological change result in increases in aggregate unemployment? Why or why not?

6. If GDP in the year 2020 is much higher than it is today, will this mean that all our material problems will be solved? Why or why not?

7. On April 5, 2000, Alan Greenspan stated, "There can be little doubt that not only has productivity picked up from its rather tepid pace during the preceding quarter century, but that the growth rate has continued to rise, with scant evidence that it is about to relent."* What could be some implications of even faster productivity growth? What could derail the process?

Problems

1. In 2003, 10 workers working 40 hours a week were able to make 2,000 units a week. In 2004, the same workers could produce 2,160 units in the same time.

   a. Find the output per hour of labor in 2003 and 2004.
   b. Find the growth in output per hour between 2003 and 2004.
   c. If output per hour rises 5 percent from 2004 to 2005, how many units of output do the 10 workers make in 2005?

2. Output per hour of labor increased by 4 percent per year in the chemical industry in country Z between January 1, 1995, and January 1, 1999.

   a. In 1999, the chemical industry's employment (in hours of labor) was equal to what it had been in 1995. How big was the percentage change in chemical output between 1995 and 1999?
   b. Suppose that the chemical industry's employment (in hours of labor) was 10 percent less in 1999 than in 1995. How big was the percentage change in chemical output between 1995 and 1999?
   c. What happened to the workers no longer needed in the chemical industry?

3. Economic growth in Palmerland, the golfer's paradise, is spurred by the production of a new supersonic golf cart. Suppose that this technological change results in an increase in full-employment GDP from $1,000 million to $1,100 million. (Net exports in Palmerland equal zero.)

   a. If the $C + I + G$ line is as follows, what is the immediate effect on unemployment of this technological change?

*www.abcnews.com/sections/business/DailyNews/neweconomy.000405.html.

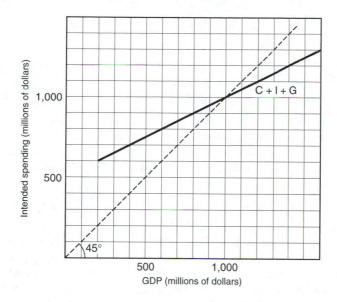

b. In what direction must the $C + I + G$ line be pushed to attain full employment? By how much must it be pushed? Draw the new $C + I + G$ line in the graph.

c. What kinds of policies might the government of Palmerland adopt to push the $C + I + G$ line in the direction indicated in part b?

4. Suppose the real GDP of country Y was $800 million in 2004. If it increases at a compound rate of 5 percent per year, what will its real GDP be in 2005? 2006? How long will it take before its GDP equals $1 billion?

5. Economy X's productive capacity is growing at 5 percent per year. In 2004, economy X had the capacity to produce $100 billion of GDP. Aggregate demand each year is also shown, all of it in billions of constant dollars:

Year	Aggregate demand	Productive capacity	Actual GDP
2004	95	100	_____
2005	100	_____	_____
2006	107	_____	_____

a. Fill in the blanks.

b. Is the rate of growth of actual GDP between 2004 and 2005 as big as it could be? Why or why not?

c. Between 2005 and 2006, is the rate of increase of actual GDP as big as it could be? Why or why not?

d. Between 2005 and 2006, is the rate of increase of actual GDP bigger or smaller than the rate of increase of productive capacity? How is this possible?

6. Suppose that the United States has 1 billion tons of iron ore and it uses 10 million tons of iron ore per year.

   a. Does this mean that the United States will run out of iron ore in 100 years? Why or why not?
   b. Does this mean that the United States will not be able to produce steel in 100 years? Why or why not?

7. According to the U.S. Bureau of Mines, potential total reserves of mercury in the United States would have been about 1.3 million flasks if the price of mercury were $1,000 per flask, but only about 140,000 flasks if the price were $200 per flask.

   a. How is it possible that the reserves of mercury are variable, not constant?
   b. According to William Baumol and Wallace Oates, "It is hard to believe that any resource whose price falls consistently without regulatory interference is really growing very scarce relative to prospective demand." Does this proposition seem reasonable in the case of mercury? Why or why not?
   c. Harold Barnett and Chandler Morse studied the unit cost of extraction of 13 minerals during 1870 and 1957 and found that the cost of each declined. Does this indicate a shortage of these minerals? Why or why not?

8. Suppose that both a haircut (a service) and a watchband (a manufactured good) can be produced by an hour of labor (and, for simplicity, no other resources) in 2004.

   a. What is the cost of a haircut and of a watchband in 2004 if the wage rate in both industries is $6 per hour?
   b. If technological change is greater in the production of watchbands than in the production of haircuts, with the result that labor productivity increases by 5 percent per year in watchband production but by only 1 percent per year in haircut production, what will be the cost of a haircut and of a watchband in 2005, if the wage rate in both industries increases by 3 percent per year?
   c. Do you think that this simple model helps explain why the costs of education, local government, and many other services have risen relative to the costs of manufactured goods in recent years? Why or why not?

Answers

Completion Questions

1. high, low   2. England, France, Germany   3. a quarter, defense, space   4. 0.2, 0.3   5. 0.5   6. technological change, technological lead   7. decreased considerably, increased considerably   8. high, less   9. tax credit   10. incremental R & D tax credit

True-False

1. True   2. False   3. True   4. True   5. False   6. False   7. True   8. False
9. False   10. True   11. False   12. True   13. False   14. True

Multiple Choice

1. a   2. d   3. e   4. d   5. d   6. c   7. d   8. b

Problems

1. 10 workers times 40 hours a week equals 400 labor hours a week.
   a. In 2003, 2000 units/400 hours = 5 units per hour of labor. In 2004, 2160 units/400 hours = 5.4 units per hour of labor.
   b. 0.4 units per hour of labor/5 units per hour of labor = 0.08 or 8 percent increase.
   c. 2160(1.05) = 2268 units in 2005.

2. a. $[(1.04)^5 - 1] \times 100$ percent, which is approximately 22 percent.
   b. $[0.9 \times (1.04)^5 - 1] \times 100$ percent, which is approximately 10 percent.
   c. Presumably they found employment in other industries.

3. a. Increased unemployment.
   b. Upward. To the point where it intersects the 45-degree line at $1,100 million.

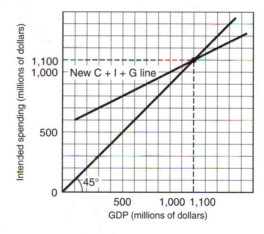

   c. Increase the money supply, reduce interest rates, increase government spending, or reduce taxes.

4. $1.05 \times \$800$ million = $840 million. $(1.05)^2 \times \$800$ million = $882 million. About five years.

5. a.

Year	Productive capacity	Actual GDP
2004	100	95
2005	105	100
2006	110	107

   b. No, because, in 2005, actual GDP is less than it could be if all capacity were utilized.
   c. No, because, in 2006, actual GDP is less than it could be if all capacity were utilized.
   d. Bigger, because the rate of utilization of capacity is higher in 2006 than in 2005.

6. a. No, because more iron ore may be discovered in the future or the United States may be able to trade for iron ore.

   b. No, because more iron ore may be discovered, the United States may trade for ore, or the United States may produce steel by recycling.

7. a. Because if the price is higher, it pays to obtain mercury that is more difficult and costly to obtain.

   b. Yes, because if it were growing scarcer relative to demand, one would expect producers to have to resort to more costly methods to obtain it, and the price would rise.

   c. No, for the reason given in part b.

8. a. $6.

   b. $6.12 for a haircut and $5.89 for a watchband.

   c. Yes, because productivity has not appeared to have risen as rapidly in some of the service industries as in manufacturing.

CHAPTER 12

Surpluses, Deficits, Public Debt, and the Federal Budget

Chapter Profile

After years of extremely large deficits, the United States started running budget surpluses in the late 1990s. The intense economic and political debates over the seriousness of the deficits turned into arguments over the permanence of the surpluses and how to spend them. By the early 2000s, the United States saw the return of large deficits—in 2004 it is projected to be a record $480 billion.

At least three policies concerning the government budget have had serious proponents. First, the budget should be balanced every year. Second, the budget should be balanced over the course of the business cycle. Third, the budget should be set in a way that promotes full employment and stable prices, whether or not this means that the budget is unbalanced over considerable periods of time.

The history of the past 50 years has seen enormous changes in the public's attitude toward the government budget. Seventy years ago, the prevailing doctrine was that the budget should be balanced each year. Now, although a balanced budget has more support than 30 years ago, the attitude seems to be that the budget should be used as a tool to reduce unemployment and inflation.

Some of the popular misconceptions concerning budget deficits can be avoided by the use of the structural deficit, which shows the difference between government expenditure and tax revenue that would result if we had full employment. When the actual budget shows a large deficit but the structural deficit is very small, most economists feel that fiscal policy is not too expansionary.

When it spends more than it receives in revenues, the government borrows money to cover the difference. It could simply print money for this purpose, but it has chosen to borrow a considerable proportion of what has been needed. The total amount owed is called the *national debt.*

One reason why the public is concerned about deficits is that they may cause inflation if the government finances the deficit by increasing the money supply. Also, government budget deficits may crowd out private investment because government borrowing may push up the interest rate.

Surpluses can create concerns when they become targets for attempts to increase government spending or cuts in taxes. If a surplus is temporary, due to unsustainable economic conditions, these policies worsen future deficits when the economy returns to more normal circumstances. If a surplus accrues in advance of a future government financial obligation, then eliminating the current surplus could create serious future problems. The U.S. government surpluses of the late 1990s were mainly due to a robust economy coupled with low interest rates and very large revenues in the Social Security System. Even if these economic conditions could have been sustained indefinitely (the "new economy" model), as the baby boomers age, retire, and start drawing on Social Security benefits, the situation would dramatically change.

Despite much public worry about the size of the national debt, as a percentage of national output, it was not much larger in 1994 than in 1939. There are important differences between government debt and private debt. Although the size of the debt is certainly of consequence, it is not true that it must somehow lead to bankruptcy. It is a concern, however, when anyone's debt rises faster than his or her income for a prolonged period of time. In recent years, the U.S. national debt has increased rapidly relative to the growth of the country's "income," or GDP; the national debt-to-GDP ratio has been rising at troubling rate.

The spending decisions of the federal government take place in the context of the budgetary process. The president submits his budget, which is a statement of anticipated expenditures and revenues, to Congress, which votes appropriations. The Ways and Means Committee of the House of Representatives and the Senate Finance Committee play important roles in the federal tax legislative process.

Concepts for Review

budget deficit	crowding-in effect	balanced budget
budget surplus	national debt	structural deficit
crowding-out effect	federal budget	Ways and Means Committee

Completion Questions

1. In addition to the crowding-out effect, there is the _____ effect.

2. The _____ is a statement of the government's anticipated expenditures and revenues.

3. Currently, Social Security is running a _____ but is projected to run a _____ as the baby boomers retire. The situation in the United States is (better, worse) _____ than in most developed countries.

4. Borrowing is not the only method the government can use to finance a deficit. It can also create _____ to cover the difference between expenditures and revenues.

5. Suppose that tax receipts and government expenditures on goods and services are related in the following way to GDP (all figures are in billions of dollars):

GDP	Tax receipts	Government expenditures
800	200	260
900	230	260
1,000	260	260
1,100	300	260

If GDP is $900 billion, the government runs a (deficit, surplus)

_____ of $_____ billion. If the full-

employment GDP is $1,100 billion, the structural deficit is $_____
billion. For this economy to achieve full employment, intended investment

must be $_____billion (greater, less) _____
than intended saving at full employment. (This assumes that net exports are zero.) This is because, in equilibrium, *intended saving plus taxes must equal intended investment plus government expenditure.* (This follows from the material in Chapter 6.)

True-False

_____ 1. If the structural deficit is $10 billion, the equilibrium value of GDP must be above the full-employment level of GDP.

_____ 2. One disadvantage to society of a government debt may be the inflation caused by the deficits producing the debt.

_____ 3. If the government's actual deficit in one year is $10 billion and its actual deficit in another year is $20 billion, fiscal policy must be more expansionary in the latter year than in the former.

_____ 4. To the extent that the national debt is held by foreigners, we must send goods and services overseas to pay the interest on it.

_____ 5. World War II would have imposed a burden on subsequent generations whether or not the national debt was increased.

_____ 6. As the national debt grows, the transfer payments required to meet interest charges grow, too, and these transfer payments are likely to encourage national output.

_____ 7. The United States has run large budget surpluses for the last six years.

_____ 8. When the actual budget shows a deficit but the structural deficit is very small, fiscal policy is probably too expansionary.

_____ 9. In 2002, the national debt-to-GDP ratio was about 60 percent.

_____ 10. The size of the deficits required to eliminate excessive unemployment always equal the size of the surpluses required to moderate the subsequent inflation.

_____ 11. A deficit occurs when the government spends more than it collects in receipts.

_____ 12. The national debt as a percent of GDP was larger in World War II than in 1999.

_____ 13. Supply-side economists want any surpluses accumulated to pay for future expansionary policies when recessions occur.

Multiple Choice

1. The most expansionary fiscal policy is a

   a. surplus saved for future needs.
   b. surplus used to reduce the public debt.
   c. deficit financed by new money.
   d. deficit financed by borrowing from the public.
   e. balanced budget.

2. The most anti-inflationary fiscal policy is a

   a. surplus saved for future needs.
   b. surplus used to reduce the public debt.
   c. deficit financed by new money.
   d. deficit financed by borrowing from the public.
   e. balanced budget.

3. If the national debt is held by foreigners,

   a. interest must be sent abroad.
   b. the debt may produce enough extra output to cover the interest payments.
   c. goods and services are sent overseas.
   d. all of the above
   e. none of the above

Discussion and Extension Questions

1. If a balanced budget for the federal government is not all that important for the economy, why have so many politicians promised to have a balanced budget?

2. Why is it important to distinguish between the actual deficit and the structural deficit? Answer in detail.

3. Evaluate the significance of a large national debt.

4. Describe the budgetary process and suggest why it is often difficult for the president to pass his budget.

5. Explain the concept of crowding out, and indicate how it differs from crowding in.

6. On the *Newshour with Jim Lehrer,* January 9, 1998, a commentator for the *Atlanta Constitution* said, "In fact it's a bit misleading to talk about that as a surplus. If I got a big raise and I'm already $100,000 in debt, I'm still in the red. I still have a negative net worth. And that's the situation we're in at the moment."* Comment on this statement.

Problems

1. The following figures (in millions of dollars) pertain to country Q's economy at various levels of GDP:

Taxes	GDP	Disposable income	Intended consumption expenditure	Intended saving
25	1,000	975	898	77
30	1,100	1,070	983	87
38	1,200	1,162	1,066	96
50	1,300	1,250	1,145	105
67	1,400	1,333	1,220	113
90	1,500	1,410	1,289	121
120	1,600	1,480	1,352	128
158	1,700	1,542	1,408	134
205	1,800	1,595	1,456	139

Suppose that intended investment is $128 million and government expenditures on goods and services are $27 million. Net exports equal zero.

a. What is the equilibrium level of GDP? What is the status of the government's budget at this value of GDP? (Hint: See Completion Question 5.)

b. Assume full employment to occur at GDP = $1,600 million. Assuming that changes in government expenditures are the country's only policy tool, how large must these expenditures be to move the economy to full employment? What will be the status of the government's budget once full employment is reached?

2. In the previous problem, suppose that intended investment increases to $143 million and government expenditures on goods and services rise to $37 million.

a. Is equilibrium GDP the same as it was in the previous problem? What is the new level of equilibrium GDP? What is the status of the government's budget at this equilibrium value of GDP?

*Transcript for January 9, 1998, "Show the Money," available at www.pbs.org/newshour/bb/budget/budget.html.

b. Assume full employment to occur at GDP = $1,600 million. How large must government expenditures be to move the company to full employment? When it gets there, will the sum of taxes and intended saving equal the sum of government expenditure and intended investment? Why or why not?

3. Consider the following model of an economy:

$$C_d = 1,000 + 0.9Y_d \qquad T = 400$$
$$G = 600 \qquad\qquad Y_d = GDP - T$$
$$I_d = 390 \qquad\qquad B = T - G,$$

where G equals government expenditure on goods and services, T equals taxes, B equals the government surplus (or deficit), C_d is intended consumption expenditures, Y_d is disposable income, and I_d is intended investment. All figures are in millions of dollars. Fill in the blanks in the following questions:

a. Equilibrium GDP = _____.

b. The multiplier for a change in G = _____.

c. The impact on GDP of a $1 increase in taxes = _____.

d. Savings at equilibrium GDP = _____.

e. If GDP at full employment is $15,000 million, savings at full employment =

_____.

f. If taxes remain constant, the level of government expenditure needed to

attain full employment = _____.

4. In economy B, GDP = $20 billion at full employment, GDP = $16 billion currently, taxes = 0.1(GDP), and government expenditures on goods and services = $1.8 billion.

a. Is the government running a surplus or a deficit? Is the budget too expansionary? Why or why not?

b. Suppose you learn that when GDP = $20 billion, intended saving = $1.8 billion and intended investment = $1.5 billion. If tax rates cannot be changed and government expenditures are altered to push the economy to full employment, will there be a surplus or deficit? How big? (Assume net exports equal zero.)

5. Consider an economy in which

$$C_d = 500 + 0.9(Y_d), \qquad I_d = 500, \qquad G = 225, \qquad T = 250,$$

where C_d equals intended consumption expenditure, Y_d equals disposable income, I_d equals intended investment, G equals government expenditure, and T equals taxes. All figures are in millions of dollars. Net exports equal zero.

a. What is equilibrium GDP?

b. The full-employment GDP = $10,400 million. President Earnest is most interested in getting the economy to full employment, but she also feels a driving need to balance the government's budget. How would you change fiscal policy (*T* and/or *G*) in an attempt to satisfy President Earnest's twin goals? Convince Ms. Earnest that your policy suggestions will work by using numerical values.

Answers

Completion Questions

1. crowding-in   2. budget   3. surplus, deficit, better   4. money   5. deficit, 30, minus 40, 40, greater

True-False

1. False   2. True   3. False   4. True   5. True   6. False   7. False
8. False   9. True   10. False   11. True   12. True   13. False

Multiple Choice

1. c   2. a   3. d

Problems

1. a. Since intended investment plus government spending equals $155 million, this should also be the sum of intended saving plus taxes. This is the case when GDP = $1,300 million, so the equilibrium GDP is $1,300 million. The government runs a surplus of $23 million.
   b. $120 million. There will be a balanced budget.
2. a. No. The new equilibrium GDP is $1,400 million. The government runs a surplus of $30 million.
   b. $105 million. Yes, because this is a necessary condition for equilibrium (if net exports are zero).
3. a. $16.3 billion
   b. 10
   c. −$9
   d. $590 million
   e. $460 million
   f. $470 million
4. a. The government is running a deficit of $.2 billion. Since it is running a structural surplus of $0.2 billion, the budget does not seem too expansionary.
   b. There will be a deficit of $0.3 billion.
5. a. GDP = 500 + 0.9(GDP − 250) + 500 + 225. Hence, 0.1GDP = 500 − 225 + 500 + 225 = 1,000, so the equilibrium value of GDP is $10,000 million.
   b. Ms. Earnest wants GDP = $10,400 million and *T* = *G*. Therefore, GDP = 500 + 0.9(GDP − *G*) + 500 + *G* = 10,400, which means that 0.1*G* = 10,400 − 500 − 500 − 9,360 = 40. Therefore, both *G* and *T* should be set equal to $400 million.

CHAPTER 13

Monetary Policy, Interest Rates,

and Economic Activity

Chapter Profile

The United States' history has seen many sharp fluctuations in the price level. Generally, severe inflations occurred because the government expanded the money supply far too rapidly. However, too small a rate of growth of the money supply can also be a mistake, resulting in excessive unemployment.

Most economists believe that the lower is the interest rate, the greater the amount of money demanded, all other things equal. Therefore, increases in the quantity of money result in lower interest rates, which result in increased investment (and other types of spending), which results in a higher GDP. Conversely, decreases in the quantity of money result in higher interest rates, which result in decreased investment (and other types of spending), which result in a lower GDP. This is the simple Keynesian approach.

The equation of exchange is $MV = PQ$, where M is the money supply, V is the velocity of circulation of money, P is the price level, and Q is gross domestic product in real terms. The velocity of circulation of money is the rate at which the money supply is used to make transactions for final goods and services. Specifically, it equals GDP in money terms divided by the money supply.

If the velocity of circulation of money remains constant and real gross domestic product is fixed at its full-employment level, it follows from the equation of exchange that the price level is proportional to the money supply. This is the crude quantity theory, which is a reasonably good approximation during periods of runaway inflation and works reasonably well in predicting long-term trends in the price level.

The monetarists, led by Milton Friedman, prefer the quantity theory to the Keynesian model. There have been many disagreements between the monetarists and the Keynesians, but both approaches agree that increases in the money supply tend to increase nominal GDP while decreases in the money supply tend to decrease nominal GDP.

As indicators of how tight or easy monetary policy is, the Fed has looked at the level of short-term interest rates, the rate of growth of the money supply, and the rate of growth of the monetary base. During the 1950s and 1960s, the Fed paid most attention to the first indicator; in the 1970s and early 1980s, the Fed increased the amount of attention it paid to the last two. More recently, the Fed has closely watched nominal GDP.

The Federal Reserve is faced with many difficult problems in formulating and carrying out monetary policy. It must try to see where the economy is heading, and whether—and to what extent—it should tighten or ease money to stabilize the economy. This task is made very difficult by the fact that there is often a long—and highly variable—lag between an action by the Fed and its effect on the economy. Also, the Fed cannot always control both its money supply and interest rate targets at the same time. Finally, should the Fed be concerned about asset inflation in addition to goods inflation and unemployment?

There has been criticism of various kinds regarding the performance of the Federal Reserve. Often, the Fed is criticized for paying too little attention to the long lags between its actions and their effects on the economy. Some monetarists, led by Milton Friedman, believe that monetary policy would be improved if discretionary policy were replaced by a rule that the Fed should increase the money supply at some fixed, agreed-on rate, such as 4 or 5 percent per year.

A more-sophisticated version of the quantity theory recognizes that real gross domestic product is often less than its full-employment value; consequently, Q is not fixed. If the velocity of circulation of money remains constant, gross domestic product in money terms should be proportional to the money supply. In fact, the velocity of circulation of money has by no means remained stable over time. However, nominal GDP has been fairly closely related to the money supply, and the monetarists have asserted that the velocity of circulation of money is predictable.

Concepts for Review

transactions demand
precautionary demand
demand curve for money
nominal GDP
velocity of circulation of money
asset inflation
monetary base
equation of exchange

crude quantity theory
easy monetary policy
tight monetary policy
speculative bubble
recessionary gap
inflationary gap
monetarists
real interest rate

Completion Questions

1. If the velocity of money is 5, and the money supply equals $200 billion, nominal

    GDP equals _____. If the velocity of money
    remains constant at 5, a $10 billion increase in the money supply results in a(n)

    _____ increase in nominal GDP, and a $5 billion decrease

    in the money supply results in a(n) _____ decrease in nominal
    GDP.

2. Economists worry that asset inflation may encourage businesses to (overinvest,

    underinvest) _____ and (overborrow, underborrow)

    _____. This can lead to a _____
    when the bubble bursts.

3. A bond pays interest of $100 per year (indefinitely). If the interest rate is 5

    percent, this bond is worth _____. If the interest rate is 10

    percent, this bond is worth _____. An increase in the interest

    rate (reduces, increases) _____ the market price of
    the bond. An increase in the market price of the bond means a(n) (decrease,

    increase) _____ in the interest rate.

4. If the demand curve for money is a vertical line, the interest rate (does, does not)

    _____ influence the quantity of money demanded.
    One reason why such a demand curve for money seems (likely, unlikely)

    _____ is that there are _____ costs of
    holding money, and these costs increase as the interest rate (rises, falls)

    _____.

5. One of the most important costs of holding money is the loss of

    _____.

6. The _____ of money is the rate at which the money supply
    is used to make transactions for final goods and services.

7. The _____ assumes that full employment exists and states
    that the price level must be proportional to the money supply.

8. The _____ shows the relationship between the interest rate

    and the quantity of money assuming the _____ and

    _____ are held constant.

9. Excessive increases in the quantity of money may result in serious

    _____, while inadequate increases in the quantity of money

    may result in excessive _____.

10. The amount of money held by individuals and firms is inversely related to the

    _____.

11. The value of a dollar is equivalent to what a dollar will _____,

    which in turn depends on the _____ level. If all

    _____ doubled, the value of a dollar would be cut in half.

12. The velocity of money tends to _____ during recessions and

    depressions and _____ during booms.

True-False

_____ 1. If the velocity of money increases at 2 percent per year and the economy's potential real GDP grows at 3 percent per year, the money supply should grow at 6 percent to maintain a constant price level.

_____ 2. If the velocity of money is constant and the economy's potential real GDP grows at 3 percent per year, the money supply should grow at 3 percent to maintain a constant price level.

_____ 3. During each war in which the United States has participated, there has been pronounced inflation followed by a postwar drop in prices.

_____ 4. The higher is a person's income, the more money he or she tends to hold for transactions demand.

_____ 5. Over the past 50 years, nominal GDP has not been correlated with the money supply in the United States.

_____ 6. In the short run, if there is an increase in the money supply, there is a tendency for the price level to fall.

_____ 7. The crude quantity theory sometimes works fairly well in predicting long-term trends in the price level and the course of runaway inflations.

_____ 8. The effect of an increase in the money supply is to decrease nominal GDP.

_____ 9. Basically, the value of currency depends on its acceptability by people and its scarcity.

_____ 10. If all prices were reduced by 50 percent, the value of a dollar would double.

_____ 11. Holding GDP constant, the amount of money demanded by individuals and firms is inversely related to the interest rate, since the cost of holding money is the interest or profit forgone.

Multiple Choice

1. A reduction in the rate of interest is likely to result in an increase in demand for

   a. capital goods.
   b. consumer durable goods.
   c. residential housing.
   d. all of the above.
   e. none of the above.

2. An increase in the quantity of money will *not* affect the interest rate if the demand curve for money is

   a. upward sloping to the right.
   b. downward sloping to the right.
   c. horizontal.
   d. vertical.
   e. all of the above.

3. If the quantity of money supplied exceeds the quantity of money demanded, the

    a.   interest rate rises.
    b.   interest rate rises, and GDP rises too.
    c.   interest rate falls.
    d.   demand curve for money shifts downward.
    e.   interest rate is not affected.

4. If next year's real GDP is expected to equal this year's and the velocity of money is expected to be 2 percent higher next year than this year, how big is the money supply expected to be next year if the price level is expected to be 3 percent higher than this year?

    a.   The money supply is expected to be 1 percent above this year's level.
    b.   The money supply is expected to equal its value this year.
    c.   The money supply is expected to be 2 percent above this year's level.
    d.   The money supply is expected to be 3 percent above this year's level.
    e.   The money supply is expected to be 4 percent above this year's level.

5. The velocity of circulation of money is

    a.   nominal GDP/M.   d.   all of the above.
    b. $(P \times Q)/M$.   e.   none of the above.
    c.   not a constant.

6. On the average, 2003 prices in the United States were about how many times what they were in 1970?

    a.   About the same   d.   10 times as high
    b.   2 times as high   e.   20 times as high
    c.   About 4 times as high

7. The money that people and firms keep to meet contingencies like illness or home and car repairs is called the _____ demand for money.

    a.   transactions   d.   investment
    b.   precautionary   e.   none of the above
    c.   speculative

Discussion and Extension Questions

1. *Business Week* quoted Allen Meltzer of Carnegie-Mellon University as saying, "Given anticipations, the level of capacity utilization in the economy makes little difference. An increase in the money supply in the 1930s would have had the same impact on prices as a similar increase in the 1960s." Explain what he means. Do you agree? Why or why not?

2. How and why does the increased used of credit cards affect the demand for money?

3. Is it always true that $MV = PQ$? Why or why not? To what extent is velocity constant over time? How does the more-sophisticated quantity theory differ from the crude quantity theory?

4. Does the fact that velocity is not constant mean that the more-sophisticated version of the quantity theory is useless? Why or why not?

5. Explain how a worried public, which begins to increase the speed with which it spends money, can create inflation without any increases in the money supply.

6. Suppose that a ceiling is placed on the interest rate. In what way, if any, would such a ceiling interfere with the effect of a reduction of the money supply on GDP?

7. Throughout 2003, the U.S. economy expanded, yet the first quarter of 2004 saw extremely low Fed funds and discount rates. Why was the Federal Reserve still so expansionary? Why were analysts expecting the Fed to start raising interest rates by the summer of 2004?

Problems

1. In nation A, the price level during various years was as follows:

Year	Price level (1950 = 100)
1950	100
1960	120
1970	140
1980	200
1990	300

a. Plot the relationship between the price level and time in the following graph:

b. By what percentage did the value of money decline in nation A from 1980 to 1990? From 1950 to 1980?

    c.   If your grandfather invested in a 40-year, $1,000 bond in nation A in 1950 and if he held it until maturity in 1990, how much did he receive in principal in 1990 dollars? In 1950 dollars?

2. Suppose that in the nation of South Isthmus the relationship between the interest rate and the quantity of money demanded, holding GDP constant, is

$$i = 20 - 2M,$$

where i is the interest rate (in percentage points) and M is the quantity of money (in trillions of dollars).

    a.   What is the name often given to this relationship?

    b.   What is the interest rate in South Isthmus if the quantity of money demanded equals $5 trillion?

    c.   Suppose that GDP in South Isthmus increases. Will the relationship between i and M remain constant? If not, in what direction will it shift?

3. a.   If nominal GDP in South Isthmus increases by 20 percent between 2001 and 2003, while the money supply increases by 10 percent, what change occurs in the velocity of circulation of money?

    b.   If nominal GDP in South Isthmus increased by 20 percent between 2001 and 2003, while velocity increased by more than 20 percent, did the money supply increase during this period or decrease?

4. a.   Suppose that the quantity of money in South Isthmus increased considerably during 2004. The next graph shows two investment functions, one of which was the one that existed before the increase in the money supply, and the other was the one that existed after the increase in the money supply. According to the Keynesian model, which one is which?

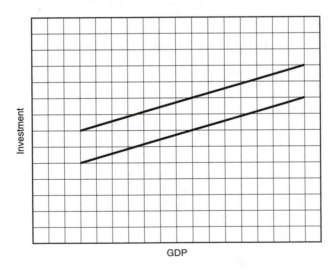

    b.   After the increase in the money supply, it was discovered that the crude quantity theory of money was applicable. The money supply was increased by 10 percent. How much did the price level increase during 2004?

5. Country Q's real GDP increased from 2000 to 2003 by 3 percent per year, and its velocity of money increased by 2 percent per year. Fill in the blanks.

Year	Price level (2000 = 100)	Money supply (2000 = 100)
2000	100	100
2001	_____	101
2002	100	_____
2003	100	_____

6. The following data come from the *Economic Report of the President:*

Year	M1 (billions of dollars)	M2 (billions of dollars)	Nominal GDP (billions of dollars)
1967	187.4	350.0	814.3
1969	209.0	392.5	959.5
1971	234.0	471.9	1,097.2
1973	270.5	571.4	1,349.6
1975	295.2	664.7	1,585.9
1977	338.5	809.5	1,974.1

When M2 is used rather than M1, was the velocity of money more stable over time during 1967–77?

7. A bond pays interest of $100 per year (forever). The following table shows the price of the bond at selected interest rates. Fill in the blanks.

Interest rate (percent)	Price of bond (dollars)
1	_____
2	_____
_____	2,500
_____	2,000
10	_____
12$^1/_2$	_____

8. Suppose that the quantity of money demanded in country X (denoted M) is related in the following way to nominal GDP (denoted Y) and the interest rate (denoted i):

$$M = \frac{Y(30 - 2i)}{50},$$

where M and Y are in trillions of dollars and i is in percentage points.

a. Is the demand curve for money in this country a straight line?
b. If the interest rate exceeds 15 percent, do you think that this equation holds? Why or why not?
c. On the basis of these data, is the crude quantity theory of money valid in country X? Explain.
d. Country X adopts a variety of devices to reduce the cost of transferring money balances from saving to checking accounts. Will this affect the validity of the equation in the previous problem? If so, what effect is it likely to have?

Answers

Completion Questions
1. $1 trillion, $50 billion, $25 billion   2. overinvest, overborrow, recession
3. $2,000, $1,000, reduces, decrease   4. does not, unlikely, opportunity, rises   5. interest or profit   6. velocity of circulation   7. crude quantity theory   8. demand curve for money, price level, real GDP   9. inflation, unemployment
10. interest rate   11. buy, price, prices   12. fall, rise

True-False
1. False   2. True   3. False   4. True   5. False   6. False   7. True   8. False
9. True   10. True   11. True

Multiple Choice
1. d   2. c   3. c   4. a   5. d   6. c   7. b

Problems
1. a.

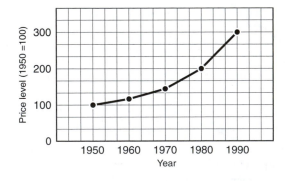

b. 33$^1/_3$ percent, 50 percent.

c. $1,000, 333^1/_3$.

2. a. Demand curve for money.

   b. 10 percent.

   c. No. It will shift upward and to the right.

3. a. It increases by about 9 percent.

   b. It decreased.

4. a. The higher one is after the increase in the money supply; the lower one is before the increase in the money supply.

   b. 10 percent.

5. The 2001 price level was 100, the 2002 money supply was 102, and the 2003 money supply was 103.

6. The velocity of money based on M1 and M2 was as follows:

Year	Based on M1	Based on M2
1967	4.35	2.33
1969	4.59	2.44
1971	4.69	2.33
1973	4.99	2.36
1975	5.37	2.39
1977	5.83	2.44

The velocity of money was more stable when M2 is used than when M1 is used.

7. The complete table is:

Interest rate (percent)	Price of bond (dollars)
1	10,000
2	5,000
4	2,500
5	2,000
10	1,000
12$^1/_2$	800

8. a. Yes.

   b. No, because if this equation holds, M is negative if i is greater than 15.

   c. No. The velocity of money equals $50/(30 - 2i)$; this means that the velocity of money is not constant if the interest rate changes.

   d. The adoption of such devices may result in less money being demanded at each level of Y and i than indicated by this equation.

CHAPTER 14

Controversies over

Stabilization Policy

Chapter Profile

The principal debate of the 1960s and 1970s was between the Keynesians and the monetarists. The Keynesians put more emphasis than the monetarists on the federal budget; the monetarists put more emphasis than the Keynesians on the money supply. In the late 1970s, supply-side economists came to prominence; their emphasis was on tax cuts to push the aggregate supply curve to the right.

The new classical macroeconomists, like Robert Lucas, also came to prominence in the 1970s. On the basis of their assumptions, the new classical macroeconomists conclude that the government cannot use monetary and fiscal policies to close recessionary and inflationary gaps in the ways described in earlier chapters, because the models presented in those chapters do not recognize that the expectations of firms and individuals concerning their incomes, job prospects, sales, and other relevant variables are influenced by government policies. If firms and individuals formulate their expectations rationally, they will tend to frustrate the government's attempts to use activist stabilization policies.

According to real business cycle models, put forth by some new classical macroeconomists like Edward Prescott, business fluctuations are due largely to shifts in the aggregate supply curve. Among the most important factors shifting the aggregate supply curve are new products, new methods of production, new sources of raw materials, and good or bad weather. Real business cycle theorists tend to ignore monetary policy and believe that changes in real GDP result in changes in the money supply, rather than the other way around.

The new Keynesians, like the old Keynesians, assume that prices and wages tend to be rigid in the short run, with the result that the quantity of output, more than price, tends to adjust to changes in aggregate demand. But, whereas the old Keynesians merely assumed that wages and prices are sticky, the new Keynesians developed theories that help to explain why such wage and price stickiness can be expected, given the rational behavior of individuals and firms.

According to the new Keynesians, prices tend to be sticky because of menu costs (costs incurred by firms when they change prices), and wages tend to be sticky because of long-term labor contracts. On the basis of the theory of implicit contracts, they conclude that wages are set according to long-term considerations. (Responding to workers' aversion to risk, firms maintain relatively rigid wages.)

The debate over the pros and cons of policy activism has been going on for decades. Opponents of policy activism tend to believe that activist monetary and fiscal policies to stabilize the economy are likely to do more damage than good. They have often favored a rigid policy rule, stipulating that the money supply should grow at a constant rate. Policy activists, while admitting that discretionary monetary and fiscal policy have sometimes been destabilizing, are much more optimistic about the efficacy of such policies in the future.

Concepts for Review

Keynesians   rigid policy rule
monetarists   discretionary policy
supply-side economics   feedback policy rule
rational expectations   menu costs
new classical macroeconomists   implicit contracts
real business cycle theorists   inflation targeting
new Keynesians   time inconsistency
supply shocks

Completion Questions

1. According to the Keynesians, although the money supply has an important

   influence on GDP, its impact on the _____ is what in turn affects spending. The Keynesians are more inclined than the monetarists to

   use the level of _____ to measure whether money is tight or

   easy. To the monetarists, the change in the quantity of _____,

   not the level of _____ rates, is most important.

2. According to some of the leading (Keynesians, monetarists)

   _____, a rule stipulating that the _____

   should grow steadily at a rate fixed somewhere between 4 and 5 percent per year would be the most-effective way to regulate the economy.

3. According to real business cycle theories, output fluctuations are due predominantly to shifts in the aggregate supply curve. Among the factors causing

   shifts in this curve are new _____, new _____

   of production, and good or bad _____.

4. According to the new classical macroeconomists, high rates of unemployment

   (are, are not) _____ evidence of a gap between actual and

   _____ output that can be reduced; instead, output fluctuations

   result from _____ errors.

5. The demand for services is _____ stable than the demand for _____. Since the U.S. economy is now dominated by the _____ sector, this makes the economy _____ stable, all other things equal.

True-False

_____ 1. During the 1940s, 1950s, and early 1960s, the Keynesian view was definitely predominant, both here and abroad. But, by the mid-1960s, it was being challenged seriously by the monetarists, led by Professor Milton Friedman and his supporters.

_____ 2. According to Keynesians, the velocity of money is more predictable than the multiplier.

_____ 3. Both the new classical macroeconomists and the new Keynesians often assume that the expectations of people and firms conform to the theory of rational expectations.

_____ 4. Real business cycle models, in contrast to new Keynesian models, assume that prices and wages are flexible and markets clear.

_____ 5. According to real business cycle theories, changes in real GDP tend to cause changes in the money supply, rather than the other way around.

_____ 6. According to the new classical macroeconomists, prices can be sticky because of menu costs.

_____ 7. The new classical macroeconomists believe that fluctuations in aggregate demand are due principally to erratic and unpredictable government policy.

_____ 8. According to Robert Lucas, people come to learn the way in which policy is made, and only unanticipated government policy changes can have a substantial effect on output or employment.

_____ 9. The Fed currently practices inflation targeting.

_____ 10. According to Lucas, excess unemployment is essentially voluntary.

_____ 11. Critics claim that the new classical macroeconomics neglects the inertia in wages and prices and is inconsistent with the evidence.

_____ 12. Better inventory control has led to a less stable economy.

Multiple Choice

1. The reason why some leading monetarists favor a growth rate of *M* of 4 to 5 percent per year is that this has been

   a. the rate of increase of *M* in the past.
   b. the rate of increase of *V* in the recent past.
   c. the average rate of increase of potential real output.
   d. the average rate of increase of real output.
   e. none of the above.

2. According to the Keynesians,

   a. prices are relatively inflexible downward.
   b. the length of time required for the economy to get itself out of a severe recession would be very long.
   c. business spending represents a substantial source of instability.
   d. governments can be trusted to establish responsible economic policies.
   e. all of the above.

3. Real business cycle theorists believe that

   a. supply shocks usually are not important causes of business fluctuations.
   b. prices and wages respond flexibly to changing economic conditions.
   c. both business fluctuations and economic growth stem from factors that shift the long-run aggregate demand curve.
   d. all of the above.
   e. none of the above.

4. The new Keynesians believe that prices and wages tend to adjust slowly because of

   a. menu costs.
   b. long-term contracts.
   c. implicit contracts.
   d. all of the above.
   e. none of the above.

5. Milton Friedman's suggestion that the money supply be set so that it grows at a fixed, agreed-on percentage rate is

   a. a rigid policy rule.
   b. a feedback policy rule.
   c. a discretionary policy.
   d. all of the above.
   e. none of the above.

6. Some economists take issue with the Fed's flexible monetary policy because

   a. it is so dependent on the chairman.
   b. it creates uncertainty.
   c. it can result in greater political pressure on the Fed.
   d. all of the above.
   e. none of the above.

Discussion and Extension Questions

1. Do the monetarists agree that fiscal policy works as the Keynesians assert? If not, what are the differences between their views?

2. "Skeptics [of real business cycle models] doubt that any conceivable supply shock could explain why output fell one-third in the Great Depression of the 1930s." Do you agree? Why or why not?

3. Do you tend to agree with the policy activists or with their critics? Explain your own position on this issue.

4. Assuming that you were a new classical macroeconomist, what policy recommendations would you make to stabilize the economy?

5. How might the different economic theories be used to explain the robust U.S. economy of the middle to late 1990s?

6. According to Franco Modigliani, "the most glaring flaw of the [new classical macroeconomics] . . . is its inconsistency with the evidence: if it were valid, deviations of unemployment from the natural rate would be small and transitory—in which case Keynes' *General Theory* would not have been written." What does he mean? Do you agree? Why or why not?

7. From the point of view of the new classical macroeconomics, criticize both the Keynesian and monetarist policy recommendations to stabilize the economy.

Problems

1. Suppose that the quantity of money demanded (M_d) depends on GDP and the interest rate (i) in the following way:

$$M_d = 0.4\text{GDP} - 2i,$$

where M_d and GDP are measured in billions of dollars and i is measured in percentage points.

   a. If GDP = $100 billion and $i = 8$, what is the quantity of money demanded?
   b. If the quantity of money demanded equals the quantity of money supplied when GDP = $100 billion and $i = 8$, what does velocity equal under these circumstances?
   c. Suppose the monetary authorities increase the money supply to $30 billion, with the result that GDP increases to $110 billion and the interest rate falls to 7 percent. What now is the quantity of money demanded? Does the quantity of money demanded equal the quantity of money supplied?
   d. Under the circumstances described in part c, what change, if any, occurs in the velocity of money?
   e. Suppose that the fiscal authorities carry out an expansionary fiscal policy, with the results that GDP increases to $115 billion and the interest rate rises to 8 percent. The money supply remains at $30 billion. What now is the quantity of money demanded? Does the quantity of money demanded equal the quantity of money supplied?

f. Under the circumstances described in part e, what change, if any, occurs in the velocity of money?
g. A Keynesian economist claims that the velocity of money is not constant in this economy. Is he correct?
h. A monetarist economist claims that the velocity of money is predictable in this economy. Is she correct? If so, how can it be done?
i. Why is it useful to try to predict the velocity of money?

2. Suppose labor contracts are negotiated evenly throughout the year and wages do not fall until a contract expires. Assume that 20 percent of workers have no contract, 20 percent have a one-year contract, 30 percent have a two-year contract, and 30 percent have a three-year contract. Aggregate demand falls in the economy.

a. After six months, approximately what percent of wages have adjusted to the new level of aggregate demand?
b. After 12 months, approximately what percent of wages have adjusted?
c. After 18 months, approximately what percent of wages have adjusted?
d. What might the Keynesians and monetarists each say about this economy and government stabilization policy?

Answers

Completion Questions
1. interest rate, interest rates, money, interest   2. monetarists, money supply
3. products, methods, weather   4. are not, potential, random forecasting
5. more, goods, service, more

True-False
1. True   2. False   3. True   4. True   5. True   6. False   7. True   8. True
9. False   10. True   11. True   12. False

Multiple Choice
1. c   2. e   3. b   4. d   5. a   6. d

Problems
1. a. $24 billion.
   b. 4.17.
   c. $30 billion. Yes.
   d. Velocity equals 3.67.
   e. $30 billion. Yes.
   f. Velocity equals 3.83.
   g. Yes.
   h. So long as the quantity of money demanded equals the quantity of money supplied, the velocity of money (= GDP/M_d) equals GDP/(0.4GDP – 2i).

      i.   Because if we know the velocity and the quantity of money, we can predict nominal GDP.

2. a. 42.5 percent.

   b. 65 percent.

   c. 77.5 percent.

   d. The Keynesians might argue that the lack of wage flexibility will create a business cycle the government needs to stabilize with the appropriate policy. Almost a quarter of wages will not have adjusted by the end of 18 months and labor unions may be unwilling to accept wage cuts even to save jobs on the initial renegotiation. The monetarists would probably point out that stabilization policy itself takes time, generally over a year, and by then most wages will have had a chance to adjust. Further, they might point out that the average economic downturn in the United States lasts less than two years, indicating little need for stabilization policy.

CASE 2

The End of the Business Cycle?

COUNCIL OF ECONOMIC ADVISERS[1]

The Changing Nature of Business Cycles in the United States

Forty-one years ago a former chairman of the Council of Economic Advisers predicted that "The business cycle is unlikely to be as disturbing or troublesome to our children as it once was for our fathers." Research quantifying the degree to which business cycles have moderated over time confirms this view. If the severity of economic fluctuations is measured in terms of the output lost during a recession, the 14 recessions between 1900 and 1953 cost on average about three times as much as the 7 recessions since then. Even if the Great Depression of the 1930s is excluded, recessions in the earlier period still were on average more than one and a half times as severe as those in the 1954–99 period.

Other evidence supports the notion that business cycle fluctuations have diminished over time. From 1982 to 1998, fluctuations in GNP and unemployment were on average about 20 percent smaller than they were from 1954 to 1981, and fluctuations in inflation were less than half as large on average. With the caveat that data from the nineteenth century and the early twentieth century are less reliable than and not directly comparable to recent data, business cycle fluctuations appear to have become less severe in the second half of the twentieth century than in earlier periods.

One other way to think about the postwar moderation of the business cycle is in terms of the length of time that the economy has spent in recession and the amount of time it has spent in expansion. The average length of expansions nearly doubled in the second half of the century, from about $2^1/2$ years during 1900–53 to about 5 years since then, and the average length of economic contractions has fallen from about 17 months to less than 11 months.

Sources of Business Cycle Moderation

One source of moderation in the business cycle is the changing nature of the U.S. economy. Historically, inventories have been one of the most volatile components of spending. Businesses now tend to operate with much leaner inventory stocks than before, and they appear to be better able to adjust these stocks to changing economic conditions. The composition of output has also tended to move from more volatile toward less volatile sectors. Spending on services, which tends to be relatively insensitive to cyclical fluctuations, made up over half of GDP in 1999, compared with less than a third in 1950. Conversely, the cyclically sensitive manufacturing sector makes up a smaller share of aggregate output and employment than in the past.

[1]*Economic Report of the President* (Washington, DC: Government Printing Office, 2000), pp. 75–79.

The growing role of stabilization policies—fiscal and monetary policies, which buffer the effects of destabilizing influences on the economy—may also have contributed to this moderation of the business cycle. Over the last century, the role of fiscal policy in affecting the business cycle not only has grown but has indeed changed fundamentally. At the beginning of the twentieth century, the Federal Government's role in the economy was tiny. In 1900 there was no Federal income tax and no Social Security, and total Federal receipts equaled a mere 3 percent of GNP. The Nation's monetary policy was generally one of simple adherence to the gold standard, which limited the use of monetary policy as a stabilizing tool.

The Federal Government's role in macroeconomic stabilization grew in importance following World War II. Although the income tax had been introduced in 1913 and Social Security in 1937, by 1940 income and payroll taxes equaled only 3 percent of GNP. Income and payroll tax revenue rose thereafter as a share of GNP and has averaged around 14 percent over the last 30 years. It amounted to over 16 percent of GNP in 1999. The role and character of monetary policy likewise underwent a fundamental transformation during the late twentieth century. Recent experience supports the view that modern monetary policy can achieve the long-run goal of price stability while aiding in the cause of short-run macroeconomic stabilization by "leaning against the wind" when macroeconomic imbalances develop.

Do Expansions Die of Old Age?

One question that has intrigued economists is whether each expansion contains the seeds of its own destruction. Is it true that the longer an expansion lasts, the more likely it is to end in the next quarter or the next year? Studies find no compelling evidence that postwar expansions possess an inherent tendency to die of old age. Instead, they appear to fall victim to specific events related to economic disturbances or government policies. For instance, the Iraqi invasion of Kuwait, which led to a doubling of oil prices in the fall of 1990, contributed to the decline in economic activity during the recession of 1990–91. American consumers, having suffered through the tripling of oil prices in 1973–74 and their subsequent doubling in 1979, anticipated negative repercussions on the U.S. economy, and consumer confidence declined sharply and consumption fell.

An example of policy affecting the end of an expansion is the Federal Reserve's successful disinflation at the end of the 1970s and in the early 1980s. In 1979 the CPI inflation rate reached 11 percent. Under a new chairman, the Federal Reserve dedicated itself to a renewed effort to reduce inflation, which fell 8 percentage points over four years, to about 3 percent by the end of 1983. As a result, the short expansion that started in July 1980 came to a halt one year later. With the Federal funds rate peaking at just over 19 percent in June 1981, the economy fell into a 16-month recession, during which the unemployment rate rose above 10 percent.

An Expansion Is Only as Old as It Feels, and This One Still Feels Young

Although the current expansion entered its 105th month in December 1999—what might be considered old age, based on the history of U.S. business cycles—it still appears young and vibrant when compared to the later stages of past long expansions. What is noteworthy in today's economy is the absence of developments that are frequently identified with the twilight of an expansion. In particular, productivity has accelerated during the last several years, rather than stagnated as in other mature expansions, and price inflation has been on a falling, not a rising, trend.

In the later stages of the two previous long expansions, productivity growth slowed to just above a 1 percent annual rate. In contrast, over the last two years, productivity has been growing nearly 3 percent a year, in part owing to rapid business investment. Strong productivity growth has enabled the economy to grow rapidly and helped restrain the cost pressures typically associated with a strong economy.

Inflation trends provide a second sign of an expansion's age and health. Late in the expansions of the 1960s and the 1980s, high rates of utilization and decelerating productivity contributed to an acceleration in prices, that is, a rising inflation rate. In the current expansion, even with unemployment well below 5 percent, the acceleration in productivity has helped keep inflation stable. In fact, inflation has fallen relative to the previous two-year period. Surveys of inflation expectations provide a further encouraging sign that inflation remains in check: These surveys show that both consumers and professional forecasters expect inflation to stay low over the next several years. Some have argued that the U.S. economy is now nearly immune to the business cycle, because of the effects of increased international competition, rapid innovation and productivity growth, and improved flexibility of the production and distribution systems.

Of course, it is premature to declare the business cycle dead. But there are reasons to believe that the economy will continue to perform as well as, if not better than, it has in the recent past, with less of the roller-coaster ride that characterized the 1970s and early 1980s (not to mention earlier decades). Unlike in the 1980s and early 1990s, fiscal discipline is now the order of the day. Projected surpluses can now be used to pay down the debt and free up capital for investment in education, business, and technology, spurring faster growth. Likewise, the Federal Reserve no longer follows the stop-and-go policies of the 1970s, but instead practices a systematic policy that fosters price stability and long-term growth.

The End of the Business Cycle Revisited[2]

The United States relies on the National Bureau of Economic Research (NBER) to define the business cycle activity of the U.S. economy and according to its assessment the last expansion in the U.S. economy lasted 10 years, the longest expansion in U.S. history. However, that expansion was showing signs of trouble within months of the February 2000 release of the preceding *Economic Report of the President.* By March 2001, the economy was officially in recession, a state that lasted for eight months, until November 2001. How do this recession and the economic events since then affect our assessment of U.S. business cycles?

Clearly, the business cycle is not dead and recessions *are* possible, even in our "new economy"; information processing and high-tech production do not eliminate the

[2]By Deborah J. Paige.

forces that regularly pressure the economy. In fact, they may have contributed to the recent recession, in that high-tech spending on Y2K both sped up investment spending in the late 1990s and dramatically slowed it down after the millennium. Businesses had largely spent their technology investment budgets for several years into the future preparing for Y2K, then had little incentive or money to spend further. This pressured technology producers and their stocks; the high sales and profits of the late 1990s had created unrealistic expectations in the tech sector and led to unsustainably high stock prices. Many analysts believe that the tech sector led the entire market to unreasonably high levels, given the underlying profit and sales fundamentals. As the stock market drops precipitously, billions of dollars of personal and corporate wealth disappear, affecting future spending by businesses and households. This was compounded by accounting scandals, such as Enron, that further undermined confidence in U.S. equity markets.

On the other hand, this last recession lasted only eight months, as did the previous recession from July 1990 to March 1991. The average length of an American recession (from peak to trough) has dropped from about 20 months (1854–1945) to 10 months (1945–2001). Both of the last recessions followed unusually long expansions, 92 months for the expansion of the 1980s and 120 months for the expansion of the 1990s. In addition, GDP fell by less than average during the recession of 2001. This does appear to support the contention that the business cycle is moderating—that recessions are shorter, milder, and less frequent than in the past. It will be interesting to observe whether the U.S. economy returns to the robust days of the middle to late 1990s in a timely manner or whether that period was due largely to special circumstances that are unlikely to be repeated.

Discussion Questions

1. How might a mature economic expansion create its own end? What economic theories are most compatible with the idea that real-world events have been a major cause of modern recessions? What economic theories are most compatible with the idea that government policies have been a major cause of modern recessions?

2. How do modern inventory controls and a service economy make the economy more stable?

3. What are the major differences between the recent expansion in the U.S. economy and other expansions that lasted a very long time? How do you believe this affects the likelihood of the current expansion's ending soon?

CHAPTER 15

The Business Firm: Organization, Motivation, and Optimal Input Decisions

Chapter Profile

There are three principal types of business firms: proprietorships, partnerships, and corporations. The corporation has many advantages over the other two: limited liability, unlimited life, and greater ability to raise large sums of money. Nonetheless, because the corporation also has disadvantages, such as the double taxation of corporate profits, many firms are not corporations. (Note: The government is currently experimenting with eliminating this double taxation by ceasing to tax dividends.)

As a first approximation, economists generally assume that firms attempt to maximize profits. In large part, this is because it is a close enough approximation to reality for many of the most important purposes of economics. Also, economists are interested in the theory of the profit-maximizing firm because it provides rules of behavior for firms that want to maximize profits.

To summarize the characteristics of existing technology at a given point in time, the economist uses the concept of the production function, which shows the maximum output rate of a given commodity that can be achieved from any specified set of usage rates of inputs.

Inputs can be classified into two categories: fixed and variable. A fixed input is one whose quantity cannot be changed during the period of time under consideration. A variable input is one whose quantity can be changed during the relevant period. Whether an input is considered variable or fixed depends on the length of the period under consideration. The longer the period, the more inputs are variable not fixed. The *short run* is defined as the period of time in which some of the firm's inputs (generally its plant and equipment) are fixed. The *long run* is the period of time in which all inputs are variable.

The average product of an input is the firm's total output divided by the amount of input used to produce this amount of output. The marginal product of an input is the addition to total output due to the addition of the last unit of input, the quantity of other inputs used being held constant.

The law of diminishing marginal returns states that, if equal increments of an input are added (and the quantities of other inputs held constant), beyond some point, the resulting increments of product decrease; that is, the marginal product of the input diminishes.

To minimize its costs, a firm must choose its input combination so that the marginal product of a dollar's worth of any one input equals the marginal product of a dollar's worth of any other input used. Put differently, the firm should combine inputs so that, for every input used, the marginal product of the input is proportional to its price. As an illustration, we showed in Exploring Further how this sort of model can be used to determine the optimal combination of fertilizer and land in the production of Kansas corn.

Concepts for Review

proprietorship
partnership
corporation
profits
profit maximization
input
production function

fixed input
variable input
short run
long run
average product
marginal product
law of diminishing marginal returns

Completion Questions

1. The _____ of an input is the change in total output due to the addition of the last unit of input.

2. The average product of an input is the firm's _____ divided by the _____.

3. A firm minimizes cost by combining inputs so that, for every input used, the _____ of the input is proportional to the input's _____.

4. The marginal product must exceed the average product when the latter is (decreasing, increasing) _____, it must equal the average product when the latter reaches a (maximum, minimum) _____, and it must be less than the average product when the latter is (decreasing, increasing) _____ .

5. An inefficient combination of inputs is one that includes (less, more) _____ of at least one input and as much of other inputs as some other combination of inputs that can produce the same _____. Inefficient combinations generally (can, cannot) _____ minimize costs or maximize profits.

6. The firm minimizes cost by combining inputs in such a way that the (average product, marginal product) _____ of a dollar's worth of any one input equals the (average product, marginal product) _____ of a dollar's worth of any other input used.

7. If the marginal product of the first unit of labor equals two units of output and the marginal product of the second unit of labor equals three units of output,

the total output produced with two units of labor equals _____ units of output. This answer remains valid only if the quantities of other

_____ are held constant and there is no change in

_____.

8. If the marginal product of the eighth unit of labor equals the marginal product of the ninth unit of labor and if total output with seven units of labor is 80 and total output with nine units of labor is 90, the marginal product of the

eighth unit of labor equals _____.

9. The average product of labor equals $3L$, where L is the number of units of labor employed per day. The total output produced per day if four units of labor

are employed per day is _____. The total output produced

per day if five units of labor are employed per day is _____. The marginal product of the fifth unit of labor employed per day is

_____.

True-False

_____ 1. If the average product of labor equals $6/L$, where L is the number of units of labor employed per day, total output is the same regardless of how much labor is used per day.

_____ 2. Corporations are the most common form of business in the United States.

_____ 3. If the average product of labor equals 4 when the number of units of labor employed per day is between one and six, the marginal product of labor also equals 4 when the amount of labor used is within this range.

_____ 4. If the average product of labor equals $5L$, where L is the number of units of labor employed per day, the law of diminishing marginal returns is violated.

_____ 5. In production processes, both the average product of the variable input and the marginal product usually rise, fall, and then rise again to infinity.

_____ 6. The law of diminishing marginal returns indicates that, if equal increments of an input are added (and quantities of others are held constant), the marginal product of the input diminishes beyond some point.

_____ 7. The long run refers to a period when all inputs are variable.

_____ 8. The average product of an input is the addition to total output due to the addition of the last unit of input, the quantity of other inputs used being held constant.

_____ 9. The marginal product curve intersects the average product curve when the latter is at a maximum.

_____ 10. If technology changes, the law of diminishing marginal returns can predict the effect of an additional unit of input.

_____ 11. The law of diminishing marginal returns is not applicable to cases where there is a proportional increase in all inputs.

_____ 12. If the price of a unit of capital is equal to the price of a unit of labor, a cost-minimizing firm chooses a combination of inputs where the marginal product of capital minus the marginal product of labor equals zero.

_____ 13. Corporate managers always choose to maximize profit.

_____ 14. If the price of a unit of capital is double the price of a unit of labor, a cost-minimizing firm chooses a combination of inputs where the marginal product of capital minus the marginal product of labor equals the marginal product of labor.

_____ 15. If labor can be obtained free, a cost-minimizing firm chooses a combination of inputs where the marginal product of capital minus the marginal product of labor equals the marginal product of capital.

Multiple Choice

1. If the marginal product of capital is negative,

    a. more capital results in less output.
    b. more capital does not affect output.
    c. more capital increases output but at a decreasing rate.
    d. more capital increases output at an increasing rate.
    e. none of the above.

2. If labor is the only input, a cost-minimizing firm, if it can hire all the labor it wants at $8 per hour and must produce 10 units of output per day,

    a. maximizes the amount of output from the labor it hires.
    b. minimizes the amount of labor used to produce the 10 units per day.
    c. operates at a point on the production function.
    d. all of the above.
    e. none of the above.

3. Between one and two units of labor, what is the marginal product of labor if the average product of labor is 20 bushels for one unit of labor and 25 bushels for two units of labor?

   a. 20 bushels
   b. 25 bushels
   c. 30 bushels
   d. 40 bushels
   e. 50 bushels

4. Which of the following statements about the law of diminishing marginal returns is *not* true?

   a. It assumes that technology remains fixed.
   b. No input should be used beyond the point where the marginal product falls.
   c. At least one input is fixed in quantity.
   d. It must be possible to vary the proportions in which various inputs are used.
   e. It generally holds in both agriculture and industry.

5. On the basis of its production function alone, a firm can determine

   a. what input combination to use.
   b. what amount of output to produce.
   c. what price to charge.
   d. all of the above.
   e. none of the above.

6. Firm A is run by a big-time spender who wants to maximize the amount he produces, regardless of the amount that it costs. Firm A should increase its employment of

   a. labor indefinitely.
   b. capital indefinitely.
   c. labor until the marginal product of labor is zero.
   d. capital until the marginal product of capital is zero.
   e. a and b.
   f. c and d.

7. You own a 10 percent share of a partnership. Your partner declares personal bankruptcy. You could be responsible for a maximum of

   a. 10 percent of the business debts.
   b. 50 percent of the business debts.
   c. 100 percent of the business debts.
   d. an amount equal to your investment.
   e. an amount equal to the net worth of the partnership.

Discussion and Extension Questions

1. "Any fool knows that a firm should not operate at a point where there are rising marginal returns." Comment and evaluate.

2. Suppose that capital and labor are a firm's only inputs. If the price of capital is held constant, how can we determine how many units of labor the firm hires at various prices of labor if the output of the firm is held constant? Show that the amount of labor that the firm hires is inversely related to the price of labor.

3. Is the production function for an auto firm the same in the long run as in the short run? Why or why not?

4. Is General Motors's production function the same as Ford's? Is General Motors' production function the same as the production function of an automobile manufacturer in Argentina? Explain.

5. Do firms have detailed, reliable information concerning the quantity of output that they receive from every combination of inputs? Or do they have such information only concerning those input combinations close to those that they have used or experimented with? Explain.

6. Do firms take their production functions as given, or do they engage in various kinds of activities to alter their production functions? If the latter is the case, what are some names commonly used to designate activities of this sort? Give some examples of cases where firms altered their production functions.

7. Is it commonly true that activities carried out by one firm alter another firm's production function? If so, is this commonly true even though the firms are in different industries? Explain, and give examples to buttress your answer.

Problems

1. Suppose that the production function for a 1-acre wheat farm is as follows:

Number of units of labor	Bushels of wheat produced per year
1	50
2	90
3	120
4	145
5	165

a. What is the average product of labor when one unit of labor is used?

b. What is the marginal product of labor when between two and three units of labor are used?

c. Does the law of diminishing marginal returns seem to hold? Why or why not?

2. Suppose that the production function for a car wash is as follows:

Hours of labor per day	Cars washed per day	Average product of labor		Marginal product of labor
0	0	_____		
1	2	_____		_____
2	5	_____		_____
3	7	_____		_____
4	8	_____		_____

a. Fill in the blanks in the table on the preceding page.
b. Why don't we compute the average product of labor when there are zero hours of labor?

3. Suppose that the marginal product of labor is as follows:

Quantity of labor per day		Marginal product of labor	Total output per day
0			0
1		3	—
2		5	—
3		8	—
4		—	23
5		2	—

a. Fill in the blanks.
b. Does this case conform to the law of diminishing marginal returns? Why or why not?

4. Suppose that the average product of capital is as follows:

Quantity of capital used per day	Average product of capital		Marginal product of capital
1	3		_____
2	8		_____
3	8		_____
4	6		_____
5	4		

a. Fill in the blanks.
b. What is the maximum amount of capital that this firm uses per day? Why?

5. The average product of labor equals 6, regardless of how much labor is used.

    a. What is the marginal product of the first unit of labor?
    b. What is the marginal product of the fiftieth unit of labor?
    c. By how much does output increase if labor is increased by 200 units?
    d. By how much does output fall if labor is reduced by 100 units?
    e. Does this case conform to the law of diminishing marginal returns? Why or why not?
    f. Does this case seem realistic? Why or why not?

6. A firm uses two inputs, labor and capital. The price of capital is $5 per unit, the price of labor is $7 per unit, and the marginal product of capital is 15.

    a. Is the firm minimizing its cost if the marginal product of labor is 20? Why or why not?
    b. If the firm is not minimizing its cost, should it use more or less labor relative to capital? Why?
    c. If the marginal product of labor is 23, is the firm minimizing its cost? Why or why not?
    d. If the firm is not minimizing its cost, should it use more or less labor relative to capital? Why?
    e. If the marginal product of labor is 21, is the firm minimizing its cost? Why or why not?

Answers

Completion Questions

1. marginal product   2. total output, quantity of input used   3. marginal product, price   4. increasing, maximum, decreasing   5. more, output, cannot
6. marginal product, marginal product   7. five, inputs, technology   8. five
9. 48, 75, 27

True-False

1. True   2. False   3. True   4. True   5. False   6. True   7. True   8. False
9. True   10. False   11. True   12. True   13. False   14. True   15. True

Multiple Choice

1. a   2. d   3. c   4. b   5. e   6. f   7. c

Problems

1. a. 50 bushels of wheat per unit of labor.
    b. 30 bushels of wheat.
    c. Yes, because as more labor is used, the marginal product of labor declines.

2. a.

Average product of labor		Marginal product of labor
—		
		2
2		
		3
2$\frac{1}{2}$		
		2
2$\frac{1}{3}$		
		1
2		

b. Because it would mean dividing zero by zero, since both output and labor are zero.

3. a.

Marginal product of labor		Total product per day
		0
3		
		3
5		
		8
8		
		16
7		
		23
2		
		25

b. Yes, because marginal product eventually falls as more labor is applied.

4. a.

Marginal product of capital
13
8
0
−4

b. Three units, since the price of capital is greater than zero, the firm would lose money on the fourth unit, where MP = 0.

5. a. 6.
   b. 6.
   c. 1,200.
   d. 600.
   e. No, because the marginal product of labor is the same regardless of how much labor is used.
   f. No, because it violates the law of diminishing marginal returns.

6. a. No, because the ratio of the marginal product of capital to its price does not equal the ratio of the marginal product of labor to its price.
   b. It should use less labor because the ratio of labor's marginal product to its price is lower than the ratio of capital's marginal product to its price.

c. No, for the same reason as in part a.

d. It should use more labor because the ratio of labor's marginal product to its price is higher than the ratio of capital's marginal product to its price.

e. Yes, because the ratio of labor's marginal product to its price equals the ratio of capital's marginal product to its price.

CHAPTER 16

Getting Behind the Demand and

Supply Curves

Chapter Profile

Utility is a number that represents the level of satisfaction derived by the consumer from a particular market basket. Market baskets with higher utilities are preferred over market baskets with lower utilities.

The model of consumer behavior recognizes that preferences alone do not determine the consumer's actions. Choices are dictated by the size of the consumer's money income and the nature of commodity prices. These factors, as well as the consumer's preferences, determine choice.

If consumers maximize utility, their income is allocated among commodities so that for every commodity purchased, the marginal utility of the commodity is proportional to its price. In other words, the marginal utility of the last dollar spent on each commodity is made equal for all commodities purchased.

The individual demand curve shows the quantity of a good demanded by a particular consumer at various prices of the good. The individual demand curve for practically all goods slopes downward and to the right. Its location depends on the consumer's income and tastes and the prices of other goods.

To derive the market demand curve, we obtain the horizontal sum of all the individual demand curves of the people in the market. Since individual demand curves for a commodity almost always slope downward to the right, it follows that market demand curves too almost always slope downward to the right.

The cost of a certain course of action is the value of the best alternative course of action that could have been pursued instead. This is the doctrine of opportunity, or alternative, cost. Economists include this opportunity cost in their calculations.

Three kinds of total cost functions are important in the short run: total fixed cost, total variable cost, and total cost. In addition, there are three kinds of average cost functions (corresponding to each of the total cost functions): average fixed cost, average variable cost, and average total cost.

Marginal cost—the addition to total cost due to the addition of the last unit of output—is of enormous significance in the firm's decision-making process. Because of the law of diminishing marginal returns, marginal cost tends to increase beyond some output level. This causes the supply curve to slope upward.

The firm's long-run average cost curve shows the minimum average cost of producing each output level when any desired type or scale of plant can be built. The shape of the long-run average cost curve is determined in part by whether there are increasing, decreasing, or constant returns to scale.

Suppose that a firm increases the amount of all inputs by the same percentage. If output increases by more than this percentage, this is a case of increasing returns to scale. If output increases by less than this percentage, this is a case of decreasing returns to scale. If output increases by this same percentage, this is a case of constant returns to scale.

Concepts for Review

model of consumer behavior

utility

marginal utility

law of diminishing marginal utility

equilibrium market basket

individual demand curve

market demand curve

opportunity or alternative cost

explicit costs

implicit costs

cost functions

short run

long run

total fixed cost

total variable cost

total cost

average fixed cost

average variable cost

average total cost

law of diminishing marginal
   returns

marginal cost

long-run average cost function

increasing returns to scale

decreasing returns to scale

constant returns to scale

Completion Questions

1. Economists assume that the consumer attempts to _____utility.

2. If the prices of goods X and Y are both $2 per unit and the marginal utility of good X is twice that of good Y, the consumer should buy (less, more)

   _____ of good X and (less, more) _____
   of good Y.

3. If the average fixed cost is triple the average variable cost and the average total

   cost is $40, the average fixed cost equals _____ and the

   average variable cost equals _____. If the marginal cost equals

   $20, the average variable cost is (rising, falling) _____ and

   average total cost is (rising, falling) _____.

4. The total cost at a given output is the sum of the _____ and

   _____.

5. The average fixed cost is the firm's total fixed cost divided by its

   _____.

6. Total fixed cost is the total expenditure per period of time by the firm for

   _____ inputs. Since the quantity of the _____

inputs does not vary (by definition), the total fixed costs are (the same, different) _____ for various levels of the firm's output. Among the firm's fixed costs in the short run are _____ taxes and _____ on bonds issued in the past.

7. The total variable cost is the total expenditure per period of time on _____ inputs. Due to the law of diminishing marginal returns, the total variable cost (decreases, increases) _____ first at a(n) (decreasing, increasing) _____ rate, then at a(n) (decreasing, increasing) _____ rate.

8. The average total cost is the total cost divided by _____. It equals the average _____ cost plus average _____ cost; and beyond a point, it increases as output _____ because of the law of diminishing marginal returns.

9. The marginal cost is the addition to the total cost resulting from the _____ of the last unit of output. Beyond a point, it _____ as output increases because of the law of diminishing marginal returns.

10. If the marginal cost of producing the first unit of output is $20, the marginal cost of producing the second unit of output is $25, and the marginal cost of producing the third unit of output is $30, the total variable cost of producing three units of output is _____. The average variable cost of producing two units of output is _____.

Average variable cost (rises, falls) _____ when output increases from one to three units.

11. If the average fixed cost of producing 10 units of output is $10, the average fixed cost of producing 20 units is _____. If the marginal cost of each of the first 20 units of output is $5, the average variable cost of producing 20 units is _____. And the average total cost of producing 20 units is _____.

True-False

_____ 1. If there are diminishing marginal returns from the variable input, the total variable cost ultimately increases at an increasing rate.

_____ 2. If the marginal cost always increases with increases in output, so must the average variable cost always increase with increases in output.

_____ 3. If the average variable cost always equals $10 when output is less than 100 units, the marginal cost is less than $10 when output is in this range.

_____ 4. There is sometimes a marked difference between social and private costs of producing a given commodity.

_____ 5. The average fixed cost must increase in the short run with increases in output.

_____ 6. Since price is not usually influenced by the amount sold, the total revenue is equal to output.

_____ 7. The average cost is at a minimum only when it is lower than the marginal cost.

_____ 8. If a payment is made to a supplier (other than the firm's owner), this is an explicit cost.

_____ 9. The total cost curve differs by a constant amount (equal to the total fixed cost) from the total variable cost curve.

_____ 10. Cost functions are used extensively by firms and other groups to estimate the effect of the sales rate on costs.

_____ 11. A principal determinant of the shape of the long-run average cost function is the law of diminishing marginal returns.

_____ 12. In the long run, a firm's fixed costs in industries like steel and autos may amount to tens of millions of dollars per year.

_____ 13. When a firm experiences diminishing marginal returns to its variable input, the marginal cost is increasing.

Multiple Choice

1. Suppose that Mary Murphy's total utility from various quantities of good X and good Y are as follows:

Good X		Good Y	
Quantity	Total utility	Quantity	Total utility
0	0	0	0
1	10	1	30
2	30	2	50
3	40	3	60
4	45	4	65
5	48	5	67
6	50	6	68

For good X, diminishing marginal utility occurs at

a. some but not all quantities consumed.
b. quantities exceeding two.
c. larger quantities than those where increasing marginal utility occurs.
d. all of the above.
e. none of the above.

2. In the previous question, the price of good X equals the price of good Y, and Murphy's income allows her to buy six units of good X. Under these circumstances, her optimal market basket is

a. four units of good X and two units of good Y.
b. three units of good X and three units of good Y.
c. two units of good X and four units of good Y.
d. five units of good X and one unit of good Y.
e. none of the above.

3. In question 2, if good X's price is $5, the marginal utility of the last dollar spent on good X is 4 if Murphy consumes

a. one unit of good X and one unit of good Y.
b. two units of good X and two units of good Y.
c. three units of good X and three units of good Y.
d. all of the above.
e. none of the above.

4. In question 2, if good X's price is $5, good Y's price is $10, and Murphy has $35 to spend on good X and good Y combined, she should purchase

a. a market basket where the marginal utility of the last dollar spent on good X equals 2.
b. a market basket where the marginal utility of the last dollar spent on good Y equals 2.
c. two units of good Y and three units of good X.
d. all of the above.
e. none of the above.

5. John Jones has eight hours to spend, during which he can either play tennis or read. The marginal utility he obtains from an hour of reading is 8 utils. The total utility he obtains from one, two, three, four, and five hours of tennis is as follows:

Hours	Total utility
1	20
2	33
3	40
4	40
5	35

If he maximizes utility (and can allocate only an integer number of hours to each activity), he spends

a. three hours playing tennis and five hours reading.
b. two hours playing tennis and six hours reading.
c. four hours playing tennis and four hours reading.
d. one hour playing tennis and seven hours reading.
e. none of the above.

6. Firms A and B have identical total variable cost functions, but firm A's total fixed costs are $10,000 per month higher than firm B's.

a. The two firms have identical marginal cost curves.
b. Firm A's marginal cost curve is parallel to, but higher than, firm B's marginal cost curve.
c. Firm A's marginal cost curve is parallel to, but lower than, firm B's marginal cost curve.
d. Firm A's marginal cost curve is higher than that of firm B.
e. None of the above.

7. Suppose that firm C's total costs per month equal $50,000 + $10Q$, where Q is the number of units of output produced per month. If firm C produces 100 units of output per month, its average fixed cost and average variable cost are

a. $500 and $20.
b. $510 and $10.
c. $490 and $10.
d. $500 and $10.
e. none of the above.

8. Under the circumstances described in the previous question, increases in output result in decreases in

a. average total cost and no change in marginal cost.
b. average variable cost and no change in average total cost.
c. average fixed cost and increases in average variable cost.
d. average fixed cost and increases in marginal cost.
e. none of the above.

9. If marginal cost is less than average cost, then with increased inputs, the average cost of production tends to

a. rise.
b. drop.
c. stay the same.
d. all of the above.
e. none of the above.

10. In measuring long-run cost functions, it is generally found that, in most industries for which we have data,

a. the long-run average cost curve tends to be L-shaped.
b. the marginal cost tends to be constant at all output levels above zero.
c. the total, average total, and marginal cost functions tend to be W-shaped.
d. the shape of the long-run average cost curve is influenced by fixed costs.
e. long-run average costs increase at all output levels.

Discussion and Extension Questions

1. The state of Virginia reimburses its employees when personal cars are used for state business. What costs should the state regard as the relevant ones? Why?

2. Universities frequently ask for student opinion about instructors and courses. The usual method is to distribute a questionnaire in class toward the end of a term. What are the costs of such programs? Be sure to think through what economists mean by costs. Try to formulate an actual dollar cost at your institution. Do you think such surveys are worth the costs?

3. If a large increase in the demand for economists by business firms and government agencies increases the salaries of such people, how can one also say that it has increased the cost of having an economist at a university?

4. "Statistical studies have shown that total cost is generally a linear function of output. This has embarrassed some economists, who insist that marginal cost must rise. In fact, marginal cost does not rise as output increases." Discuss and evaluate.

5. Consulting firm X claims that the minimum point on the long-run average cost curve occurs at an output level of 1,000 tons of output per week in a certain industry. As evidence for this claim, they say that firms of this size reap the biggest profits. Is this conclusive evidence? Why or why not?

6. "The concept of marginal cost is a purely academic concept. In the real world, no one can possibly tell what the value of marginal cost is." Comment and evaluate.

7. What is the cost of a certain course of action? Be specific.

8. Why does the marginal cost curve intersect both the average variable cost curve and the average total cost curve at their minimum points? Can there be cases where this is not true?

9. Suppose that two firms have exactly the same marginal cost curve, but their average fixed cost curve is not the same. Will their average variable cost curve be the same?

10. According to the *New York Times*, the cost of producing a barrel of oil from shale was thought by experts to be about $4.40 in 1972, about $10 in 1978, and about $25 in 1979. What factors can account for such great increases? Did productivity decrease in the industry? Did input prices change?

Problems

1. Suppose that the Chicago plant of the Bolton Press Company's fixed costs are $1,000 per month, and its variable costs are as follows.

a. Fill in the blanks.

Output (presses per month)	Total fixed cost (dollars)	Total variable cost (dollars)	Total cost (dollars)
0	_____	0	_____
1	_____	500	_____
2	_____	1,000	_____
3	_____	2,000	_____
4	_____	3,500	_____
5	_____	5,000	_____

b. Fill in the blanks. These blanks indicate the average cost functions of the Chicago plant of the Bolton Press Company.

Output (presses per month)	Average fixed cost (dollars)	Average variable cost (dollars)	Average total cost (dollars)
1	_____	_____	_____
2	_____	_____	_____
3	_____	_____	_____
4	_____	_____	_____
5	_____	_____	_____

c. Fill in the blanks.

Output (presses per month)	Marginal cost (dollars)
0 to 1	_____
1 to 2	_____
2 to 3	_____
3 to 4	_____
4 to 5	_____

2. Suppose that the Wilson Press Company's short-run total cost function is as follows:

Output (number of units per year)	Total cost (dollars per year)
0	20,000
1	20,100
2	20,200
3	20,300
4	20,500
5	20,800

a. What are the firm's total fixed costs?
b. What are its total variable costs when it produces four units per year?
c. What is the firm's marginal cost when between four and five units are produced per year?
d. Does marginal cost increase beyond some output level? Why?

3. Farm A is a profit-maximizing, perfectly competitive producer of wheat. It produces wheat using 1 acre of land (price = $1,000) and varying inputs of labor (price = $500 per person-month). The production function is as follows:

Number of person-months (per month)	Output per month (in truckloads)
0	0
1	1
3	2
7	3
12	4
18	5
25	6

Show that the production of farm A is subject to increasing marginal cost.

4. The production function, the price of the variable input, and the total fixed costs of the ABC Company follow. (Prices and costs are in dollars.) Fill in the blanks.

Units of variable input	Units of output produced	Average product	Marginal product	Unit price of variable input	Total variable cost	Average variable cost	Total fixed cost	Total cost	Average total cost	Marginal cost
0	0	___		2	___	___	100	___	___	
1	4	___	⟩—	2	___	___	100	___	___	⟩—
2	9	___	⟩—	2	___	___	100	___	___	⟩—
3	15	___	⟩—	2	___	___	100	___	___	⟩—
4	22	___	⟩—	2	___	___	100	___	___	⟩—
5	30	___	⟩—	2	___	___	100	___	___	⟩—
6	37	___	⟩—	2	___	___	100	___	___	⟩—
7	43	___	⟩—	2	___	___	100	___	___	⟩—
8	48	___	⟩—	2	___	___	100	___	___	⟩—
9	52	___	⟩—	2	___	___	100	___	___	⟩—

5. A firm can build plants of three types: D, E, and F. The short-run average cost curve with each type follows:

Type D		Type E		Type F	
Output	Average cost (dollars)	Output	Average cost (dollars)	Output	Average cost (dollars)
20	10	80	6	140	3.00
40	8	100	4	160	2.00
60	6	120	2	180	0.50
80	4	140	1	200	0.40
100	6	160	1	220	0.75

a. Draw the firm's long-run average cost curve in this graph:

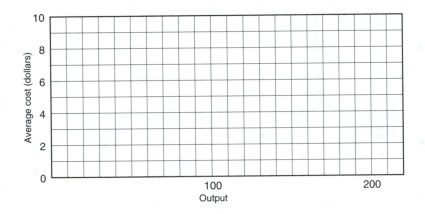

b. What is the minimum price at which the firm stays in the industry?

6. Firm S hires a consultant to estimate its long-run total cost function. The consultant, after a long study, concludes that for firm S, long-run cost equals $2 million + $4 × Q, where Q is annual output.

a. What does this equation imply about the long-run total cost of producing nothing? Is this reasonable? Why or why not?

b. What is the minimum value of long-run average cost?

c. What size of plant results in the minimum value of long-run average cost? Is this reasonable? Why or why not?

7. Firm P's total cost curve follows:

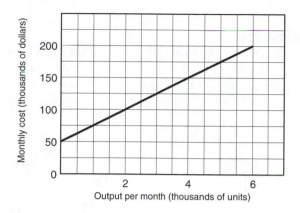

a. Draw the firm's marginal cost function in this graph:

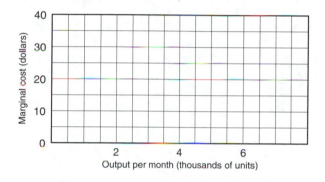

b. Suppose that it is impossible for firm P to produce more than 6,000 units of output per month. What is marginal cost at outputs above 6,000?

8. On the basis of the graph in the previous problem, fill in the blanks in this table for firm P.

Output (thousands)	Average fixed cost (dollars)	Average variable cost (dollars)	Average total cost (dollars)
1	____	____	____
2	____	____	____
3	____	____	____
4	____	____	____
5	____	____	____
6	____	____	____

Answers

Completion Questions
1. maximize   2. more, less   3. $30, $10, rising, falling   4. total fixed cost, total variable cost   5. output   6. fixed, fixed, the same, property, interest   7. variable, increases, decreasing, increasing   8. output, fixed, variable, increases   9. addition, increases   10. $75, $22.50, rises   11. $5, $5, $10

True-False
1. True   2. True   3. False   4. True   5. False   6. False   7. False   8. True
9. True   10. True   11. False   12. False   13. True

Multiple Choice
1. d   2. b   3. c   4. d   5. b   6. a   7. d   8. a   9. b   10. a

Problems

1. a.

Total fixed cost (dollars)	Total cost (dollars)
1,000	1,000
1,000	1,500
1,000	2,000
1,000	3,000
1,000	4,500
1,000	6,000

b.

Average fixed cost (dollars)	Average variable cost (dollars)	Average total cost (dollars)
1,000	500	1,500
500	500	1,000
333	667	1,000
250	875	1,125
200	1,000	1,200

c.

Marginal cost (dollars)
500
500
1,000
1,500
1,500

2. a. $20,000.
   b. $500.
   c. $300.
   d. Yes. The law of diminishing marginal returns.

3. Since the services of each person cost $500 per month, the total variable cost of each output level (per month) is

Output	Total variable cost (dollars)
0	0
1	500
2	1,500
3	3,500
4	6,000
5	9,000
6	12,500

Therefore, the marginal cost is $500 between 0 and 1 units of output, $1,000 between 1 and 2 units of output, and so forth. Clearly, marginal cost increases as output increases.

4.

Average product	Marginal product	Total variable cost	Average variable cost	Total cost	Average total cost	Marginal cost
—		0	—	100	—	
	4					0.50
4		2	$^1/_2$	102	$25^1/_2$	
	5					0.40
$4^1/_2$		4	$^4/_9$	104	$11^5/_9$	
	6					0.33
5		6	$^6/_{15}$	106	$7^1/_{15}$	
	7					0.29
$5^1/_2$		8	$^8/_{22}$	108	$4^{10}/_{11}$	
	8					0.25
6		10	$^1/_3$	110	$3^2/_3$	
	7					0.29
$6^1/_6$		12	$^{12}/_{37}$	112	$3^1/_{37}$	
	6					0.33
$6^1/_7$		14	$^{14}/_{43}$	114	$2^{28}/_{43}$	
	5					0.40
6		16	$^1/_3$	116	$2^{20}/_{48}$	
	4					0.50
$5^7/_9$		18	$^{18}/_{52}$	118	$2^{14}/_{52}$	

5. a.

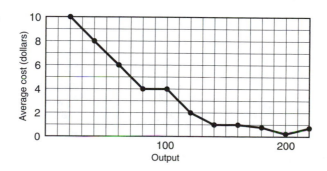

  b. $0.40.

6. a. It implies it equals $2 million. No, because there are no fixed costs in the long run.

  b. $4.

  c. An infinite size of plant. No, because one would expect that eventually the long-run average cost function would turn up.

  b. Infinite.

7. a.

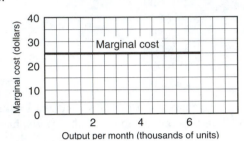

8.

Average fixed cost (dollars)	Average variable cost (dollars)	Average total cost (dollars)
50	25	75
25	25	50
$16^2/_3$	25	$41^2/_3$
$12^1/_2$	25	$37^1/_2$
10	25	35
$8^1/_3$	25	$33^1/_3$

CHAPTER 17

Market Demand and Price Elasticity

Chapter Profile

The market demand curve, which is the relationship between the price of a commodity and the amount of the commodity demanded in the market, is one of the most important and frequently used concepts in economics. The shape and position of a product's market demand curve depend on consumers' tastes, consumers' income, the price of other goods, and the number of consumers in the market.

The price elasticity of demand, defined as the percentage change in quantity demanded resulting from a 1 percent change in price, measures the sensitivity of the amount demanded to changes in price. Whether a price increase results in an increase or decrease in the total amount spent on a commodity depends on the price elasticity of demand.

The market demand curve for a commodity is not the same as the demand curve for the output of a single firm that produces the commodity, unless the industry is composed of only one firm. In general, the demand curve for the output of a single firm is more elastic than the market demand curve for the commodity. Indeed, if many firms are selling a homogeneous commodity, the individual firm's demand curve becomes horizontal.

The income elasticity of demand, defined as the percentage change in quantity demanded resulting from a 1 percent increase in total money income, measures the sensitivity of the amount demanded to changes in total income. A commodity's income elasticity of demand may be positive or negative. Luxury items are generally assumed to have higher income elasticities of demand than necessities.

The cross elasticity of demand, defined as the percentage change in the quantity demanded resulting from a 1 percent change in the price of another commodity, measures the sensitivity of the amount demanded to changes in the price of another commodity. If the cross elasticity of demand is positive, two commodities are substitutes; if it is negative, they are complements.

*Agriculture in the United States has been plagued by relatively low incomes. Until 1973, the demand for farm products grew slowly, while rapid technological change meant that the people and resources currently in agriculture could supply more and more farm products. Because people and resources did not move out of agriculture as rapidly as the price system dictated, farm incomes tended to be relatively low.

*The starred item pertains to material covered in Exploring Further.

*In response to political pressures from the farm blocs, the government set in motion a series of programs to aid farmers. A cornerstone of these programs was the concept of parity, which said that the prices farmers receive should increase at the same rate as the prices of the goods and services farmers buy. The government instituted price supports to keep farm prices above their equilibrium level. But, since the support prices exceeded the equilibrium prices, the government had to purchase and store the surplus of the commodities. To help reduce these surpluses, the government tried to restrict the output of farm products and expand the demand for them.

*Since both the supply and demand of agricultural products are relatively inelastic, prices fluctuate significantly with shifts in demand or supply. Periods of farm prosperity tend to alternate with periods of losses. In 1973, farm prices increased greatly, due partly to very great increases in foreign demand for U.S. agricultural products. By 1975, many people felt that U.S. agriculture no longer suffered from overcapacity. But subsequently farmers complained bitterly of low prices and their need for government assistance. In the early 1990s, American farms showed improving incomes and household wealth and attempts were made to reduce government support of agriculture. Unfortunately, by the late 1990s, American farmers were hard hit by falling agricultural prices worldwide, and the Clinton administration reversed its position on reducing farm aid.

Concepts for Review

market demand curve	income elasticity of demand
price elasticity of demand	cross elasticity of demand
arc elasticity of demand	substitutes
price elastic	complements
price inelastic	parity
unitary elasticity	price supports

Completion Questions

1. When income increases from $80 billion to $81 billion, the quantity demanded of good X increases from 3,000 to 3,050. The income elasticity of demand for good X equals _____. When computing the income elasticity of demand, the price of good X is held _____.

2. When the price of good X rises from $2.00 to $2.10, the quantity demanded of good X falls from 3,000 to 2,800. The price elasticity of demand for good X equals _____. The demand for good X is (elastic, inelastic) _____.

*The starred items pertain to material covered in Exploring Further.

3. The total amount spent on a good is not affected by its price if the price elasticity of demand equals _____. The total quantity demanded of a good is not affected by its price if the price elasticity of demand equals _____.

4. If the government imposes a $1 tax on a commodity, it will obtain the most revenue from the tax if the commodity's price elasticity of demand equals _____. The largest burden of the tax is borne by consumers if the price elasticity of demand equals _____.

5. Whether a price cut results in an increase in the total amount spent on a commodity depends on the _____.

6. The total amount spent on a commodity is the _____ times _____.

7. If the demand for a commodity is price inelastic, then the price elasticity of demand is _____.

8. The income elasticity of demand is the percentage change in the quantity demanded resulting from _____ increase in total _____.

9. If the cross elasticity of demand is positive, two commodities are _____.

10. The demand for a commodity is _____ when the price increase or decrease results in no difference in the total amount spent on the commodity.

11. The _____ is the percentage change in quantity demanded resulting from a 1 percent change in price.

12. During a (long, short) _____ period, demand for a nondurable good is likely to be more sensitive to price than over a (long, short) _____ one. The longer the period, the (easier, harder) _____ it is for consumers to substitute one good for another.

13. The demand curve for the output of a particular firm is generally (less, more) _____ price elastic than the market demand curve for the commodity, because the products of other firms in the industry are close (substitutes, complements) _____ for the product of this firm.

True-False

_____ 1. An increase in the price of fishing licenses reduces the quantity of fishing poles demanded.

_____ 2. An increase in the subway fare in Philadelphia increases the ridership on buses in Philadelphia.

_____ 3. Holding constant the demand curve of a perfectly competitive firm, the total amount spent on the firm's product is proportional to the number of units of output it produces and sells.

_____ 4. The demand for an appendectomy is likely to be less price elastic than the demand for aspirin.

_____ 5. If the price elasticity of demand of product Y equals infinity and the government imposes a tax of $1 per unit on product Y, none of the tax is shifted to consumers.

_____ 6. If the quantity demanded of product Z falls by five units whenever the price of product Z increases by $1, the price elasticity of demand for product Z is 5.

_____ 7. The consumer generally tends to respond to an increase in a commodity's price by reducing the amount of it he or she consumes.

_____ 8. If the demand for a commodity is price elastic, an increase in its price leads to an increase in the total amount spent by consumers on the commodity.

_____ 9. A commodity's income elasticity of demand may be positive or negative.

_____ 10. The income elasticity of demand for food is very high.

_____ 11. The price elasticity of demand is expressed in terms of relative, not absolute, changes in price and quantity demanded.

_____ 12. The price elasticity of demand is a measure of the sensitivity of the quantity demanded to the price of other commodities.

_____ 13. Since the market demand curve reflects what consumers want and are willing to pay for, when the market demand curve for wheat shifts upward to the right, this indicates that consumers want more wheat at the existing price.

_____ 14. The demand for a particular brand of oil is more price elastic than the demand for fuel as a whole.

_____ 15. The demand for a commodity is price elastic if the price elasticity of demand is less than 1.

_____ 16. If the demand for the commodity is price elastic, an increase in its price leads to a decrease in the total amount spent by consumers on the commodity.

_____ 17. The demand for a commodity is price inelastic if the price elasticity of demand is greater than 1.

Multiple Choice

1. If $R = 30 + 2P$, where R is the total amount spent on good A and P is the price of good A, the price elasticity of demand for good A is

   a. less than 1.
   b. 1.
   c. 2.
   d. more than 2.
   e. none of the above.

2. A representative of organized labor says that an increase in the wage rate would have no effect on the total amount of wages paid to labor. If this is true, the price elasticity of demand for labor is

   a. less than 1.
   b. 1.
   c. 2.
   d. more than 2.
   e. none of the above.

3. The supply curve for product Q is a vertical line. The government establishes a floor under the price of product Q; this floor is $1 above the equilibrium price. The surplus of product Q is greatest if the price elasticity of demand of product Q is

   a. 0.25.
   b. 1.
   c. 1.25.
   d. 2.50.
   e. 3.

4. The amount of strawberries available on any given day is 3 tons in Baltimore and 5 tons in Philadelphia. The equilibrium price is the same in both cities, but the government establishes a price ceiling that is 50¢ per box below the equilibrium price of both cities. The price elasticity of demand for strawberries is 2 in Baltimore and 3 in Philadelphia. The size of the shortage in Baltimore is

   a. 0.50 tons.
   b. $(1 - 0.50)/2 = 0.25$ tons.
   c. $2/(1 - 0.50) = 4$ tons.
   d. zero.
   e. indeterminate from the information given.

5. In question 4, the relative size of the shortage in Baltimore

   a. will exceed that in Philadelphia.
   b. will equal that in Philadelphia.
   c. will be less than that in Philadelphia.
   d. will be less than or equal to that in Philadelphia.
   e. may or may not be greater than that in Philadelphia.

6. (Advanced.) Along any straight-line demand curve, the price elasticity of demand

   a. increases as the price falls.
   b. decreases as the price falls.
   c. remains constant as the price falls.
   d. equals the slope of the line.
   e. first increases then decreases as the price falls.

7. The quantity of Velasquez paintings increases by 2 percent because a number of such paintings is discovered in a cave by Basque revolutionaries. If the price elasticity of demand for Velasquez paintings is 0.3, the result is a reduction in the price of Velasquez paintings of

   a. 0.3 percent.
   b. 0.6 percent.
   c. $3^{1}/_{3}$ percent.
   d. $6^{2}/_{3}$ percent.
   e. none of the above.

8. A 1 percent increase in the price of good X results in a 2 percent increase in the quantity demanded of good Y. A 1 percent increase in the price of good Y results in an increase in the quantity demanded of good X that is

   a. 2 percent.
   b. $^{1}/_{2}$ percent.
   c. more than 2 percent.
   d. less than $^{1}/_{2}$ percent.
   e. indeterminate from the information given.

9. If two goods are substitutes, a decrease in the price of one results in

   a. a shift to the right in the other good's supply curve.
   b. a shift to the left in the other good's supply curve.
   c. a shift to the right in the other good's demand curve.
   d. a shift to the left in the other good's demand curve.
   e. an increase in the quantity demanded of the other good.

10. If two goods are complements, a decrease in the price of one results in

   a. a shift to the left in the other good's demand curve.
   b. a shift to the right in the other good's demand curve.
   c. a decrease in the quantity demanded of the other good.
   d. no change in the quantity demanded of the other good.
   e. none of the above.

11. In general, the individual demand curve do not remain fixed if there is a change in

   a. preferences.
   b. income.
   c. prices of other goods.
   d. any of the above.
   e. none of the above.

12. If a great many firms sell a homogeneous product, an individual firm's demand curve becomes

   a. of unitary elasticity.
   b. price inelastic.
   c. cross elastic.
   d. close to horizontal.
   e. income elastic.

13. If the cross elasticity of demand is negative, two commodities are

   a. complements.
   b. substitutes.
   c. positive elastomers.
   d. negative elastomers.
   e. none of the above.

14. If the income elasticity of demand for a product is zero and incomes increase considerably during a 10-year period, then the effect of this change in income on the product's sales should be

    a. positive.   d. infinite.
    b. negative.   e. none of the above.
    c. impossible to predict.

15. Which of the following goods is most likely to have a negative income elasticity?

    a. milk
    b. gasoline
    c. a high-mileage used car
    d. 48″ plasma TV
    e. a Caribbean cruise

Discussion and Extension Questions

1. According to the *New York Times*, "Coffee drinking, drip or perk, isn't as popular as it once was. Per capita consumption has dropped from 3.12 cups a day in 1962 to 2.2 cups. . . . The decline hasn't kept prices down, though." Does the information given here prove that there has been a shift to the left in the demand curve for coffee? Why or why not?

2. In fall 1973, there was talk of a beef shortage; in winter 1974, there was talk of a gasoline shortage. Why did government officials talk more about rationing to solve the gasoline shortage than the beef shortage?

3. If a family budgets a fixed amount of money for certain expenditures during the coming year, such as $800 a month for food and $200 a month for clothing purchases, what is that family's price elasticity of demand for food? Clothing? Be careful!

4. How could a state government use the information that the price elasticity of demand for cigarettes is about 0.4 when considering an increase in the state cigarette tax as a means of providing additional revenue? How might the information that New Hampshire has per-capita sales of cigarettes twice that of any neighboring state affect the decision by the government of New Hampshire to use the number 0.4 as the estimate of price elasticity in its calculations?

5. "If the demand curve for coffee is linear, the price elasticity of demand for coffee is the same at all prices." Discuss and evaluate.

6. "The theory of demand is based entirely on the supposition that individualism should reign supreme. Yet it is obvious that people often do not know what is good for them. Consequently, the state should play a greater role in determining what consumers should have." Comment and evaluate.

7. What are some ways to measure market demand curves? Why might there be problems with some of these?

8. According to results obtained by Professor William Vickrey, the demand for passenger service on the New York subways is price inelastic. Does this mean that fare increases would result in greater revenues for the New York subways?

9. What is meant by a market? How can one derive the market demand curve from the demand curves of the individuals composing the market?

10. According to the Department of Agriculture, the income elasticity of demand for coffee is about 0.23. If incomes rise by 1 percent, what effect would this have on the quantity demanded of coffee? Do you think that the income elasticity for a latte from Starbucks is higher or lower than 0.23? Why?

11. What different policies has the U.S. government tried to help raise farm income? How successful do you think they have been?

Problems

1. Suppose that the relationship between the price of aluminum and the quantity of aluminum demanded is as follows:

Price (dollars)	Quantity
1	8
2	7
3	6
4	5
5	4

What is the arc elasticity of demand when price is between $1 and $2? Between $4 and $5?

2. Suppose that the price elasticity of demand for gasoline is 0.50. About how big a price increase is required to reduce the consumption of gasoline by 1 percent?

3. Suppose that the income elasticity of demand for automobiles is 2.5 in the United States and 3.0 in the United Kingdom. If incomes in the United States rise by 2 percent next year and incomes in the United Kingdom rise by 1 percent, what will be the effect in each country on the quantity of automobiles purchased?

4. If a 1.5 percent reduction in the price of Nike running shoes results in a 3.0 percent reduction in the quantity demanded of New Balance running shoes, what is the cross elasticity of demand for these two commodities? Are they substitutes or complements?

5. Suppose that the market demand curve for mink coats is as follows:

Price (dollars)	Quantity of mink coats
500	500
1,000	300
1,500	200
2,000	100

a. What is the price elasticity of demand for mink coats when the price is between $1,500 and $2,000?

b. What is the price elasticity of demand when the price is between $500 and $1,000?

c. According to the text, an increase in price results in increased total expenditures on a product if its price elasticity of demand is less than 1 and less total expenditure on a product if its price elasticity of demand is greater than 1. Show that this proposition is true if the price of mink coats is raised from $500 to $1,000.

d. Show that the proposition in part c is true if the price of mink coats is raised from $1,500 to $2,000.

6. Suppose only three people are in the market for sable coats: Ms. Smith, Ms. Kennedy, and Ms. Jones. Suppose that their demand curves are as follows. Fill in the blank spaces for the market demand curve for sable coats.

Price of a sable coat (dollars)	Quantity demanded			Market demand
	Smith	Kennedy	Jones	
500	3	2	5	_____
1,000	2	1	4	_____
1,500	2	1	3	_____
2,000	1	0	2	_____

7. Every time the price of a pint of beer falls by a dime, Tom buys three more pints per week, but Jean buys five more. The price is now $1, and we observe Tom buying 25 pints per week while Jean is buying 10 pints.

a. Draw each person's demand curve for beer.

b. Whose price elasticity of demand for beer is higher when the price is between $1 and $0.90 per pint?

8. Suppose the price elasticity of demand for zambowies is unity when the price is $40. Suppose further that, when the price is $40, 100 zambowies are sold each week in Sommersville. Assuming no change in the elasticity for a small rise in zambowie prices, how many will be sold next week if price should rise to $42 per zambowie?

9. Suppose that the Brazilian government destroys a substantial portion of its coffee harvest to increase its revenue from coffee exports. What conditions are essential to make this type of policy economically beneficial for the country? Why would the conditions you identify increase export revenues?

10. a. On the basis of the diagram that follows, which would be more expensive for the government:
    (1) Set a minimum wage at $4 per hour and hire all the people the market does not hire at that wage.
    (2) Let the market determine an equilibrium wage ($3 per hour in the diagram) and pay everyone who works a subsidy of $1 to make up the difference between what the market pays and what is deemed a fair wage ($4 per hour).

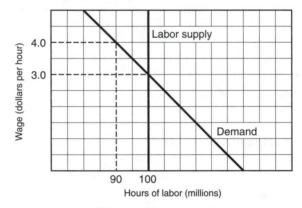

b. Would the answer be different if the demand for labor were price elastic with the result that an increase in the wage rate to $4.00 cut the quantity of labor demanded to a greater extent than shown here? Why or why not?

11. A firm estimates that the demand curves for its two products are given by

$$Q_1 = 200 - 2P_1 - 3P_2 \quad \text{and} \quad Q_2 = 450 + 6P_1 - 2P_2,$$

where Q_1 is the quantity demanded of the first product, P_1 is its price, Q_2 is the quantity demanded of the second product, and P_2 is its price. Compute the following elasticities at $P_1 = \$2$ and $P_2 = \$2$:

a. Price elasticity of demand for the first product
b. Cross elasticity of demand for the second product with respect to variation in the price of the first product

Answers

Completion Questions

1. 1.3, constant   2. 1.4, elastic   3. 1, zero   4. zero, zero   5. price elasticity of demand   6. quantity demanded, price   7. less than 1   8. a 1 percent, money income   9. substitutes   10. of unitary elasticity   11. price elasticity of demand   12. long, short, easier   13. more, substitutes

True-False

1. True   2. True   3. True   4. True   5. True   6. False   7. True   8. False   9. True   10. False   11. True   12. False   13. True   14. True   15. False   16. True   17. False

Multiple Choice

1. a   2. b   3. e   4. e   5. c   6. b   7. d   8. e   9. d   10. b   11. d   12. d   13. a   14. e   15. c

Problems

1.
$$-\frac{Q_2 - Q_1}{(Q_1 + Q_2)/2} \div \frac{P_2 - P_1}{(P_1 + P_2)/2} = -\frac{7-8}{(8+7)/2} \div \frac{2-1}{(1+2)/2} = \frac{3}{15} = 0.20$$

$$-\frac{Q_2 - Q_1}{(Q_1 + Q_2)/2} \div \frac{P_2 - P_1}{(P_1 + P_2)/2} = -\frac{4-5}{(5+4)/2} \div \frac{5-4}{(4+5)/2} = \frac{9}{9} = 1.00$$

2. 2 percent.

3. The quantity of automobiles demanded will increase by 3 percent in the United Kingdom and by 5 percent in the United States (assuming other factors are constant).

4. 2. Substitutes.

5. a.
$$-\frac{200-100}{150} \div \frac{1,500-2,000}{1,750} = \frac{100}{150} \div \frac{500}{1,750}$$

$$= \frac{2}{3} \div \frac{2}{7} = \frac{2}{3} \times \frac{7}{2} = \frac{7}{3} = 2\frac{1}{3}$$

b.
$$-\frac{500-300}{400} \div \frac{500-1,000}{750} = \frac{200}{400} \div \frac{500}{750} = \frac{1}{2} \div \frac{2}{3} = \frac{1}{2} \times \frac{3}{2} = \frac{3}{4}$$

c. As indicated in part b, the price elasticity of demand is less than 1 in this range. Therefore, an increase in price should increase the total expenditure on the product. Looking at the figures, this is the case. When the price is $500, total expenditure is $250,000; when it is $1,000, total expenditure is $300,000.

    d. As indicated in part a, the price elasticity of demand is greater than 1 in this range. Therefore, an increase in price should decrease the total expenditure on the product. Looking at the figures in part a, this is the case. When the price is $1,500, total expenditure is $300,000; when it is $2,000, total expenditure is $200,000.

6. *Market demand*

    10
    7
    6
    3

7. a.

    b. For each person we can compute the arc elasticity of demand between $1 per pint and $.90. For Tom it is

$$-\frac{28-25}{26.5} \div \frac{90-100}{95} = 1.08.$$

For Jean it is

$$-\frac{15-10}{12.5} \div \frac{90-100}{95} = 3.8.$$

Therefore, Jean's is higher.

8. About 95.

9. The price elasticity of demand must be less than 1. Export revenues would increase because, if the price elasticity of demand is less than 1, increases in price (and reductions in quantity) increase revenue.

10. a. The cost of the first alternative would be 10 million $\times$ $4, or $40 million. The cost of the second alternative would be 100 million $\times$ $1, or $100 million. Therefore, the second alternative would be more expensive.

    b. If the demand for labor were price elastic, the answer would be the opposite. Let Q_1 be the quantity of labor demanded (in millions of hours) when the wage is $4. Under the first alternative, the cost to the government is $4 \times (100 - Q_1)$ million. Under the second alternative, the cost is $100 million. If $4 \times (100 - Q_1) > 100$, the cost under the first alternative would be higher. In other words, if $Q_1 < 75$, this is the case. If the demand for labor is price elastic, Q_1 is less than 75, because an increase in the wage rate reduces the total amount spent on labor.

11. a. If $P_2 = 2$, $Q_1 = 194 - 2P_1$. Therefore, if $P_1 = 2$, $Q_1 = 190$. And if $P_1 = 2.02$, $Q_1 = 189.96$. Consequently, a 1 percent increase in price (from 2 to 2.02) results in about a 0.02 percent decrease (from 190 to 189.96) in the quantity demanded, so the price elasticity of demand is about 0.02.

   b. If $P_2 = 2$, $Q_2 = 446 + 6P_1$. Hence, if $P_1 = 2$, $Q_2 = 458$. And if $P_1 = 2.02$, $Q_2 = 458.12$. Consequently, a 1 percent increase in price (from 2 to 2.02) results in about a 0.03 percent increase (from 458 to 458.12) in the quantity demanded, so the cross elasticity of demand is about +0.03.

CHAPTER 18

Economic Efficiency, Market Supply,

and Perfect Competition

Chapter Profile

Economists generally classify markets into four types: perfect competition, monopoly, monopolistic competition, and oligopoly. Perfect competition requires that the product of any seller be the same as the product of any other seller, no buyer or seller be able to influence the price of the product, and resources be able to switch readily from one use to another.

If it maximizes profit, a perfectly competitive firm should set its output rate in the short run at the level where the marginal cost equals the price, so long as the price exceeds the average variable cost. If there is no output rate at which the price exceeds the average variable cost, the firm should discontinue production.

The firm's supply curve coincides with its marginal cost curve for prices exceeding the minimum value of the average variable cost. For prices less than or equal to the minimum value of the average variable cost, the firm's supply curve coincides with the price axis as the firm shuts down and makes zero units.

As a first approximation, the market supply curve can be viewed as the horizontal summation of the supply curves of all of the firms producing the product. This assumes that increases or decreases in output by all firms simultaneously do not affect input prices.

Price and output under perfect competition are determined by the intersection of the market supply and demand curves. In the short run, the price influences as well as rations the amount supplied.

In the long run, equilibrium is achieved under perfect competition when enough firms—no more, no less—are in the industry that economic profits are eliminated. In other words, the long-run equilibrium position of the firm is at the point where its long-run average cost equals price. But, since the price must also equal the marginal cost (to maximize profit), it follows that the firm must be operating at the minimum point on the long-run average cost curve.

In a perfectly competitive economy, prices are the signals used to guide the reallocation of resources in response to changes in consumer tastes, technology, and other factors.

At times, the government sets how high or low the price of a good can be. A price ceiling limits how high price can go. If this maximum is set below equilibrium, it causes a shortage (the quantity demanded greater than the quantity supplied). A price floor, also known as a *price support,* limits how low price can go. If this minimum is set above equilibrium, it causes a surplus (the quantity demanded less than the quantity supplied).

Concepts for Review

perfect competition	firm's supply curve
monopoly	market supply curve
monopolistic competition	economic profits
oligopoly	price ceiling
barriers to entry	price floor or price support
Golden Rule of Output Determination	

Completion Questions

1. If a firm cannot affect the price of its product and it can sell any amount it wants, the firm is said to be _____.

2. If a perfectly competitive firm's marginal cost of producing the Qth unit of output per month equals $5Q$ dollars and the price of a unit of output is

   $30, the firm, if it maximizes profit, should produce _____ units of output per month. If it does so, its profits per month equals

   _____ if its fixed costs per month equal $100. If its fixed

   costs are $300 per month, the firm (would, would not) _____ be better off to shut down in the short run.

3. Maximum profit under perfect competition is achieved usually at the output rate

   where the _____ equals the _____.

4. A firm's _____ shows how much it wants to produce at each price.

5. The _____ is the horizontal summation of the supply curves of all the firms producing the product, assuming that industry output does not influence input prices.

6. If there is an output rate where the price exceeds the average _____ cost, it pays the firm to produce, even though price does not cover average

   _____ cost. If there is no such output rate, the firm is

   better off to produce _____.

7. Under perfect competition the firm's supply curve is exactly the same as the

   firm's _____ cost curve for prices above the minimum value

   of the average _____ cost. For prices at or below the

   minimum value of the average _____ cost, the firm's supply

   curve corresponds to the _____ axis, the desire to supply at

   these prices being uniformly _____.

8. In perfect competition, each firm has (no, little, much) _____ control over the price of its product.

9. A perfectly competitive firm is (likely, unlikely) _____ to advertise its product.

10. In the short run, the _____ determines the amount of a product supplied. For instance, according to Hubert Risser of the University of Kansas, the short-run supply curve for bituminous coal is very price

(elastic, inelastic) _____ when output is within the range of existing capacity. In other words, if output is less than the existing capacity,

small variations in price result in (large, small) _____ variations in output.

11. Under perfect competition, long-run equilibrium requires that the price equals

the (highest, lowest) _____ value of long-run average total costs. In other words, firms must be producing at the (maximum,

minimum) _____ point on their long-run average cost curves,

because to maximize their _____, they must operate where the

price equals the long-run (average, marginal) _____ cost. Also,

they must operate where the price equals the long-run _____

cost. But, if both conditions are satisfied, the long-run _____

cost must equal the long-run _____ cost, since both equal the

price. And we know that the long-run _____ cost equals the

long-run _____ cost only at the point at which the long-run

average cost is a (maximum, minimum) _____.

12. Firm X is a perfectly competitive firm in long-run equilibrium. The price of its product is $10 more than the value of its economic profit; this

means that the price of its product equals _____. Its long-

run average cost (equals, exceeds, is less than) _____ $10.

Its short-run marginal cost (equals, exceeds, is less than) _____ $10. In this situation, firm X's economic profit (does, does not)

_____ equal its accounting profit.

True-False

_____ 1. If the short-run marginal cost curve of every firm in an industry slopes upward and to the right, the industry's long-run supply curve must slope upward and to the right.

_____ 2. Firm Y, a perfectly competitive firm, produces at an output rate where its marginal cost is $1 less than its average cost (which equals its price). To increase its profit, firm Y should increase its output rate.

_____ 3. At all points where the total revenue curve lies below the total cost curve, profits are negative.

_____ 4. If price is fixed, then increases in output have little effect on the firm's profits.

_____ 5. The Golden Rule of Output Determination for a perfectly competitive firm is this: Choose the output rate at which the marginal cost is equal to the price.

_____ 6. The firm maximize profits by producing nothing if there is no output rate at which the price exceeds the average variable cost.

_____ 7. No industry, now or in the past, has met all the requirements of perfect competition.

_____ 8. In the short run, output is set by demand alone.

_____ 9. Under perfect competition, the product of any one seller must be the same as the product of any other seller.

_____ 10. A perfectly competitive firm in long-run equilibrium earns normal profits (that is, profits equal to those obtainable elsewhere).

_____ 11. If firm X's marginal cost curve intersects its average variable cost curve at $4 per unit of output, firm X will shut down in the short-run if the price of its product falls below $4 per unit.

_____ 12. A price ceiling causes a surplus or excess supply.

Multiple Choice

1. The supply curve of each firm in industry X is a vertical line. The government dictates that no firm can enter or leave industry X. The market supply curve

   a. slopes upward to the right.
   b. may or may not slope upward to the right.
   c. is a vertical line.
   d. does not exist.
   e. none of the above.

2. The output of industry S does not affect input prices in the industry. The industry contains 1,000 firms, and for each firm, the marginal cost of producing five units per month is $2, the marginal cost of producing six units per month is $3, and the marginal cost of producing seven units per month is $5. If the price per unit of the industry's product is $3, the industry output is

   a. no more than 5,000 units per month.
   b. 5,000 units per month.

    c.   6,000 units per month.
    d.   7,000 units per month.
    e.   at least 7,000 units per month.

3. In question 2, if the price per unit of the industry's product is $6, the industry output is

    a.   no more than 5,000 units per month.
    b.   5,000 units per month.
    c.   6,000 units per month.
    d.   7,000 units per month.
    e.   at least 7,000 units per month.

4. If a firm has no fixed costs, it follows that

    a.   the firm ceases production if the price is less than average total cost.
    b.   the average variable cost equals the average total cost.
    c.   the average variable cost achieves a minimum at the same point that the average total cost achieves a minimum.
    d.   all of the above.
    e.   none of the above.

5. If the marginal cost exceeds the average total cost at its profit-maximizing output, a competitive firm

    a.   makes positive profits.
    b.   operates at a point to the right of the minimum point on the average total cost curve.
    c.   does not discontinue production.
    d.   all of the above.
    e.   none of the above.

6. A firm is better off in the short run to produce when

    a.   the loss from production is less than fixed costs.
    b.   the fixed costs are less than the loss from production.
    c.   the average total cost minus the price is greater than the average fixed cost.
    d.   the average total cost is greater than the average fixed cost plus the price.
    e.   none of the above.

7. For an individual firm, the simultaneous expansion or contraction of output by all firms is likely to alter

    a.   input prices.   d.   all of the above.
    b.   cost curves.   e.   none of the above.
    c.   the supply curve.

8. The shape of the short-run market supply curve may be influenced by

    a.   changes in input prices.
    b.   the number of firms in the industry.
    c.   the size of the firm's plants.
    d.   the nature of technology.
    e.   all of the above.

9. The following graph shows the total revenue and total cost of a firm:

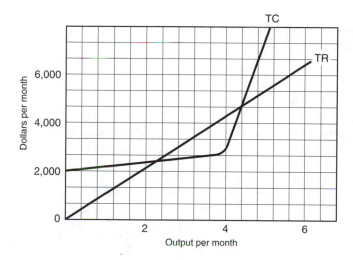

On the basis of this graph, it is clear that

a. the firm is perfectly competitive.
b. the firm's fixed costs equal $2,000 per month.
c. the firm maximizes its profit if it produces about four units of output per month.
d. all of the above.
e. a and b.

10. On the basis of the graph in question 9, it is clear that

a. the marginal cost is less than the marginal revenue when output is less than three units per month.
b. the marginal cost is greater than the marginal revenue when output is greater than four units per month.
c. there is only one output rate at which the average total cost equals the average revenue. (The average revenue is the total revenue divided by the output.)
d. all of the above.
e. a and b.

11. Oligopoly is a kind of market where there is (are) _____ sellers.

a. one
b. few
c. many
d. no
e. too many

12. If the demand curve shifts to the right (and the supply curve slopes upward), the equilibrium price

a. decreases.
b. increases.
c. stays the same.
d. is impossible to determine.
e. none of the above.

13. The market demand curve for product R is as follows:

Price (dollars)	Quantity demanded
30	200
20	300
10	400
5	600
3	800

Firms in the industry can expand or contract their output without affecting input prices. Each firm has the following long-run total cost curve:

Output	Total cost (dollars)
1	10
2	12
3	15
4	30

The total number of firms in the industry in the long run is approximately

a.   100.
b.   200.
c.   300.

d.   400.
e.   none of the above.

14. In question 13, the price of product R in the long run is approximately

a. $10.
b. $12.
c. $15.

d. $30.
e.   none of the above.

Discussion and Extension Questions

1. In the *New York Times*, Henry Ford II wrote that, "The main reason more oil hasn't been found is that, with a 34-year inventory on hand, there has been little incentive to look farther or deeper for still more. . . . As the easily recovered supply of petroleum is depleted, the cost of finding and extracting new supplies will go up and up." On the basis of this statement, what, according to Ford, is the shape of the long-run supply curve for oil? Do you agree? Why or why not?

2. Suppose you are currently enrolled for five courses this term. Use the principles presented in this chapter to illustrate how much time you will devote to studying for the final exam in each course. What is the cost to you of an hour's study for your economics final exam? Under what circumstances would it pay you not to study at all for a particular course, and what is the counterpart for the competitive firm?

3. Suppose the Pentagon is interested in expanding our military force by 10 percent. Describe why it is important for the Pentagon and other agencies to have some idea of the elasticity of supply of military personnel when contemplating an increase in their numbers.

4. "There is a learning curve in many industries; that is, unit costs go down as more units are produced. This is a major reason why supply curves slope downward to the right." Comment and evaluate.

5. "Higher prices do not result in greater supplies; they result in higher profits." Comment and evaluate.

6. Show why a firm continues to produce in the short run so long as the price exceeds the average variable cost, even if price is smaller than average total cost.

7. Distinguish among diminishing marginal returns, diseconomies of scale, and increasing cost industries.

8. According to Kenneth Boulding, "From the point of view of society as a whole, the inability of agriculture to reduce output in a depression is an almost unmixed blessing." Why can't agriculture reduce output? Why is this a blessing, and why is this blessing not quite unmixed? What are the effects of government farm programs on the validity of this statement?

9. "Competition is all very well in theory, but in practice it generally is a disaster, leading to low profits and eventual government intervention. Agriculture is a case in point." Comment and evaluate.

10. Explain why equilibrium in the long run under perfect competition requires that price must be equal to the lowest value of long-run average total cost.

Problems

1. Suppose that the total costs of a perfectly competitive firm are as follows:

Output rate	Total cost (dollars)
0	40
1	60
2	90
3	130
4	180
5	240

Assume that the output rate can only assume integer values.

a. If the price of the product is $50, what output rate should the firm choose?

b. On the following graph, draw the short-run supply curve of the firm.
c. Draw the firm's demand curve.
d. Draw the firm's average total cost curve.

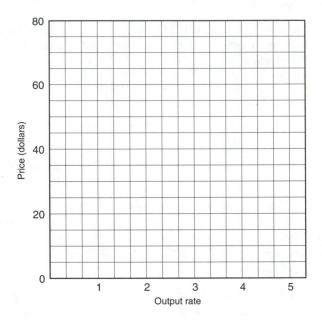

e. What will be the firm's total profit?

2. You are the owner of a firm that currently loses $1,000 per month, with fixed costs per month of $800. A management consultant advises you to cease production. Should you accept the advice? Why or why not?

3. Suppose that the total cost curve of the Rem Sofa Company is as follows:

Output (sofas per month)	Total cost (dollars per month)
1	1,000
2	1,100
3	1,200
4	1,300
5	1,500
6	1,700
7	2,000
8	2,500

Assume that the output rate must be an integer amount per month.

a. If the price of a sofa is $300, how many sofas should Rem produce per month?
b. Suppose that Rem's fixed costs increase by $100 per month. What effect does this have on the optimal output?
c. If its fixed costs increase by $100 per month, what is the maximum profit rate that the Rem Sofa Company can earn?

    d. Does the Rem Sofa Company exhibit increasing marginal cost? What is the value of marginal cost when between seven and eight units of output are produced per month?

4. Data follow concerning the Allied Peanut Company, a firm producing peanut brittle.

    a. Supposing that this firm is a member of a perfectly competitive industry, complete the table that follows, with price, costs, revenue, and profit in dollars:

Daily output of peanut brittle (tons)	Price per ton of peanut brittle	Total cost	Total Revenue	Profit	Marginal cost
0	200	100	____	____	
					____
1	____	200	____	____	
					____
2	____	310	____	____	
					____
3	____	500	____	____	
					____
4	____	700	____	____	
					____
5	____	1,000	____	____	

Assume that the output rate must equal an integer number of tons per day.

    b. If the price of a ton of peanut brittle falls to $50, does Allied continue producing or shut down?

    c. What is the minimum price at which Allied continues production (assuming that it cannot produce fractions of tons of output)?

    d. If the price of a ton of peanut brittle is $200, what output rate does Allied choose? Does the price equal the marginal cost at this output rate?

5. The following graph shows the total cost and total revenue curves of a hypothetical competitive firm:

    a.   How much is the price of the firm's product?
    b.   How much is the firm's total fixed cost?
    c.   At what output levels are the firm's profits zero?
    d.   At what output levels are the firm's profits at a maximum?

6. Suppose that a perfectly competitive firm has this short-run total cost function:

Output	Total cost (dollars)
0	10
1	12
2	16
3	22
4	30
5	40

    a.   If the firm can produce only integer amounts of output, what output level does it choose when the price of its product is $3? $5? $7? $9?
    b.   What are the firm's profits when the price of its product is $3? $5? $7? $9?
    c.   If 1,000 firms are in this industry and all have the cost function shown in the table, the market supply curve is given. Fill in the blanks.

Price (dollars)	Quantity supplied
3	_____
5	_____
7	_____
9	_____

    d.   If the market demand curve is as shown here, what is the equilibrium price of the product?

Price (dollars)	Quantity demanded
3	3,000
5	2,000
7	1,500
9	1,000

    e.   What is the output of each firm?
    f.   How much profit does each firm make?
    g.   Will firms tend to enter or leave this industry in the long run?

7. As of midnight, December 13, National Agriculture, a recently formed farmers' lobby group, is calling for a nationwide strike by farmers. The goal is to raise the price of the crops enough to cover production costs and provide some profit. Suppose that the current price of wheat is $1.50 per bushel, which is about one-half of the cost of growing that bushel.

    a.   Depict the current plight of a typical wheat farmer graphically. (Treat him or her as a perfect competitor.) Your diagram should correctly depict both variable and total costs relative to today's market price, given that the typical farmer chooses to continue producing despite losses.

b. In perfect competition, no single firm has any market power. Suppose that through an organization such as National Agriculture, all farmers could coordinate the selling of their produce. What would be the effect on the price of their produce? What would be the effect on the amount they would sell?

8. Assume that perfect competition exists. Assume that the marginal cost increases with increases in output. In the following table, fill in all spaces that do not contain a number. An asterisk on an entry means that *ATC* or *AVC* is at a minimum level at that output. *Treat each horizontal row in the table as a separate problem.* Enter in the last column one of the following responses:

Number	Response
1	Firm is now at the correct output.
2	Firm should increase the price.
3	Firm should decrease the price.
4	Firm should increase the output.
5	Firm should decrease the output.
6	Firm should shut down operations.

The symbols are as follows: P = price, Q = quantity, TR = total revenue, TC = total cost, TFC = total fixed cost, TVC = total variable cost, ATC = average total cost, AVC = average variable cost, MC = marginal cost.

P	Q	TR	TC	TFC	TVC	ATC	AVC	MC	Response
10	—	800	—	500	—	10	—	—	1
—	—	400	—	100	—	2	1	5	—
—	10	30	—	20	—	—	0.30	0.25	—
10	100	—	—	200	—	—	10*	—	—
—	50	300	—	—	—	7*	5	—	—

Answers

Completion Questions

1. perfectly competitive   2. 6, –$25, would not   3. price, marginal cost
4. supply curve   5. market supply curve   6. variable, total, nothing
7. marginal, variable, variable, price, zero   8. no   9. unlikely
10. price, elastic, large   11. lowest, minimum, profits, marginal, average,
marginal, average, marginal, average, minimum   12. $10, equals, equals, does not

True-False

1. False   2. True   3. True   4. False   5. True   6. True   7. True   8. False
9. True   10. True   11. True   12. False

Multiple Choice

1. c   2. c   3. e   4. d   5. d   6. a   7. d   8. e   9. d   10. e   11. b   12. b
13. b   14. e

Problems

1. a.   Three or four units of output per period of time.
    b, c, d.

    e. $20.
2. Yes. Because you lose less money ($800) if you cease production than at present.
3. a.   Six or seven.
    b.   No effect.
    c.   Zero profits.
    d.   Yes. $500.

4. a.

Price per ton	Total revenue	Profit	Marginal cost
	0	−100	
			100
200	200	0	
			110
200	400	90	
			190
200	600	100	
			200
200	800	100	
			300
200	1,000	0	

b. It will shut down.
c. $100.
d. Either 3 or 4 tons per day. Yes; as shown in the answer to part a, the marginal cost is $200 when the output is between 3 and 4 tons per day. The price too equals $200.

5. a. $2 per unit of output.
b. $30.
c. 25 and 45 units of output.
d. 35 to 40 units of output.

6. a. 1, 2, 3, 4.
b. −$9, −$6, −$1, +$6.
c. *Quantity supplied*

  1,000
  2,000
  3,000
  4,000+

d. $5.
e. 2.
f. −$6.
g. They will leave it.

7. a.

b. The price would increase. The quantity they would sell would decrease.

8.

P	Q	TR	TC	TFC	TVC	ATC	AVC	MC	Response
10	80	800	800	500	300	10	3.75	10	1
4	100	400	200	100	100	2	1	5	5
3	10	30	23	20	3	2.3	0.30	0.25	4
10	100	1,000	1,200	200	1,000	12	10*	10	6
6	50	300	350	100	250	7*	5	7	5

CHAPTER 19

Monopoly and Its Regulation

Chapter Profile

A pure monopoly is a market with only one seller. Monopolies may occur because of patents, control over basic inputs, and government action as well as decreasing average costs up to the point where the market is satisfied.

If average costs reach their minimum at an output rate large enough to satisfy the entire market, competition cannot be maintained; and the public often insists that the industry (a natural monopoly) be regulated by the government.

Since the monopolist is the only seller of the product, the demand curve facing the monopolist is the market demand curve, which slopes downward (rather than being horizontal, as in perfect competition). The unregulated monopolist maximizes profit by choosing the output where marginal cost equals marginal revenue, which is defined as the addition to the total revenue attributable to the addition of one unit to sales. This rule for output determination also holds under perfect competition, since the price equals the marginal revenue under perfect competition.

If monopolists cannot prevent losses from exceeding fixed costs, they, like perfect competitors, discontinue production even in the short run. In contrast to the case in perfect competition, the long-run equilibrium of a monopolistic industry may not be marked by the absence of economic profits.

The output of a monopoly tends to be smaller and the price higher than under perfect competition. Economists tend to believe that society would be better off if more resources were devoted to the production of the good than under monopoly and often regard the competitive output as best.

One way society attempts to reduce the harmful effects of monopoly is through public regulation. Commissions often set the price at the level at which it equals the average total cost, including a "fair" rate of return on the firm's investment.

There has been a great deal of controversy over the practices of the regulatory commissions. Many economists viewed them as lax or ill conceived. According to many studies, their decisions resulted in substantial costs and inefficiencies, particularly since they can be dominated or "captured" by special interest groups, especially the industry being regulated.

Regulatory commissions try to prevent a monopoly from earning excessive profits; the firm is allowed only a "fair" rate of return on its investment. One difficulty with this arrangement is that, since the firm is guaranteed this rate of return (regardless of how well or poorly it performs), there is no incentive for the firm to increase its efficiency.

*In defense of monopoly power, some economists, such as John Kenneth Galbraith, asserted that the rate of technological change is likely to be greater in an imperfectly

*The starred item pertains to material covered in Exploring Further.

competitive industry than under perfect competition. It seems unlikely that a perfectly competitive industry would be able—and would have the incentive—to carry out the research and development required to promote a rapid rate of technological change in many sectors of the economy.

*However, contrary to the allegations of Galbraith and others, there is little evidence that giant firms are needed to ensure rapid technological change in a great many sectors of the economy. The situation is much more complex than such statements indicate, and the contributions of smaller firms are much greater than is commonly recognized.

Concepts for Review

monopoly	Golden Rule of Output Determination
patent	public regulation
natural monopolies	historical cost
network effect	reproduction cost
total revenue	deregulation
marginal revenue	

Completion Questions

1. A monopolist can sell 12 units of output when it charges $10 a unit, 11 units of output when it charges $11 a unit, and 10 units of output when it charges $12 a unit. The marginal revenue from the eleventh unit of output equals

   _____. The marginal revenue from the twelfth unit of

   output equals _____.

2. If the marginal revenue from the first unit of output is $5 and the marginal revenue from the second unit of output is $4, the total revenue from the first

   two units of output is _____. The average revenue when one

   unit of output is produced and sold equals _____. The average revenue when two units of output are produced and sold equals

   _____.

3. For the monopolist, if demand is price _____, the marginal

   revenue is positive; if demand is price _____, the marginal revenue is negative.

4. The output of a perfectly competitive industry tends to be _____ and

   the price tends to be _____ than under monopoly.

5. Commissions often set the price at the level at which it equals _____ including a fair return.

*The starred item pertains to material covered in Exploring Further.

6. A firm's _____ is the addition to total revenue attributable to the addition of one unit of the quantity sold.

7. The firm under _____ has no direct competitors; it is the sole _____. However, such a firm is not entirely free of rivals but is affected by certain indirect and potential forms of_____.

8. A firm may become a monopolist because it is awarded a(n) _____by a government agency. The government may give a particular firm the franchise to sell a particular product in a(n) _____ or the right to provide a(n) _____, such as telephone service, to people in a particular area. In exchange for this right, the firm agrees to allow the government to _____ certain aspects of its operation.

9. A firm may become a monopolist because the average costs of producing the product reach a(n) _____ at an output rate great enough to satisfy the entire market (at a price that is _____). Under such circumstances, the firm obviously has an incentive to _____to the point where it produces all the market will buy of the good, because its costs (increase, decrease) _____ as it continues to expand. Competition cannot be maintained in such a case.

10. A company's assets can be valued by _____ cost or _____ cost, that is, at what the company paid for them or at what it would cost to replace them. If the _____ does not change much, these two approaches are interchangeable. But if prices are rising, _____ cost will be greater than _____ cost.

11. If a monopolist's demand curve is of unitary elasticity, the marginal revenue equals _____. In such a case, it would be (possible, impossible) _____ for the monopolist to set marginal cost equal to marginal revenue. The monopolist would try to make its output as _____ as possible, since _____ in output reduce its total cost but not its total revenue.

12. If a monopolist's demand curve is price elastic, its marginal revenue is (positive, negative, zero) _____. If a monopolist's demand curve is price inelastic, its marginal revenue is (positive, negative, zero) _____. A monopolist will not operate at a point on its demand curve where demand is price (elastic, inelastic) _____.

True-False

_____ 1. A profit-maximizing monopolist that does not shut down always sets the average revenue higher than the marginal cost if the demand curve for its product slopes downward to the right.

_____ 2. A profit-maximizing monopolist always sets the average revenue higher than the average total cost in the short run.

_____ 3. If a monopolist does not maximize its profit per unit of output, it is not setting the marginal cost equal to the marginal revenue.

_____ 4. Cost-plus-fixed-fee contracts provide less incentive for efficiency than fixed-price contracts, but where the risk to the contractor is very great, they may be the only type of contract feasible.

_____ 5. The monopolist's demand curve must always be horizontal.

_____ 6. A monopolist discontinues production if its losses exceed its fixed costs.

_____ 7. Because price levels have been rising in the past 40 years, most regulatory commissions use replacement cost to value a firm's assets.

_____ 8. A monopolist seeks to maximize its profit per unit of output.

_____ 9. Monopoly, like perfect competition, seldom corresponds more than approximately to conditions in real industries, but it is a very useful model.

_____ 10. A monopolist has to take into account the possibility that new firms might arise to challenge its monopoly if it attempted to extract conspicuously high profits. Thus, even the monopolist is subject to some restraint imposed by competitive forces.

_____ 11. Many firms with monopoly power achieved it in considerable part through patents.

_____ 12. When an industry is a natural monopoly, the public often insists that its behavior be regulated by the government.

_____ 13. For both the monopolist and the perfectly competitive firm, profits are maximized by setting the output rate at the point where the price equals the marginal cost.

_____ 14. A consumer might be better off using a lesser-quality product if it is widely used and there is a network effect in the market.

Multiple Choice

1. If a firm's marginal cost curve always lies below its average total cost curve, it is likely to be

   a. a perfectly competitive firm.
   b. a monopolistically competitive firm.
   c. a monopoly.
   d. any of the above.
   e. none of the above.

2. An industry that formerly was perfectly competitive is monopolized. The monopoly's demand curve is

   a. the same as the demand curve for an individual firm when the industry was competitive.
   b. the same as the demand curve for the industry's product when the industry was competitive.
   c. more price elastic than either of the demand curves in a and b.
   d. less price elastic than either of the demand curves in a and b.
   e. none of the above.

3. To maximize profit, a monopoly should set its

   a. marginal cost equal to the price.
   b. marginal cost equal to the input costs.
   c. marginal revenue equal to the marginal cost.
   d. marginal revenue equal to the input costs.
   e. average cost equal to the price.

4. Economists often regard the socially optimal output of an industry as the output

   a. where the marginal cost equals the price.
   b. that a perfectly competitive industry would produce.
   c. where the social value of an extra unit of the good is equal to the social cost of an extra unit of the good.
   d. all of the above.
   e. none of the above.

5. If the marginal cost to society of producing an extra unit of good X is $5 and the extra value to society of an extra unit of good X is $15 when 10 units or less are produced and $4 when more than 10 units are produced, the socially optimal output of good X is

   a. less than 10 units.
   b. 10 units.
   c. more than 10 units.
   d. unobtainable from the information given.

6. Under monopoly, the marginal cost ordinarily is less than the price because

   a. the price is less than the marginal revenue.
   b. the price is greater than the marginal revenue.
   c. the marginal cost is less than the average cost.
   d. the marginal cost is greater than the average cost.
   e. none of the above.

7. A country's economy consists of two industries, one perfectly competitive and one a monopoly. To improve the allocation of resources, it is likely that

   a. the output of the competitive industry should be reduced.
   b. the output of the monopoly should be increased.
   c. both a and b should occur.
   d. neither a nor b should occur.
   e. a tax should be imposed on the output of the monopoly.

8. A monopolist's total cost equals $100 + 3Q$, where Q is the number of units of output it produces per month. Its demand curve is $P = 200 - Q$, where P is the price of the product. If it produces 20 units of output per month, its total revenue equals

   a. $4,000.   d. $180.
   b. $3,600.   e. none of the above.
   c. $400.

9. In question 8, the marginal revenue from the twentieth unit of output per month equals

   a. $3,600.   d. $400.
   b. $3,439.   e. none of the above.
   c. $180.

10. In question 8, if the monopolist produces 19 units of output per month, its profit

   a. increases by $158 if it increases output by 1 unit per month.
   b. increases by $3 if it increases output by 1 unit per month.
   c. decreases by $3 if it increases output by 1 unit per month.
   d. decreases by $158 if it increases output by 1 unit per month.
   e. none of the above.

Discussion and Extension Questions

1. "Monopoly prices do not reflect true opportunity costs to society." Explain.

2. "Even if a monopolist earns no economic profits whatsoever, it may harm society." Do you agree? If so, how does the harm come about? Be specific.

3. Is the trucking industry a natural monopoly? Why has the trucking industry been regulated by the Interstate Commerce Commission? What advantages have accrued from deregulation of the trucking industry? Why might some trucking companies be opposed to such deregulation?

4. "Whether one considers a firm a monopolist depends on how the relevant market is defined. If the market is very narrow, many firms would be classified as monopolists; using a very broad definition, there may be no such thing as a monopolist." Explain.

5. Define what is meant by *monopoly*. Is a monopolist free of all indirect and potential forms of rivalry? What are the most important reasons for monopoly?

6. Prove that a monopolist, to maximize profit, should choose an output rate such that marginal revenue equals marginal cost.

7. How do the price and output set by a monopolist compare with those that would prevail if the industry were perfectly competitive? Why do many economists argue that the allocation of resources under perfect competition is likely to be more socially desirable than under monopoly? Use diagrams to illustrate your arguments.

8. What are some criticisms directed at the regulatory commissions and the principles they use? Why did Congress say in 1962 that the Food and Drug Administration has to be shown that a new drug is effective as well as safe?

9. In the late 1990s, the Department of Justice tried to break up Microsoft. How else could the Department of Justice have handled Microsoft's domination of the computer industry, and what would be some of the challenges it would face?

Problems

1. The Uneek Corporation is the only producer of battery-powered soup ladles. Suppose that the demand curve facing the firm is as follows:

Quantity of soup ladles produced per day	Price (dollars per soup ladle)
1	30
2	20
3	10
4	6
5	1

a. Using these data fill in the following table for the Uneek Corporation:

Quantity	Total revenue (dollars)	Marginal revenue (dollars)
1	_____	
2	_____	_____
3	_____	_____
4	_____	_____
5	_____	_____

b. Suppose that the Uneek Corporation has a horizontal marginal cost curve, with a marginal cost of $9 per soup ladle (see the following graph). Its fixed costs are zero.

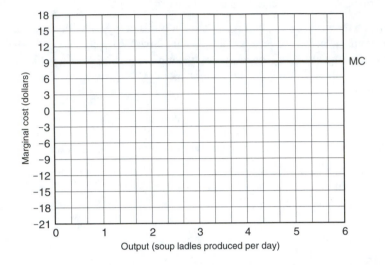

If the Uneek Corporation's costs are as just described and it produces one unit of output, how much will a second unit of output (that is, a second ladle) add to its costs? How much will it add to its revenue? Is it profitable to produce a second unit?

c. On the basis of the data given, what price should the Uneek Corporation charge?

d. What output should it choose?

e. What is the Uneek Corporation's profit if it produces at the optimal output rate?

f. Suppose that its fixed costs are $10, rather than zero. Will this affect the optimal output rate? Will this affect the firm's profit? If so, how?

2. In a particular industry, the minimum value of the average cost is reached when a firm produces 1,000 units of output per month. At this output rate, the average cost is $1 per unit of output. The demand curve for this product is as follows:

Price (dollars per unit of output)	Quantity (produced per month)
3.00	1,000
2.00	8,000
1.00	12,000
0.50	20,000

a. Is this industry a natural monopoly? Why or why not?

b. If the price is $2, how many firms, each of which produces an output such that average cost is at a minimum, can the market support?

3. The following graph pertains to a monopolist. One of the curves is its demand curve, one is its marginal revenue curve, and one is its marginal cost curve.

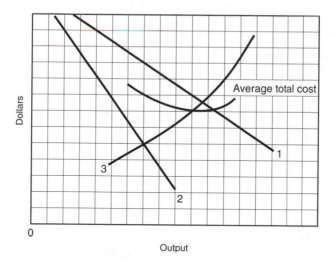

a. Which is curve 1?
b. Which is curve 2?
c. Which is curve 3?
d. Show the output that the monopolist chooses and the price it sets.
e. Does the monopolist choose the output at which average total cost is at a minimum? Do perfectly competitive firms choose such an output rate in the long run?
f. In the graph, show the total profit earned by the monopolist.
g. If the monopolist set the price equal to the marginal cost, what would be its output rate?

4. Suppose that a hypothetical monopoly has the following demand curve and total costs; all prices, revenues, costs, and profits are in dollars:

Output sold (per month)	Price	Total revenue	Total cost (per month)	Average total cost	Marginal cost	Marginal revenue	Profit
0	50	_____	40	_____			_____
1	45	_____	50	_____	_____	_____	_____
2	40	_____	70	_____	_____	_____	_____
3	35	_____	95	_____	_____	_____	_____
4	30	_____	125	_____	_____	_____	_____
5	25	_____	165	_____	_____	_____	_____
6	20	_____	225	_____	_____	_____	_____

a. Fill in the blanks.
b. What output (or outputs) maximizes the monopolist's profits?
c. What price does the monopolist choose?

5. Suppose that a monopolist has five units of output on hand. It can sell this output in one of two markets. The demand curve for the product in each market follows.

Market A		Market B	
Price (dollars)	Quantity demanded	Price (dollars)	Quantity demanded
70	1	50	1
65	2	45	2
60	3	40	3
50	4	30	4
40	5	20	5

There is no way a unit of the good sold in one market can be resold in the other market.

a. Suppose that the monopolist sells four units in market A and none in market B. Should it sell the fifth unit in market A or market B? Why?
b. Suppose that the monopolist sells four units in market B and none in market A. Should it sell the fifth unit in market A or market B? Why?
c. Prove that the monopolist should allocate the goods between markets so that the marginal revenues in the two markets are equal or as close as possible.
d. What is the profit maximizing combination of sales in the two markets? Explain how this satisfies the rule in part c.

6. A monopolist's demand curve is as follows:

Price (dollars)	Quantity demanded
20	0
15	1
10	2
5	3

The monopolist's total cost (in dollars) equals $3 + 20Q$, where Q is its output rate. What output rate maximizes the monopolist's profit?

7. In industry X, a firm's long-run average cost (in dollars) equals $5 + 3/Q$, where Q is the firm's output per year.

    a.   Is this industry a natural monopoly? Why or why not?

    b.   If this industry is monopolized and the monopoly maximizes profit, what is the value of marginal revenue in the long run?

    c.   In the long run, under the circumstances described in part b, we can be sure that the price exceeds a certain amount. What is this amount, and why must price exceed it?

8. A labor union can be viewed as a monopoly for supplying labor services. Use diagrammatic analysis together with the concept of price elasticity of demand to apply what you learned about monopoly to the way in which a union sets the wage. Your analysis should respond to two specific questions:

    a.   How do the union-set wage and the wage that would be set by competition differ?

    b.   Even though wages for each working union member might rise when the union sets the wage, how is it possible that total wages to all members taken together might, in fact, fall when wages are raised to the union level?

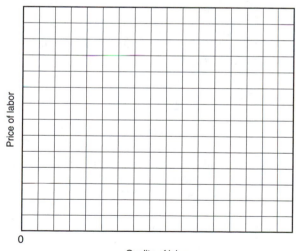

Quality of labor

9. Suppose a firm produces quarks and has a complete monopoly over quarks. The following information is given:

$$\text{Marginal revenue} = 1{,}000 - 20Q$$
$$\text{Total revenue} = 1{,}000Q - 10Q^2$$
$$\text{Marginal cost} = 100 + 10Q$$

where Q = output of quarks and P = price of a quark. How many quarks would be sold and at what price if

a. The firm sets price as a monopoly?
b. The industry (firm) behaves perfectly competitively?

Answers

Completion Questions
1. +$1, –$1   2. $9, $5, $4.50   3. elastic, inelastic   4. greater, lower
5. average total cost   6. marginal revenue   7. monopoly, supplier, competition
8. market franchise, public facility, service, regulate   9. minimum, profitable, expand, decrease   10. historical, reproduction, price level, replacement, historical
11. zero, impossible, small, decreases   12. positive, negative, inelastic

True-False
1. True   2. False   3. False   4. True   5. False   6. True   7. False
8. False   9. True   10. True   11. True   12. True   13. False   14. True

Multiple Choice
1. c   2. b   3. c   4. d   5. b   6. b   7. c   8. b   9. e   10. a

Problems
1. a.

Total revenue	Marginal revenue
30	
	10
40	
	–10
30	
	–6
24	
	–19
5	

b. The second ladle adds $9 to its costs and $10 to its revenue. Yes.
c. $20.
d. Two soup ladles per day.
e. $22.
f. No. Yes. It will decrease its profit by $10.

2. a. No. If price is $1, 12 firms of optimal size can exist in the market.
   b. 8.
3. a. Its demand curve.
   b. Its marginal revenue curve.
   c. Its marginal cost curve.
   d. It will choose an output of *OQ and set* a price of *OP.*

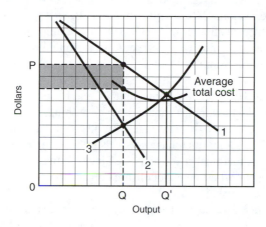

   e. No. Yes.
   f. The shaded area in the graph in the answer to part d equals this profit.
   g. *OQ′* in the graph in the answer to part d.
4. a.

Total revenue	Average total cost		Marginal cost	Marginal revenue	Profit
0	—				−40
			10	45	
45	50				−5
			20	35	
80	35				10
			25	25	
105	$31^2/_3$				10
			30	15	
120	$31^1/_4$				−5
			40	5	
125	33				−40
			60	−5	
120	$37^1/_2$				−105

   b. Two or three units per month.
   c. $40 or $35.
5. a. The marginal revenue from the fifth unit in market A is zero. The marginal revenue from the first unit in market B is $50. Therefore, it should be sold in market B.
   b. The marginal revenue from the fifth unit in market B is −$20. The marginal revenue from the first unit in market A is $70. Therefore, it should be sold in market A.

c. If the marginal revenue in one market is less than in the other, it pays the monopolist to allocate one more unit to the latter market and one fewer to the former market. Hence, the monopolist maximizes profit only when the marginal revenue in each market is equal.

d. Three in market A and two in market B. The marginal revenue of the last unit sold in each market is less than the marginal revenue of the next unit in the other market. In other words, the MR of unit 3 in market A is greater than the MR of unit 3 in market B, so it would do no good to switch production from A to B. The MR of unit 2 in market B is greater than the MR of unit 4 in market A, so it would do no good to switch production from B to A.

6. The marginal cost equals $20. The marginal revenue from the first unit of output is $15, from the second unit $5, and from the third unit –$5. Therefore, the monopolist should produce nothing.

7. a. Yes, because long-run average cost falls continually as output increases.

b. The firm's long-run total cost equals $Q(5 + 3/Q) = 3 + 5Q$. Therefore, its long-run marginal cost equals $5. Since the marginal revenue equals the marginal cost if the monopolist maximizes profit, the long-run marginal revenue equals $5.

c. The price exceeds $5, because the price exceeds the marginal revenue so long as the product's demand curve slopes downward to the right.

8. a. The demand and supply curves of labor follow. The marginal revenue curve corresponding to the demand curve is also given.
If the union behaves as a monopolist, it will set a wage of P_M. Under competition, the wage would be P_c.

b. If the demand curve for labor is price elastic, an increase in the wage reduces the total wages. That is, it reduces the quantity of labor demanded times the wage.

9. a. Since marginal revenue = marginal cost,

$$1,000 - 20Q = 100 + 10Q;$$

this means that $900 = 30Q$, or $Q = 30$.
Since $PQ = 1,000Q - 10Q^2$, the demand curve must be

$$P = 1,000 - 10Q.$$

And, if $Q = 30$, P must equal 700.

b.   Since the industry's supply curve is the same as the monopolist's marginal cost curve, the supply curve is

$$P = 100 + 10Q.$$

As pointed out in part a, the demand curve is

$$P = 1,000 - 10Q.$$

In a competitive market,

$$100 + 10Q = 1,000 - 10Q$$
$$20Q = 900$$
$$Q = 45.$$

And $P = 1,000 - 10(45) = 550$.

CHAPTER 20

Monopolistic Competition,

Oligopoly, and Antitrust Policy

Chapter Profile

Monopolistic competition occurs where there are many sellers whose products are somewhat different. The demand curve facing each firm slopes downward to the right. The conditions for long-run equilibrium are that each firm maximizes profits and economic profits are zero.

The firm under monopolistic competition is likely to produce less and charge a higher price than under perfect competition. Relative to pure monopoly, monopolistically competitive firms are likely to have lower profits, greater output, and lower prices. Firms under monopolistic competition offer a wider variety of styles, brands, and qualities than firms under perfect competition.

Oligopoly is characterized by a small number of firms and a great deal of interdependence, actual and perceived, among them. Oligopoly is a common market structure in the United States.

Game theory is often used to analyze oligopoly. A game is described in terms of its players, rules, payoffs, and information conditions. The relevant features of a two-person game can be shown by the payoff matrix. A dominant strategy is a strategy that is the player's best choice regardless of what the other player does.

Conditions in oligopolistic industries tend to promote collusion. A cartel is an open formal collusive arrangement. A profit-maximizing cartel acts like a monopolist with a number of plants or divisions, each of which is a member firm. In practice, it appears that the members of a cartel often divide markets geographically or in accord with each firm's level of sales in the past.

Price leadership is quite common in oligopolistic industries: One or a few firms apparently set the price and the rest follow their lead. Two types of price leadership are the dominant-firm model and the barometric-firm model.

Relative to perfect competition, it seems likely that both price and profits are higher under oligopoly. Moreover, oligopolistic industries tend to spend more on advertising, product differentiation, and style changes than perfectly competitive industries.

In 1890, the Sherman Act was passed. It outlawed any contract, combination, or conspiracy in restraint of trade and made it illegal to monopolize or attempt to monopolize. In 1914, Congress passed the Clayton Act, and the Federal Trade Commission was created. A more recent antitrust development was the Celler-Kefauver Anti-Merger Act of 1950.

The real impact of the antitrust laws depends on the interpretation placed on these laws by the courts. In its early cases, the Supreme Court put forth and used the famous rule of reason: that only unreasonable combinations in restraint of trade, not all trusts, required conviction under the Sherman Act. The situation changed greatly in the 1940s when the Court decided that Alcoa, because it controlled practically all the nation's aluminum output, was in violation of the antitrust laws.

Many observers seem to feel that the antitrust laws have not been as effective as they might—or should—have been, largely because they lack sufficient public support. At the same time, many feel that the evidence, although incomplete and unclear, suggests that they have had an effect on business behavior and markets. Two important cases decided in the past 30 years involved AT&T and IBM, while a third case, involving Microsoft, has not yet been entirely settled at the state level.

Concepts for Review

monopolistic competition	game	dominant strategy
oligopoly	cartel	Sherman Act
pure oligopoly	price leader	Clayton Act
differentiated oligopoly	dominant firm	Federal Trade
product differentiation	barometric firm	Commission Act
product group	antitrust laws	price discrimination
collusion	rule of reason	tying contract
payoff matrix	game theory	nonprice competition

Completion Questions

1. The demand and cost curves of a monopolistically competitive firm follow.

   If the firm charges a price of $4, its profits equal about _____.

   If the firm charges a price of $6, its profits equal about _____.

   If it charges a price of $8, its profits equal about _____. In the

   long run, (entry, exit) _____ will occur in this industry.

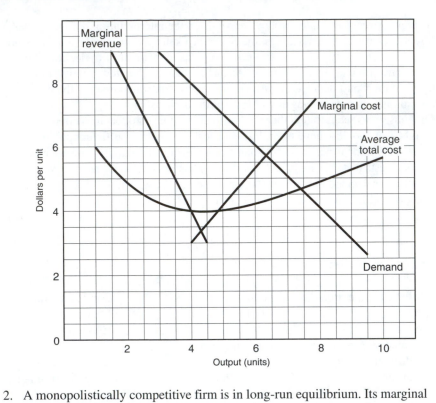

2. A monopolistically competitive firm is in long-run equilibrium. Its marginal revenue equals $5. If its marginal revenue plus its economic profit equal

   one-half of its price, its price equals $_____ and its

   marginal cost equals $_____. In game theory, a strategy is

   a _____ of what a player will do under each contingency.

3. All firms in an industry have marginal cost curves that are horizontal lines at $5 per unit of output. If they combine to form a cartel, the cartel's marginal

   cost (will, will not) _____ be $5 per unit of output. If the car-
   tel maximizes profit, its marginal revenue will be (greater than, smaller

   than, equal to) _____ $5 per unit of output, and its price

   will be (greater than, smaller than, equal to) _____ $5 per unit
   of output.

4. Under monopolistic competition, the firm is likely to produce (more, less)

   _____ and charge a (higher, lower) _____
   price than under perfect competition.

5. Relative to pure monopoly, monopolistically competitive firms are likely to have

   (greater, lower) _____ profits, (greater, lower)

   _____ output, and (higher, lower) _____
   prices.

6. If the demand curve is the same under oligopoly as under perfect competition, then under oligopoly, prices tend to be (higher, lower)

    _____ and output (higher, lower) _____ than under perfect competition.

7. Oligopoly occurs in markets where there are (few, many) _____ sellers and it has two forms: one in which all sellers produce an identical product and another in which the sellers produce somewhat different

    products. Examples of _____ are the markets for steel,

    cement, tin cans, and petroleum. Examples of _____ are the markets for automobiles and machinery.

8. Under monopolistic competition, the demand curve slopes (downward, upward)

    _____ to the right. Consequently, the marginal revenue must

    be (less, more) _____ than the price. Therefore, under monopolistic competition, the marginal cost must also be (less, more)

    _____ than the price, since the marginal revenue must (equal,

    exceed) _____ the marginal cost at the firm's profit-maximizing

    output rate. But, if the marginal cost is (less, more) _____

    than the price, the firm's output rate must be (less, more) _____

    —and the price (higher, lower) _____—than if the marginal cost equals the price, which is the case under perfect competition.

9. A(n) _____ is an open, formal collusive arrangement among

    firms. In many countries in Europe, _____ are common and

    legally acceptable. In the United States, most

    _____arrangements, whether secret or open, were declared

    illegal by the Sherman Antitrust Act, which was passed in _____.

10. There is always a temptation for oligopolists to _____ on any collusive agreement. So long as the other firms stick to the agreement,

    any firm that _____ its price below that agreed to under the collusive arrangement can take a lot of business away from the other

    firms and (decrease, increase) _____ its profits substantially, at least in the short run.

11. Hollywood film studios used to require theater owners to buy the rights to

    second-rate films to get a top film. This is an example of a _____.

12. To coordinate their behavior without outright collusion, some industries contain a(n) _____. It is quite common in oligopolistic industries for one or a few firms to _____ the price and for the rest to follow their lead. Two types of _____ leadership are the _____ model and the _____ model.

13. The _____ Act was passed in 1914 because the _____ Act was considered too weak.

True-False

_____ 1. Under perfect competition, firms offer a greater variety of styles, brands, and qualities than under monopolistic competition.

_____ 2. Monopolistic competition occurs in markets where there are few sellers, and oligopoly occurs where there are many sellers.

_____ 3. In an oligopoly, any change in one firm's price or output generally influences the sales and profits of its rivals.

_____ 4. In all games, every player has a dominant strategy.

_____ 5. Under monopolistic competition, a large number of firms must be in the product group.

_____ 6. The number of firms in the product group must be large enough under monopolistic competition that each firm expects its actions to go unheeded by its rivals and is unimpeded by possible retaliatory moves on their part.

_____ 7. A firm under monopolistic competition may be somewhat efficient because it tends to operate with excess capacity.

_____ 8. A cartel may act like a monopolist with a number of plants or divisions, each of which is a member firm.

_____ 9. In practice, it appears that cartels often divide markets geographically or in accord with a firm's level of sales in the past.

_____ 10. During the 1950s, there was widespread collusion among about 30 firms selling turbine generators, switchgears, transformers, and related products with total sales of about $1.5 billion per year.

_____ 11. Collusion is often difficult to achieve and maintain because an oligopoly contains an unwieldy number of firms, the product is quite heterogeneous, or the cost structures of the firms differ considerably.

_____ 12. Oligopolists tend to compete less aggressively through advertising and product differentiation than through direct price reduction.

_____ 13. Oligopolistic industries tend to spend more on advertising, product differentiation, and style changes than perfectly competitive industries.

_____ 14. A monopolistically competitive firm's short-run demand and cost curves are as follows:

Price (dollars)	Quantity demanded	Total cost (dollars)	Output
8	1	5	1
7	2	7	2
6	3	9	3
4	4	11	4
3	5	20	5

This firm, if it maximizes profit, chooses an output rate of 4.

_____ 15. In question 14, the number of firms in this industry tends to increase if all firms in the industry are like this one.

_____ 16. In question 14, if the firm's fixed cost rises by $5, the firm's short-run output rate is unaffected.

_____ 17. Under deregulation, airline fares increased while safety decreased.

Multiple Choice

1. The graph below pertains to a monopolistically competitive firm.

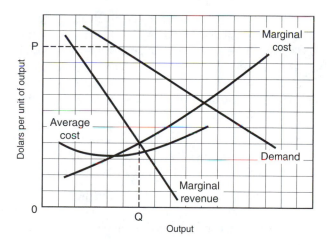

This firm would be foolish to set a price of 0P because

a. the marginal revenue exceeds the marginal cost at this price.
b. it exceeds the profit-maximizing price.
c. it results in an output that is lower than the profit-maximizing output.
d. all of the above.
e. b and c.

2. In question 1, if the firm chooses an output rate of $0Q$,

   a. other firms tend to enter the industry, since entry is easy.
   b. the firm makes an economic profit.
   c. the firm sets a price of $0P$.
   d. all of the above.
   e. a and b.

3. A major assumption of Chamberlin's theory of monopolistic competition is that

   a. demand curves are the same for each firm but cost curves are different.
   b. each firm's product is a fairly close substitute for the others in the group.
   c. just a few firms are in each group.
   d. each firm expects its actions to influence those of its rivals.
   e. all of the above.

4. In 1998, industry A was a perfectly competitive industry in long-run equilibrium. In 2000, it was cartelized, with the result that its economic profit was $10 million higher than in 1998. In 2000, its economic profits were

   a. zero.
   b. less than $10 million.
   c. $10 million.
   d. more than $10 million.
   e. indeterminate on the basis of the available data.

Discussion and Extension Questions

1. Suppose your economics professor states publicly that he grades on a curve (i.e., the top 10 percent of the students get an A, the next 20 percent a B, the next 40 percent a C, the next 20 percent a D, and the lowest 10 percent fail). The whole class could save itself a lot of work then by agreeing privately not to study at all (assuming the love of knowledge is negligible) for the final exam and just let the rankings thus far determine the final grades. Why might such an agreement be difficult to maintain and enforce?

2. In the middle of the 1970s, there was considerable debate in Congress and elsewhere concerning the desirability of breaking up the major oil firms. Do you believe such a step would be socially desirable? Why or why not?

3. "A cartel merely redistributes income. It takes from the cartel's customers and gives to the cartel members. So long as the latter are as worthy as the former, there are no adverse social consequences." Comment and evaluate.

4. Under monopolistic competition, does the firm produce less than the minimum-cost output in the long run? Why or why not? How does the level of price under monopolistic competition compare with that under perfect competition? Under monopoly?

5. What is a cartel? How does a profit-maximizing cartel set its price? What is meant by *price leadership*? Does it occur frequently?

6. What parts of the discussed antitrust laws do you see as relevant to the Microsoft case? If the rule of reason were to be used, do you believe it would support Microsoft or the government? Why?

7. Some economists claim that firms will never cooperate with each other to raise prices because any firm will see that short-run profits will rise if they "cheat" on the agreement and moderately lower the price. Do you agree or disagree? Can you think of conditions that would make it more likely that firms could cooperate?

Problems

1. The cost curves and demand curve of the Jones Manufacturing Company, a monopolistically competitive firm, follows:

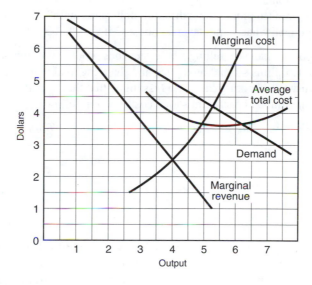

a. What output rate does this firm choose?
b. What price does it charge?
c. How great are its profits?
d. Is this a long-run equilibrium situation?

2. The India Company and the China Company are duopolists. Each firm has two possible strategies. The payoff matrix follows:

Possible strategies for the China Company	*Possible strategies for the India Company*	
	Strategy A	*Strategy B*
Strategy 1	China's profit: $6 million India's profit: $5 million	China's profit: $7 million India's profit: $6 million
Strategy 2	China's profit: $5 million India's profit: $6 million	China's profit: $6 million India's profit: $7 million

a. Does the China Company have a dominant strategy?

    b.   Does the India Company have a dominant strategy?

    c.   What strategy does the China Company choose?

    d.   What strategy does the India Company choose?

3. Suppose an industry is composed of 20 firms, each with a horizontal marginal cost curve. In particular, each firm can produce at a marginal cost of $2 per unit of output. Variation in industry output does not affect the cost curve of the individual firms.

    a.   If the industry is cartelized, what will the marginal cost curve of the cartel look like?

    b.   The marginal revenue for the cartel is $3 when it produces 100 units of output, $2 when it produces 200 units of output, and $1 when it produces 300 units of output per month. Will it produce more or less than 100 units of output per month?

    c.   Will it produce more or less than 300 units per month?

    d.   Can you tell what output level it chooses? If so, what is it?

4. An oligopolistic industry selling a homogeneous product is composed of two firms. The two firms set the same price and share the total market equally. The demand curve confronting each firm (assuming that the other firm sets the same price as this firm) and each firm's total cost function follow:

Price (dollars)	Quantity demanded	Output	Total cost (dollars)
10	5	5	45
9	6	6	47
8	7	7	50
7	8	8	55
6	9	9	65

    a.   Assuming that each firm is right in believing that the other firm will charge the same price that it does, what price should each charge?

    b.   Under the assumptions in part a, what output rate should each firm set?

    c.   Is there bound to be entry into this industry in the long run?

    d.   Is there any incentive for each firm to cut its price to somewhat below its rival's price? If so, what is it?

5. Suppose that, if industry A sets its price above $5 per unit, a swarm of new firms enter the industry and take a very large proportion of the sales away from the established firms.

    a.   What effect does this have on the shape of the demand curve confronting the established firms in the industry?

    b.   What effect do you think this will have on the industry's pricing practices?

Answers

Completion Questions
1. –$6, $11, $16, entry   2. $10, $5, complete specification   3. will, equal to, greater than   4. less, higher   5. lower, greater, lower   6. higher, lower   7. few, pure oligopoly, differentiated oligopoly   8. downward, less, less, equal, less, less, higher   9. cartel, cartels, collusive, 1890   10. cheat, cuts, increase   11. tying contract   12. price leader, set, price, dominant-firm, barometric-firm   13. Clayton, Sherman

True-False
1. False   2. False   3. True   4. False   5. True   6. True   7. False   8. True
9. True   10. True   11. True   12. False   13. True   14. False   15. True
16. True   17. False

Multiple Choice
1. d   2. e   3. b   4. c

Problems
1. a. Four units of output.
    b. $5.
    c. $4.
    d. No.
2. a. Yes.
    b. Yes.
    c. Strategy 1.
    d. Strategy B.
3. a. A horizontal line at $2 = MC$.
    b. More.
    c. Less.
    d. Yes. 200 units of output if it maximizes profit.
4. a. $9.
    b. 6.
    c. Not necessarily; it depends on the extent of the barriers to entry.
    d. Yes, because its demand curve is likely to be very elastic if the other firm does not match its price cut.
5. a. The demand curve may have a kink at the price of $5; it may be much more price elastic above this price than below it.
    b. The established firms may avoid raising the price above $5, since this would encourage entry.

CHAPTER 21

Pollution and the Environment

Chapter Profile

A major social issue of recent years has been environmental pollution. To a considerable extent, environmental pollution is an economic problem. Waste disposal and other pollution-causing activities result in external diseconomies.

Firms and individuals that pollute the water and air (and other facets of the environment) often pay less than the true social costs of disposing of their wastes in this way. Part of the true social cost is borne by other firms and individuals, that must pay to clean up the water or air or live with the consequences.

Because of the divergence of private from social costs, the market system does not result in an optimal allocation of resources. Firms and individuals create too much waste and dispose of it in excessively harmful ways. Because the polluters do not pay the full cost of waste disposal, their products are artificially cheap, with the result that they produce too much of these products.

The government can intervene in several ways to help remedy the breakdown of the market system in this area. One way is to issue regulations for waste disposal and other activities influencing the environment. Another is to establish effluent fees, charges a polluter must pay to the government for discharging wastes, or transferable emissions permits. In recent decades, government programs designed to control pollution have grown considerably.

It is extremely difficult to determine how clean the environment should be. The sensible goal for society is to permit the level of pollution that minimizes the sum of the costs of pollution and the costs of controlling pollution; but no one has a very clear idea of what these costs are, and to a large extent, the choices must be made through the political process.

Concepts for Review

external diseconomy
private costs
social costs
zero economic growth
transferable emissions permits
Clean Air Act of 1970
Environmental Protection Agency

zero population growth
direct regulation
effluent fees
tax credits
Kyoto agreement
optimal pollution level

Completion Questions

1. When important external diseconomies are present, government can try to reduce pollution through _____, _____, and/or _____. Also, tax credits can be used.

2. A(n) _____ occurs when one person's or firm's use of a resource imposes damages on others that cannot obtain proper compensation.

3. _____ are charges a polluter must pay to the government for discharging waste. Faced with these fees, a polluter finds it profitable to reduce waste discharge to the point where the cost of reducing an additional unit of waste is _____ the effluent fee.

4. An agency that establishes standards for air and water quality is the _____.

5. The sensible goal for our society is to minimize the sum of the costs of pollution and the _____.

6. A major contributor to air pollution is the combustion of _____ fuels, particularly _____ and _____ products.

7. If a paper mill uses water then treats it to restore its quality, there is no divergence between the _____ and _____ cost. In other words, there are no _____.

8. Some power companies (do, do not) _____ pay the full cost of disposing of wastes in the atmosphere. Thus, they may set an artificially (high, low) _____ price, and the public may be induced to use (less, more) _____ electric power than is socially desirable.

True-False

_____ 1. When polluters do not pay the true cost of waste disposal, too little of their products is produced.

_____ 2. The price system is unlikely to allocate resources efficiently in the presence of significant external diseconomies.

_____ 3. As national output goes up, it is most likely that pollution levels fall considerably.

_____ 4. If polluters are forced to pay the social costs of disposing of their wastes, the prices of many goods we buy must rise.

_____ 5. The price system is based on the supposition that the full cost of using each resource is borne by the person or firm that uses it.

_____ 6. Immediately after cans and no-deposit bottles were introduced, the consumer of beverages no longer had to pay directly for the cost of disposing of the cans or bottles.

_____ 7. Technological change is a potential hero in the fight against pollution, because the creation of new technology is an important way to reduce the harmful side effects of existing techniques.

_____ 8. The average American is responsible for much less pollution than the average citizen of most other countries.

_____ 9. Economists favor effluent fees or transferable emissions permits because this approach requires far less information in the hands of the relevant government agencies than direct regulation.

_____ 10. Subsidies to promote the purchase of particular types of pollution control equipment may result in relatively inefficient and costly reductions in pollution.

_____ 11. The sensible goal for our society is to minimize the sum of the costs of pollution and the costs of controlling pollution.

_____ 12. The United States is currently bound by the Kyoto agreement to reduce greenhouse emissions by 7 percent from 2000 levels.

Multiple Choice

1. If a chemical firm pollutes a river and forces fishing firms downstream to install devices to clean up the water, from the point of view of society as a whole,

   a. chemical output and fish output are too high.
   b. chemical output and fish output are too low.
   c. chemical output is too low and fish output is too high.
   d. chemical output is too high and fish output is too low.
   e. none of the above.

2. Suppose that, at the current level of pollution, the social cost of reducing pollution by one unit is less than the social benefit of reducing pollution by one unit. If so,

   a. the current level of pollution is optimal.
   b. there is too little pollution from society's point of view.
   c. there is too much pollution from society's point of view.
   d. all pollution should be eliminated.
   e. existing pollution control measures should be dropped.

3. Taylor Bingham and Allen Miedema estimated that the cost of reducing sulfur emissions to current standards in St. Louis, Missouri, would be about $50 million per year if direct controls were used and about $29 million if effluent fees were used. The lower cost with effluent fees is because

    a.   there are large differences in abatement costs among polluters.
    b.   effluent fees induce larger reductions in sulfur emissions among steam-electric power plants (where such reductions are cheap) than among oil refineries (where such reductions are expensive).
    c.   direct controls do not result in the cost of reducing emission by one unit being the same for polluters.
    d.   all of the above.
    e.   none of the above.

4. Bingham and Miedema estimated that an effluent fee of 13 cents per pound of sulfur discharge would induce the required curtailment of emissions in St. Louis, while in Cleveland the effluent fee would have to be 19 cents per pound. Such differences in the effluent fee may be due to differences between cities in

    a.   the amount by which the total emission of sulfur is to be reduced.
    b.   industrial composition.
    c.   the technology used in each industry.
    d.   all of the above.
    e.   none of the above.

Discussion and Extension Questions

1. The optimal amount of pollution is not zero; we are quite sure of that. However, how do we know that, given some pollution is necessary for a social optimum, we currently have too much pollution? Is it possible that we do not have enough pollution yet? Is more, not less, the direction in which we should be moving?

2. Can you utilize your understanding of cost-benefit analysis, opportunity costs, and other economic principles you absorbed to analyze roughly how one would decide whether a particular state should pass legislation to ban throwaway or disposable bottles and cans for soft drinks and beer? Should manufacturers also be forbidden to use throwaway containers for macaroni? Detergents? Baby food? Should consumers have to pay a deposit on egg cartons?

3. Show how too much pollution, from society's point of view, is likely to arise if the private costs of using water and air for waste disposal are less than the social costs. Is it likely that the output rate of heavy polluters is too high from a social point of view? Why or why not? Show how, once cans and no-deposit bottles were introduced, an external diseconomy arose with regard to disposal of these items. Are there any states that now require a deposit on bottles?

4. Must economic growth necessarily result in increased pollution? Should the rate of technological change be slowed in order to reduce pollution? Explain.

5. Explain how transferable emissions permits can be used to reduce pollution. What are their advantages? Why do many economists prefer them over direct regulation? Over tax credits for pollution control equipment?

Problems

1. a. Suppose that the cost to society of various levels of pollution is as follows:

Pollution (millions of tons per year)	Cost (billions of dollars per year)
1	3
2	6
3	10
4	15
5	22
6	30
7	40
8	60

Plot this relationship in the following graph.

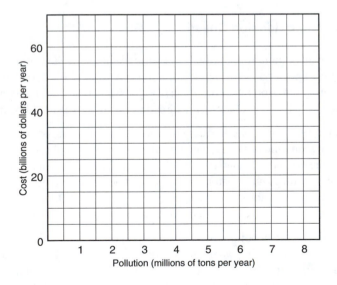

b. Suppose that the cost to society of pollution control varies as follows with the level of pollution:

Pollution (millions of tons per year)	Cost (billions of dollars per year)
1	50
2	40
3	32
4	25
5	19
6	14
7	9
8	5

Plot this relationship in the following graph.

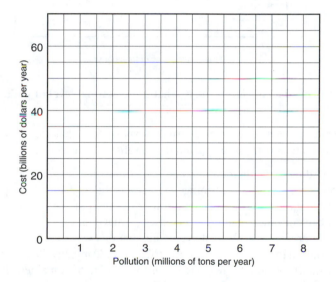

c. Does it make sense to plot the sum of the costs in parts a and b against the level of pollution? If so, plot this relationship on the following graph and tell what this relationship means.

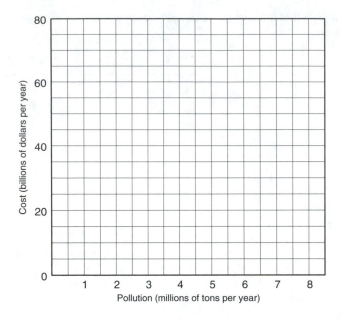

d. Given the data in parts a and b, what is the optimal level of pollution? Why isn't it sensible to aim for zero pollution?

2. Some states, such as Oregon and Vermont, passed laws that all carbonated-beverage containers must carry a minimum refundable deposit.

    a. According to the director of communications services for American Can Company, "What *is* happening in Oregon is that consumers are paying $10 million more a year for beer and soft drinks than they did before the bottle bill became law. Retail price increases . . . have far exceeded those in neighboring states." Why do you think that this was true?

    b. According to this executive of American Can Company, "Oregon [and Vermont] consumers are denied their free choice of container." Is this true? According to William Baumol and Wallace Oates, this amounts to "a denial of . . . the freedom to pollute unpenalized." Do you agree?

3. According to one study of the Delaware River, the extra social costs involved in going from one level of pollution abatement to another are as follows. Also shown are the extra benefits to society in going from one level of pollution to another, both in millions of dollars.

Transition	Extra cost	Extra benefit
From abatement level 1 to 2	35	200
From abatement level 2 to 3	20	20
From abatement level 3 to 4	130	10
From abatement level 4 to 5	245	25

    a. If abatement level 1 is currently achieved, is it socially worthwhile to advance to abatement level 2? Why or why not?

b. Is it socially worthwhile to advance to abatement level 3? Why or why not?
c. Is it socially worthwhile to advance to abatement level 4? Why or why not?
d. Is it socially worthwhile to advance to abatement level 5? Why or why not?

Answers

Completion Questions

1. direct regulation, effluent fees, transferable emissions permits   2. external diseconomy   3. Effluent fees, equal to   4. Environmental Protection Agency   5. costs of controlling pollution   6. fossil, coal, oil   7. private, social, external diseconomies   8. do not, low, more

True-False

1. False   2. True   3. False   4. True   5. True   6. True   7. True   8. False
9. True   10. True   11. True   12. False

Multiple Choice

1. d   2. c   3. d   4. d

Problems

1. a.

b.

c.

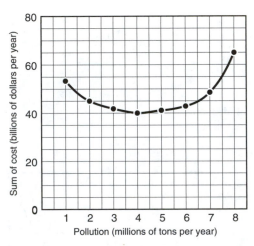

Yes. This relationship shows how the total costs (both pollution costs and pollution control costs) vary with the amount of pollution.

d. 4 million tons. Because it costs more to reduce the pollution (below 4 million tons) than it is worth.

2. a. Because of increased costs of handling, sorting, washing, returning, and refilling bottles, according to this executive.

b. The issue is too complex to permit a very brief answer, but many economists would agree with Baumol and Oates.

3. a. Yes, because the benefit exceeds the cost.

b. No, because the benefit does not exceed the cost.

c. No, because the benefit does not exceed the cost.

d. No, because the benefit does not exceed the cost.

CASE 3

Microsoft versus the Department of Justice

The latest and most serious legal battle involving the United States government and Microsoft started in 1997 because the computer giant had bundled its Web browser with its Windows 95 operating system. A settlement appeared to have resolved the issue when Microsoft agreed to allow its Internet Explorer to be removed from the desktop or even completely deleted by PC manufacturers. In 1998, Microsoft announced that its new Windows 98 software had been thoroughly integrated with the Web browser and that the latter should no longer be removed as it was now necessary to parts of the system software. The Department of Justice and 20 states then joined in one of the largest, most-publicized antitrust cases since early this century, ranking only with the AT&T case in recent years. As with AT&T, the government has requested the breakup of the company.

On November 1999, Judge Jackson released his findings, outlining the events and facts as the court saw them but delayed his conclusions on how those events and facts violated antitrust law, hoping to push Microsoft into a settlement. When an appointed mediator failed to bring the two sides together, Judge Jackson issued his judgment on April 3, 2000, that Microsoft had violated the Sherman Act as well as a host of state laws:

> Most harmful of all is the message that Microsoft's actions have conveyed to every enterprise with the potential to innovate in the computer industry. Through its conduct toward Netscape, IBM, Compaq, Intel, and others, Microsoft has demonstrated that it will use its prodigious market power and immense profits to harm any firm that insists on pursuing initiatives that could intensify competition against one of Microsoft's core products. Microsoft's past success in hurting such companies and stifling innovation deters investment in technologies and businesses that exhibit the potential to threaten Microsoft. The ultimate result is that some innovations that would truly benefit consumers never occur for the sole reason that they do not coincide with Microsoft's self-interest.[1]

In response to Microsoft's motion that the reorganization be rejected and additional time granted in regard to the other remedies, the court responded:

> First, despite the Court's Findings of Fact and Conclusions of Law, Microsoft does not yet concede that any of its business practices violated the Sherman Act.
>
> Second, there is credible evidence in the record to suggest that Microsoft, convinced of its innocence, continues to do business as it has in the past, and may yet do to other markets what it has already done in the PC operating system and browser markets.

[1]www.dcd.uscourts.gov/ms-findings2.pdf, pp. 205–206.

Third, Microsoft has proved untrustworthy in the past. In earlier proceedings in which a preliminary injunction was entered, Microsoft's purported compliance with that injunction while it was on appeal was illusory and its explanation disingenuous.[2]

On June 7, 2000, Judge Jackson issued his final ruling that set out two types of remedies to increase competition in the software industry and reduce Microsoft's dominance. The first and most publicized was the "structural remedy" breaking up the company:

i. The separation of the Operating Systems Business from the Applications Business, and the transfer of the assets of one of them (the "Separated Business") to a separate entity along with (a) all personnel, systems, and other tangible and intangible assets (including Intellectual Property) used to develop, produce, distribute, market, promote, sell, license and support the products and services of the Separated Business, and (b) such other assets as are necessary to operate the Separated Business as an independent and economically viable entity.[3]

Microsoft appealed the case. Steve Ballmer of Microsoft summed up the corporation's position:

It's a reflection of the fundamental issue that we have the right and the obligation, even, to add value to Windows. The court disagreed with us on that, several times.

When you believe in the propriety, integrity and righteousness of what you've done, I don't think the thing to do is have a *mea culpa*. The thing to do, at least in the United States, is to argue your position, your innocence.[4]

In June 2001, a Federal Court of Appeals upheld much of the original judgment on Microsoft's monopoly status and violation of the Sherman Antitrust Act but reversed the breakup order of Judge Jackson. The court was concerned about the lack of evidentiary hearings, which would have allowed Microsoft to present expert testimony contradicting the government's experts as well as improprieties in Judge Jackson's behavior, particularly that his interactions with the media may have tainted the proceedings. The Department of Justice then turned to settlement discussions and, by November 2001, reached an agreement with Microsoft.

The settlement would prevent Microsoft from participating in exclusive deals that could hurt competitors; require uniform contract terms for computer manufacturers; allow manufacturers and customers to remove icons for some Microsoft features; and require that the company release some technical data so software developers can write programs for Windows that work as well as Microsoft products do.[5]

[2]www.dcd.uscourts.gov/ms-final.pdf, pp. 3–4.
[3]www.dcd.uscourts.gov/ms-final2.pdf, p. 3.
[4]S. Levy, "Steve Ballmer on What Lies Ahead," *Newsweek,* June 19, 2000, p. 31.
[5]www.money.cnn.com/2002/11/01/technology/microsoft_remedy/.

A number of states eventually rejected this settlement and proceeded with class actions suits of their own, however, by spring 2004, these cases had largely been dismissed or settled in separate negotiations. As of May 2004, only six state cases remained, although three further states were appealing the dismissal of their cases. The European Union had also brought an antitrust suit against Microsoft in their jurisdiction, and in March 2004, the company received a record $613 million fine as well as other penalties.

Discussion Questions

1. Is the purpose of antitrust law to protect competitors or consumers of a powerful company or both? Should the courts consider this in an antitrust case? If so, do you believe that Microsoft has harmed consumers or not?

2. Do you believe that the main reason Microsoft bundled its Internet browser with its operating system was to enhance the latter or to cut into Netscape's market share of the browser market?

3. The new settlement requires Microsoft to share less technical data than the original remedy set by Judge Jackson; this sharing is meant to enable the ability of others to write software compatible with Windows-run computers. Do you believe that the new settlement is adequate? How much does this decision help the consumers of Microsoft products? How much does this decision help the competitors of Microsoft?

4. By the time the courts decided the IBM antitrust case in the early 1980s, IBM no longer was close to monopoly power. Some people use this as evidence that the computer industry changes too quickly for one firm to dominate unless it always remains on the cutting edge, producing the best product for the best price. How does the network effect relate to this claim? Can you think of any ways the Microsoft and IBM examples are different?

CHAPTER 22

The Supply and Demand for Labor

Chapter Profile

Assuming perfect competition, a firm employs each type of labor in such an amount that its marginal product times the product's price equals its wage. In other words, the firm employs enough labor that the value of the marginal product of labor equals labor's price, so that the benefit of the last worker hired equals the cost of the last worker.

The firm's demand curve for labor, which shows the amount of labor the firm uses for each price of labor, is the firm's value of marginal product curve (if labor is the only variable input). The market demand curve for labor shows the relationship between its price and the total amount of labor demanded in the market.

Labor's price depends on its market supply curve as well as on its market demand curve. Labor's market supply curve is the relationship between the price of labor and the total amount of labor supplied in the market. (Labor's market supply curve may bend backward.)

An input's price is determined under perfect competition in essentially the same way a product's price is determined, by supply and demand. The price of labor in equilibrium tends to be at the level at which the quantity of labor demanded equals the quantity of labor supplied. By the same token, the equilibrium amount of labor utilized is also given by the intersection of the market supply and demand curves.

There are about 200 national unions in the United States, the biggest being the National Education Association. Each national union is composed of local unions, which operate within the context of the constitution of the national union.

The AFL-CIO is a federation of national unions created by the merger in 1955 of the American Federation of Labor and the Congress of Industrial Organizations. The AFL-CIO is very important in speaking for the U.S. labor movement, but because the national unions in the AFL-CIO have given up relatively little of their power to the federation, its authority is limited.

Unions can increase wages in several ways: by shifting the supply curve of labor to the left, shifting the demand curve for labor to the right, and influencing the wage directly. Collective bargaining is the process of negotiation between union and management over wages and working conditions.

Wages, jobs, and the very power of unions can be affected by government policies. Some conservative economists credit our current robust economy and low unemployment to the decline in the power of unions and the real minimum wage seen over the 1970s and 1980s. They, and others, point to European policies that support high wages and powerful unions as a significant factor in high European unemployment.

Concepts for Review

firm's demand curve for labor

value of the marginal product of labor

market demand curve for labor

derived demand

market supply curve for labor

backward-bending supply curve

noncompeting groups

national unions

local unions

AFL-CIO

yellow-dog contracts

NEA

checkoff

featherbedding

collective bargaining

closed shop

union shop

open shop

Norris-LaGuardia Act of 1932

Wagner Act of 1935

Taft-Hartley Act of 1947

Landrum-Griffen Act of 1959

Completion Questions

1. A perfectly competitive firm's demand curve for labor slopes downward and to the right because of the law of _____. This is because the firm's demand curve for labor is the same as its _____ curve, and the _____ is equal to the price of the product times the marginal product of labor.

2. In competitive firm X, the marginal product of the first unit of labor is three units of output, the marginal product of the second unit of labor is two units of output, and the marginal product of the third unit of labor is one unit of output.

   If the price of a unit of output is $15, the firm demands _____ unit(s) of labor when the price of a unit of labor is $40, _____ unit(s) of labor when the price of a unit of labor is $25, and _____ unit(s) of labor when the price of a unit of labor is $20.

3. The profit-maximizing competitive firm uses each input in an amount such that the input's _____ multiplied by the _____ equals the input's _____.

4. Since inputs are demanded to produce other things, the demand for labor and other inputs is called a(n) _____ demand.

5. Labor's _____ is the relationship between the price of labor and the total amount of labor supplied in the market.

6. The supreme governing body of the national union is the _____.

7. An agreement whereby a worker agrees with his or her employer not to join a union is called a(n) _____.

8. The Wagner Act established the _____ and made it an unfair labor practice for employers to _____ to bargain collectively with a union representing a(n) _____ of their workers or interfere with their workers' _____ to organize.

9. In 1947, despite bitter labor opposition, the _____ Act was passed. Its aim was to redress the balance between labor and employers. The act established standards of conduct for _____ as well as _____, defined unfair union practices, and stated that unions can be _____ for acts of their agents.

10. In a(n) _____ shop a worker must be a union member before she or he can be hired. This gives the union more power than a(n) _____ shop, in which the employer can hire nonunion workers who must then become union members in a certain length of time after being hired. In a(n) _____ shop, the employer can hire both union and nonunion workers, and the latter need not join a union once employed.

True-False

_____ 1. If a union shifts the supply curve of labor to the left and the price elasticity of demand for labor is infinite, the price of labor rises.

_____ 2. If a technological change increases the marginal productivity of labor and, at the same time, the supply curve of labor shifts to the right, the price of labor must fall.

_____ 3. The Norris-LaGuardia Act permitted state legislatures to pass right-to-work laws.

_____ 4. If the value of the marginal product is greater than the input's price, the perfectly competitive firm can increase its profit by decreasing its utilization of the input.

_____ 5. An example of a backward-bending supply curve might be that for labor.

_____ 6. Union growth was most rapid during the 1920s.

_____ 7. A firm's demand curve for an input shows the relationship between the input's price and the amount of the input utilized by the firm. That is, it shows, for each price, the amount of the input that the firm uses.

_____ 8. Beyond some point, increases in wages may result in the supply of smaller amounts of labor.

_____ 9. The reason for a backward-bending supply curve for labor is that, as the price of labor increases, it is more profitable for employers to hire fewer workers.

_____ 10. The wage for surgeons is higher than for unskilled labor because the demand curve for surgeons is farther to the right and the supply curve for surgeons is farther to the left than the corresponding curves for unskilled labor.

_____ 11. The Taft-Hartley Act said that, unless workers agree in writing, the employer may not deduct union dues from each worker's paycheck and give them to the union.

Multiple Choice

1. Suppose that the production function of a hypothetical competitive firm is as follows:

Number of workers employed per day	Output per day
1	0
2	5
3	20
4	35
5	38

If the value of the marginal product of a worker is $150 when two or three workers are employed per day, the price of a unit of output must be

a. $1,000.
b. $100.
c. $20.

d. $10.
e. none of the above.

2. The price elasticity of demand for a particular input is greater

a. the more easily other inputs can be substituted for it.
b. the smaller the price elasticity of demand for the product the input helps to produce.
c. in the short run than in the long run.
d. all of the above.
e. none of the above.

3. If the supply curve bends backward, increases in price (beyond some point) may result in _____ of the input being supplied.

a. amounts increasing quickly to zero
b. an imaginary quantity

c. smaller amounts
d. a negative amount
e. none of the above

4. The president of the United States tells the attorney general to obtain an injunction forbidding a strike for 80 days. He is acting on the basis of

    a. the Norris-LaGuardia Act.
    b. the Taft-Hartley Act.
    c. the Wagner Act.
    d. the Landrum-Griffin Act.
    e. none of the above.

5. Which of the following methods could a labor union use to increase the demand for labor?

    a. Negotiate an above equilibrium wage.
    b. Restrict union membership.
    c. Require that only union members be hired.
    d. Support laws to limit imports.
    e. All of the above.

6. If a union tries to force firms to hire only workers who are already union workers, this is illegal on the basis of

    a. the Wagner Act.
    b. the Landrum-Griffin Act.
    c. the Taft-Hartley Act.
    d. the Norris-LaGuardia Act.
    e. none of the above.

7. If firm X refuses to bargain collectively with a union that represents a majority of its workers, this is an unfair labor practice on the basis of

    a. the Wagner Act.
    b. the Landrum-Griffin Act.
    c. the Taft-Hartley Act.
    d. the Norris-LaGuardia Act.
    e. none of the above.

8. Which of the following is *not* a provision of the Taft-Hartley Act?

    a. Standards of conduct for unions established
    b. Unions could be sued for acts of their agents
    c. Federal Mediation Service established
    d. The closed shop outlawed
    e. Union elections held by secret ballot

9. The European labor market has

    a. low unemployment and high wages.
    b. high unemployment and high wages.
    c. low unemployment and low wages.
    d. high unemployment and low wages.
    e. similar unemployment and wages to the United States.

Discussion and Extension Questions

1. Pro football salaries are about half of those in pro baseball and basketball. What factors help to account for this difference?

2. One study suggests that, over the last several decades, union workers earned wages that are 10 to 20 percent higher than the wages paid to nonunion labor. Does that imply that, on average, wages in the United States would be lower if there were no unions?

3. How might a consumer boycott of grapes or lettuce work to the detriment of Mexican-American farm laborers in California?

4. "Keynes regarded wages as fixed; Milton Friedman regards them as flexible. Neither is really correct, and it is important that unions, with their immense power, be willing to settle for limited wage increases to prevent ruinous inflation. Unfortunately, there is no evidence they will do so." Discuss and evaluate.

5. "Unions of state and local workers have far too much power. They can shut down entire regions." Comment and evaluate.

6. Why is the Wagner Act often called U.S. labor's Magna Charta?

7. Describe three ways unions can increase wages. Give examples where each has occurred.

8. If you were an employer, would you prefer a closed shop, an open shop, or a union shop? Why? Which would you prefer if you were president of the union? Why?

9. Labor unions today do not have the political or economic power that they had in the 1950s and 1960s. What do you think might account for this?

Problems

1. Suppose that the demand curve for lawyers is as follows:

Annual wage (thousands of dollars)	Quantity of labor demanded (thousands of person-years)
40	200
60	180
80	160
100	140
120	120
140	100
160	80

   a. Draw the demand curve for lawyers on the following graph.

b. Suppose that the supply curve for lawyers is as follows:

Annual wage (thousands of dollars)	Quantity of labor supplied (thousands of person-years)
40	80
60	100
80	120
100	140
120	160
140	180
160	200

Draw the supply curve for lawyers on the graph for part a.

c. What is the equilibrium wage for lawyers if the market is perfectly competitive?

d. Suppose that lawyers form a union and the union forces the wage up to $140,000 a year. How many person-years of labor will be supplied but will be unable to find work?

2. Suppose that the relationship between the number of laborers employed per day in a car wash and the number of cars washed per day is as follows:

Number of laborers	Cars washed
1	15
2	40
3	50
4	55

a. Suppose that the owner of the car wash receives $2 for each car wash and that the price of labor is $20 per day. How many laborers does the owner hire per day?

b. What is the value of the marginal product of labor when one or two laborers per day are used? When two or three laborers per day are used? When three or four laborers per day are used?

c. If the owner of the car wash hires three laborers per day, does the value of the marginal product of labor equal the wage?

3. Suppose that the Ace Manufacturing Company is a member of a perfectly competitive industry. Suppose that the relationship between various amounts of labor input and output is as follows:

Product price	Units of labor	Units of output	Marginal product of labor	Value of marginal product (dollars)
10	0	0		
10	1	2 ½	____	____
10	2	5	____	____
10	3	7	____	____
10	4	8	____	____

a. Fill in the blanks.

b. If you are told that the Ace Manufacturing Company is hiring three units of labor, you can establish a range for the value of the wage rate prevailing in the labor market (assuming that the firm maximizes profit). What is this range? Why?

c. Suppose that the Ace Manufacturing Company must pay $22 for a unit of labor. How many units of labor will it hire? Why?

d. In this graph, draw the Ace Manufacturing Company's demand curve for labor.

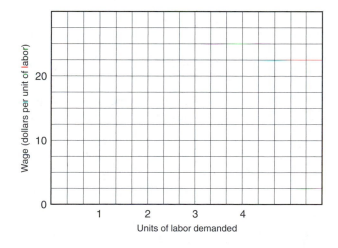

4. The demand and supply curves for musicians in a particular area in 1994 are as shown in the graph.

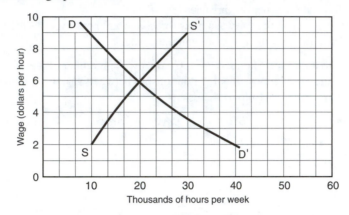

a. If a union makes the employers of musicians demand 50 percent more hours per week of musicians' time than in 1994 at each wage rate, draw the new demand curve in the graph.

b. After the union shifts the demand curve, perhaps due to featherbedding, what is the new equilibrium wage? What is the new equilibrium quantity employed?

5. A perfectly competitive firm has the following value-of-marginal-product curve:

Number of units of labor per day	Value of marginal product (dollars)
1	
	52
2	
	47
3	
	42
4	
	37
5	
	32
6	

a. If there are 1,000 firms, all of which have the same value-of-marginal-product curve, the market demand curve for labor is as follows:

Price of a unit of labor per day (dollars)	Number of units of labor demanded per day
50	_____
45	_____
40	_____
35	_____

Fill in the blanks. (Assume that only integer numbers of units of labor can be used.)

b. The supply curve for labor is as follows:

Price of a unit of labor per day (dollars)	Number of units of labor supplied per day
35	3,000
40	4,000
45	5,000
50	6,000

What is the equilibrium price of a unit of labor per day?

c. What is the total amount of labor demanded in the market? What is the amount demanded by each firm?

d. What will be the extra cost that a firm would incur if it added an extra unit of labor per day?

e. What is the value of the marginal product of labor for this firm?

f. If a minimum wage of $45 per day for a unit of labor were established, what would be the total amount of labor demanded in the market?

6. Four very important labor laws are listed, after which are listed various provisions of these laws. In the space before each provision, put the letter (A to D) corresponding to the relevant labor law.

A. Landrum-Griffin Act
B. Taft-Hartley Act
C. Wagner Act
D. Norris-LaGuardia Act

_____ a. Makes it an unfair labor practice for employers to interfere with their workers' right to organize.

_____ b. Makes yellow-dog contracts unenforceable in federal courts.

_____ c. Requires unions to file financial reports.

_____ d. Makes the checkoff illegal, except if workers agree in writing.

_____ e. Established the National Labor Relations Board.

_____ f. Established the Federal Mediation Service.

_____ g. Contains a "bill of rights" for labor.

_____ h. Outlaws the closed shop.

Answers

Completion Questions
1. diminishing marginal returns, value of marginal product, value of the marginal product   2. one, two, two   3. marginal product, product's price, price   4. derived   5. market supply curve   6. convention   7. yellow-dog contract   8. National Labor Relations Board, refuse, majority, right   9. Taft-Hartley, unions, employers, sued   10. closed, union, open

True-False
1. False   2. False   3. False   4. False   5. True   6. False   7. True   8. True   9. False   10. True   11. True

Multiple Choice
1. d   2. a   3. c   4. b   5. d   6. c   7. a   8. e   9. b

Problems

1. a, b.

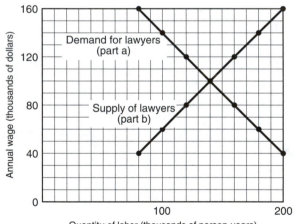

c. $100,000.
d. 80,000.
2. a. Two or three.
b. $50, $20, $10.
c. Yes.
3. a.

Marginal product of labor	Value of marginal product (dollars)
$2^1/_2$	25
$2^1/_2$	25
2	20
1	10

b. The wage must be above $10 and $20 or less, because, if it were more than $20, the firm would hire only two units of labor and, if it were $10 or less, the firm would hire four units of labor.

c. Two units of labor. Because this will maximize its profit.

d.

4. a.

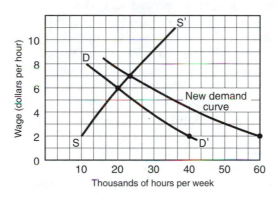

b. About $7. About 23,000 hours per week.

5. a. *Number of units of labor*
        demanded per day

            2,000
            3,000
            4,000
            5,000

b. $40.

c. 4,000 units, four units.

d. $40.

e. $42.

f. 3,000 units.

6. a. C

b. D

c. A

d. B

e. C

f. B

g. A

h. B

CHAPTER 23

Interest, Rent, and Profit

Chapter Profile

Interest is a payment for the use of money. Interest rates vary a great deal, depending on the nature of the borrower and the type and riskiness of the loan. One very important function of interest rates is to allocate the supply of loanable funds.

The pure interest rate (the interest rate on riskless loans), like any price, is determined by the interaction of supply and demand. However, because of the influence of the government on both the demand and supply sides of the market, it is clear that the pure interest rate is to a considerable extent a matter of public policy.

In a capitalist system, each asset has a market value that can be determined by capitalizing its earnings. If its annual return is held constant, the asset's worth is higher the lower is the rate of return available on other investments. Actual interest rates in the economy are adjusted off this underlying pure rate to reflect risk and other costs.

Any asset has a rate of return, which indicates its net productivity. An asset's rate of return is like an interest rate earned on the investment in the asset. If firms maximize profits, they must carry out all projects where the rate of return exceeds the interest rate at which they can borrow.

Rent is the return derived by inputs that are fixed in supply. Since the supply of the input is fixed, its price can be lowered without influencing the amount supplied. Therefore, if the government imposes taxes on rents, there is no effect on the supply of resources to the economy.

Another important type of property income is profits. Available statistics on profits are based on the accountant's concept, not the economist's, with the result that they include the opportunity costs of the labor, capital, and land contributed by the owners of the firm. Profits play a very important and legitimate role in a free enterprise system.

Two important factors responsible for the existence of profits are innovation and uncertainty. Profits are the rewards earned by innovators and a payment for bearing risk. Still another reason for the existence of profits is monopoly power; because of contrived scarcity, profits are made by firms in imperfectly competitive markets.

Concepts for Review

interest	bond
interest rate	present value
pure rate of interest	land
demand curve for loanable funds	rent
rate of return	innovators
supply curve for loanable funds	risk
anti-usury laws	profit
capitalization	

Completion Questions

1. Mr. Smith buys a bond for $1,000. If the bond pays interest of $50 per year indefinitely, the interest rate is _____ percent. If the price of the bond increases to $1,500, the interest rate is _____ percent. If the price of the bond falls to $500, the interest rate is

   _____ percent.

2. A bond yields $100 per year in interest indefinitely. If the rate of interest is 8 percent, the bond is worth _____. The price of the bond (rises, falls, is unaffected) _____ if the interest rate rises. For example, if the interest rate rises to 10 percent, the price of the bond is

   _____.

3. If the interest rate is 10 percent, a dollar received a year from now is currently worth _____, and a dollar received two years from now is currently worth _____. Therefore, a business venture that pays you both a dollar a year from now and a dollar two years from now is

   currently worth _____.

4. If the present value of a dollar received two years from now is 85.7 cents, the interest rate must be _____ percent. If the present value of $2 received three years from now is $1.78, the interest rate must be

   _____ percent. If the interest rate is more than

   _____ percent, one dollar received 20 years from now is worth less than 15 cents now.

5. Interest rates vary as a function of the loan's _____, its

   _____, and the cost of _____.

6. The equilibrium pure interest rate is given by the intersection of the

   _____ and _____ curves for loanable funds.

7. Holding an asset's annual returns constant, the asset's worth is higher, the (lower, higher) is _____ the rate of return available on other investments.

8. _____ is a process of computing an asset's worth.

9. The _____ for loanable funds is the relationship between the quantity of loanable funds supplied and the pure interest rate.

10. The price of an input that has a fixed supply is _____.

    A(n) _____ is a payment above the minimum necessary to attract this amount of the input.

11. Were the government to impose a tax on rents, there would be (some, no)

_____ effect on the supply of resources to the economy.

Because he felt rent was _____ and the supply of land (would,

would not) _____ be affected by such a tax, Henry George felt

that it was justifiable to _____ rent.

12. Critics of George's position argued that land can be improved; therefore, the

supply (is, is not) _____ completely price inelastic. They

further argued that if land rents are _____, many other
kinds of income are likewise.

13. In the accountant's definition, the money the owner of a firm has left after
paying wages, interest, and rent and providing proper allowance for the

depreciation of buildings and equipment is _____. The
economist's definition differs in that he or she would also deduct the

_____ costs of the labor, capital, and land contributed by the
owner.

True-False

_____ 1. If Pennsylvania has a usury law that puts a limit of 10 percent on
interest rates and a bond yielding $100 per year indefinitely sells for
$800 on Wall Street, the quantity of loanable funds supplied is likely to
be less than the quantity of loanable funds demanded in Pennsylvania.

_____ 2. If people become more willing to postpone consumption to future time
periods and very profitable new investment opportunities are opened up,
the interest rate must rise.

_____ 3. If the Federal Reserve pursues a policy of easy money and, at the same
time, profitable new investment opportunities open up, the equilibrium
quantity of loanable funds increases.

_____ 4. The pure rate of interest is the rate on a riskless loan.

_____ 5. A firm that maximizes profit accepts investments where the interest rate
exceeds the rate of return.

_____ 6. Interest rates serve to allocate the supply of loanable funds.

_____ 7. If a firm borrows money to buy equipment at an interest cost that is less
than the rate of return from the equipment, it loses money.

_____ 8. *Capital budgeting* refers to decisions concerning a firm's choice of
investment projects.

_____ 9. One reason for the existence of profits is "contrived scarcity" due to monopoly power.

_____ 10. Before taxes, corporation profits average about 50 percent of gross national income.

_____ 11. A very large demand for loanable funds stems from firms that want to borrow money to invest in capital goods like machine tools, buildings, and so forth.

_____ 12. An asset's rate of return is the rate earned on the investment in the asset.

_____ 13. The lower is the interest rate, the smaller the amount firms are willing to borrow.

_____ 14. The government is an important factor on the demand side of the market for loanable funds, because it is a big borrower, particularly during wartime and recent years.

Multiple Choice

1. Ms. X can either pay $50 now (for the coming year) and $50 a year from now (for the next year) for a service that protects against termites. Alternatively, she can pay $100 now (for the coming two years) for this service. Ms. X should be indifferent between these two alternatives if the rate of interest is

   a. zero.
   b. 2 percent.
   c. 5 percent.
   d. 10 percent.
   e. none of the above.

2. In question 1, if the rate of interest is 10 percent, the cost of the second alternative exceeds that of the first alternative by

   a. zero.
   b. $5.
   c. −$5.
   d. $4.55.
   e. none of the above.

3. In question 1, if the rate of interest is 8 percent, Ms. X should be indifferent between the first alternative and paying _____ now (for the coming two years) for this service.

   a. $96
   b. $96.30
   c. $100
   d. $104
   e. none of the above.

4. All other things equal, higher than normal profit rates in an industry

   a. decrease the number of firms; profits continue to rise.
   b. increase the number of firms; profits continue to rise.
   c. increase the number of firms; profits fall.
   d. decrease the number of firms; profits fall.

5. Karl Marx viewed profit as

    a. "surplus value."
    b. exploitation of workers.
    c. a necessary but disagreeable part of the incentive system.
    d. b and c but not a.
    e. a and b but not c.

6. Suppose that the rate of return on alternative investments is 6 percent and a particular asset yields $1,500 per year indefinitely. The asset is worth

    a. $9,000.   d. $250,000.
    b. $25,000.   e. $100,000.
    c. $90,000.

7. If a firm maximizes profit, the rate of return of the least productive project accepted by the firm must be _____ the interest rate at which the firm can borrow.

    a. less than   d. twice
    b. half   e. less than or equal to
    c. greater than or equal to

8. Profits are

    a. a reward for efficiency.
    b. an incentive for innovation.
    c. an indicator of where resources are needed.
    d. all of the above.
    e. none of the above.

Discussion and Extension Questions

1. "Interest rates are set largely by New York financiers and Washington politicians, not by the market. To a considerable extent, they are set to maximize the profits of the big banks, who control much of the American economy." Discuss and evaluate.

2. "Money really does not produce anything. You can stick a dollar bill in the earth, and it will not grow. You cannot wear it or eat it. Why should it receive any return? Interest is merely a trick to obtain unearned income for the moneyed classes." Discuss and evaluate.

3. Suppose your paternalistic (and rich) uncle promises you a gift of $10,000 when you "grow up," which he defines as 10 years from right now. If the interest rate is currently 6 percent and it is expected to remain at that level, how much could he give you now instead of $10,000 in 10 years, so that the two gifts have equal value?

4. What is the relationship between the concept of rent and the concept of opportunity cost?

5. According to Richard Freeman's calculations, the present value of lifetime income (in the 1960s) was about $230,000 for a Ph.D. in electrical engineering but about $208,000 for a B.A. (or B.S.) in electrical engineering. Discuss the relevance of this finding for the decision of whether to do graduate work in electrical engineering.

6. Define what is meant by the rate of interest. What difference, if any, is there between interest and usury?

7. What is the relationship between the riskiness of a loan and the rate of interest?

8. What are the social functions of the interest rate?

9. If the government imposes a tax on economic rent, does this affect the supply of resources to the economy? Why or why not?

Problems

1. Suppose that the demand curve for loanable funds in the United States is as follows:

Interest rate (percent)	Quantity of loanable funds (billions of dollars)
4	60
6	50
8	40
10	30
12	20

a. Draw the demand curve in this graph:

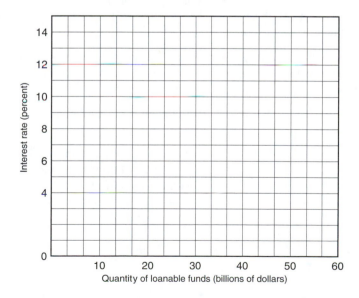

    b.   Suppose that the existing supply of loanable funds in the United States is $40 billion. What is the equilibrium interest rate, given the data presented in this problem?

    c.   If the interest rate is the one indicated in part b, what is the worth of an asset that yields $500 a year permanently?

    d.   If the interest rate is the one indicated in part b and you are considering putting your money into an investment with a rate of return of 7 percent, should you accept the investment? Why or why not?

2. Suppose that the supply curve for a particular type of mineral is as follows.

    a.   Is the price of this mineral a rent?

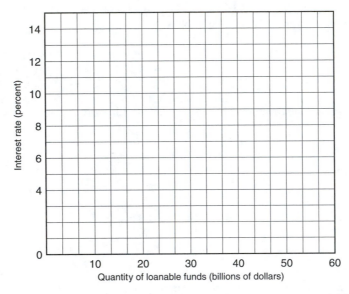

    b.   Suppose that a tax of $2 per ton is imposed on the producers of this mineral. What effect will this have on the quantity supplied? Does the answer depend on the demand curve for the mineral?

3. Suppose the Jones Construction Company can borrow money at 15 percent per year and it is willing to accept only those (riskless) investments that yield 20 percent per year or more. Is this firm maximizing profit?

4. Suppose that the Jones Construction Company has the following investment opportunities:

Rate of return (percent)	Amount of money the firm can invest at the given rate of return (millions of dollars)
35	5
30	10
25	8
20	9
17	4

a. If it has to pay 15 percent interest, which investment opportunities should it accept?

b. How much less should it invest in these projects if it has to pay 18 percent interest?

5. Ms. Smith buys a very long term bond that pays annual interest of $50 per year. It is a 5 percent bond that has a face value of $1,000. Ms. Smith bought it in 1955 when the prevailing interest rate was 5 percent, and she paid $1,000 for it. In 1985, the prevailing interest rate was about 10 percent. Approximately how much was the bond worth then?

6. a. Suppose you will receive $10,000 in three years. How much is it worth now? (Assume that the interest rate is 6 percent.)

b. How much is it worth to you to get the $10,000 one year earlier, that is, in two years, not three?

7. Mr. Q owns 100 acres of farm land which he rents at $100 per acre.

a. If the interest rate is 10 percent, how much is Mr. Q's land worth?

b. Because of a fall in the price of wheat, Mr. Q can rent his land for only $75 per acre. Now how much is Mr. Q's land worth?

c. Oil is found on Mr. Q's property, with the result that he can rent his land for $400 an acre. Now how much is Mr. Q's land worth?

8. Ms. R, if she does not undergo any further training, can expect to earn $30,000 per year for the indefinite future. If she takes this year off and goes to school rather than works, she can expect to earn $32,000 a year for the indefinite future. The school is free, but she is unable to work at all while going to school.

a. If Ms. R expects to live and work forever, what rate of return will she earn from this investment in her own education?

b. Suppose that Ms. R can obtain 10 percent on alternative investment opportunities. Is this investment worthwhile?

c. To make this investment worthwhile, how much must she be able to earn per year after the year in school?

9. Firm X must choose between investing in machine A or machine B. The machines do exactly the same work, but their purchase prices and maintenance costs differ. The purchase price of machine A is $10,000, while the purchase price of machine B is $5,000. The maintenance cost each year with machine A is $1,000, while the maintenance cost each year with machine B is $1,600. Both machines last so long that it is reasonable to assume (for simplicity) that they last forever.

a. If the interest rate is 5 percent, which machine should firm X buy? Why?

b. If the interest rate is 10 percent, which machine should firm X buy? Why?

c. If the interest rate is 15 percent, which machine should firm X buy? Why?

d. At what interest rate would firm X be indifferent between the two machines? Why?

Answers

Completion Questions

1. 5, 3¹/₃, 10   2. $1,250, falls, $1,000   3. 90.9 cents, 82.6 cents, 173.5 cents
4. 8, 4, 10   5. riskiness, term, bookkeeping and collection   6. demand, supply
7. lower   8. Capitalization   9. supply curve   10. rent, rent   11. no, unearned
income, would not, tax away   12. is not, "unearned"   13. profit, opportunity

True-False

1. True   2. False   3. True   4. True   5. False   6. True   7. False   8. True
9. True   10. False   11. True   12. True   13. False   14. True

Multiple Choice

1. a   2. d   3. b   4. c   5. e   6. b   7. c   8. d

Problems

1. a.

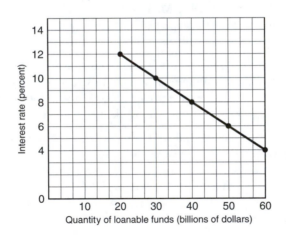

    b. 8 percent.
    c. $6,250.
    d. No, because you can get 8 percent if you lend your money elsewhere.
2. a. Yes.
    b. None. No.
3. No.
4. a. All shown in the table.
    b. $4 million less.
5. About $500.
6. a. Using Table 23.1 in the text, we see that it is worth 0.839 × $10,000, or
        $8,390.
    b. Using Table 23.1, we see that it is worth 0.89 × $10,000, or $8,900, to get
        it in two years. Therefore, it is worth $510 more than if you get the
        money in three years.

7. a. $100,000.
   b. $75,000.
   c. $400,000.
8. a. 2,000/30,000 = 6.7 percent.
   b. No.
   c. $33,000.
9. a. If firm X buys machine A rather than machine B, it is investing an additional $5,000 now to reduce annual maintenance costs by $600. Thus, the rate of return on the extra $5,000 investment is $600/$5,000, or 12 percent. Since the interest rate is 5 percent, firm X should make this extra investment; it should buy machine A.
   b. Machine A. See part a.
   c. Machine B. See part a.
   d. 12 percent. See part a.

CHAPTER 24

Poverty, Income Inequality, and Discrimination

Chapter Profile

Many factors are responsible for existing income differentials. Some people are abler, better educated, or luckier than others. Some people inherit more property or have more monopoly power than others.

Critics of income inequality argue that it lessens total consumer satisfaction because an extra dollar given to the poor provides them with more extra satisfaction than the loss of a dollar taken away from the rich. Also, they argue that at least some income inequality leads to social and political inequality.

Defenders of income inequality point out that it is scientifically impossible to make interpersonal comparisons of utility and argue that income inequality is needed to provide incentives for people to work and create and it permits greater capital formation.

There is no well-defined income level that can be used in all times and all places to determine poverty. Perhaps the most widely accepted definition of poverty in the United States today is the one developed by the Social Security Administration, according to which approximately 12 percent of the U.S. population in 2001, about 33 million people, fall below the poverty line. Over the long run, the incidence of poverty has declined in the United States.

Nonwhite families, families headed by a woman, and very large families are more likely than others to be poor. To a considerable extent, the reasons for their poverty lie beyond the control of the poor people. About one-third of poor adults suffered a disability of some sort or the premature death of the family breadwinner or family dissolution. Most heads of poor families do not have jobs.

Because private charity is judged to be inadequate, the nation authorized its government to carry out various public programs to aid the poor. Some programs to provide them with goods and services, food-stamp programs, for instance. Other programs, like aid to families with dependent children, give them cash. When these programs are taken into account, the percentage of the population falling below the poverty line is reduced considerably.

There is widespread dissatisfaction with existing antipoverty (or welfare) programs. They are judged to be inefficient, their costs increased at an alarming rate, and they provide little incentive for people to get off welfare. One suggestion to remedy these problems is a negative income tax. In most of the forms put forth, it involves a transfer of income that may be beyond the realm of political feasibility. Because of these concerns, Congress passed welfare reform, which limits the time someone can receive welfare, encourages the creation of jobs and job training programs, and offers financial incentives to work. Welfare rolls since dropped sharply, but some question whether the working poor can adequately support their families.

Despite recent improvements, the sad fact is that racial discrimination occurs in many walks of life in many areas of the United States. Nonwhites often are cut off from educational and job opportunities; and even when nonwhites do essentially the same kind of work as whites, there is sometimes a tendency to pay them less. The effects of discrimination are to reduce the wages of nonwhites relative to whites and to lower the nation's total output.

There is also much discrimination against women, making them less likely than men to enter the better-paying occupations. Even after adjusting for factors such as education and work experience, women earn about 20 percent less than men.

Concepts for Review

income inequality
progressive tax
regressive tax
poverty
Social Security Act
old-age insurance
Medicare
unemployment insurance
Medicaid
food programs

welfare
Temporary Assistance for Needy
   Families
negative income tax
breakeven income
discrimination
comparable worth
Equal Pay Act of 1963
Civil Rights Act of 1964

Completion Questions

1. The top 20 percent of households make about _____ of national income.

2. Suppose that families earning $4,000 or less per year pay no taxes and receive a welfare payment equal to the difference between their earned income and $4,000. If such a family earns $3,000, its total income is

   _____. If such a family earns $4,000, its total income is

   _____. There is (considerable, little, no) _____ incentive to earn more income up to $4,000.

3. The proposal calling for poor families to receive a payment, while families with incomes above a certain minimum would pay a graduated tax, is called

   a(n) _____.

4. The federal income tax is (progressive, regressive) _____,

   whereas the sales tax is (progressive, regressive) _____.

5. The _____ Act, passed in 1935, established a government-

   sponsored _____ system providing compulsory old-age
   insurance for both workers and self-employed people, as well as

   _____ insurance. By 1998, about _____
   million Americans were receiving old-age and survivors' insurance benefits.

6. Under discrimination, the demand curve for white labor is (different from, the

   same as) _____ that for African American labor, and the supply

   curve of white labor is (different from, the same as) _____
   that of African American labor.

7. Assume that a negative income tax exists, whereby the government pays
   each family (of four people) an amount equal to $3,000 – I/3$, where I is the

   family's earned income. Families earning less than _____ per
   year receive some payment from the government. The maximum amount

   any family can receive from the government is _____

   per year. If the poverty line is $5,000, a family must earn _____ to
   reach this line.

8. The amount that a family pays for a given tax follows, at each of a
   number of income levels of the family. This tax is progressive when a

   family's income is between _____ and _____,

   and regressive when a family's income exceeds _____.

Income (dollars)	Tax (dollars)
1,000	10
5,000	100
10,000	300
20,000	600
30,000	900
50,000	1,200
100,000	2,000

True-False

_____ 1. The demand curve for unskilled labor is $P = 5 – 2Q$, and the supply
curve for unskilled labor is $P = 3Q$, where P is the wage rate (in dollars
per hour) and Q is the quantity of labor (in millions of hours). If a
minimum wage of $5 an hour is established, all unskilled labor are
unemployed.

_____ 2. Under a negative income tax, a family that earns more income would
not necessarily receive more money (both in earned income and
payments from the government) than if it did not earn more income.

_____ 3. In question 1, if a minimum wage of $4.50 an hour is established, the quantity of unskilled labor supplied exceeds the quantity demanded by 1.50 million hours.

_____ 4. One effect of discrimination against African Americans is to lower the nation's total output.

_____ 5. There has been little reduction in the past 20 years in the amount of racial discrimination in businesses.

_____ 6. There has been little reduction in income inequality in the United States in the past 25 years.

_____ 7. Every industrialized country has greater income inequality than every developing country.

_____ 8. In the United States, inequality of after-tax income is more than inequality of before-tax income.

_____ 9. To finance old-age insurance, payroll taxes must be paid by each worker and her or his employer.

_____ 10. If the government gives all families of four persons $4,000 per year and imposes a tax of 25 percent on earned income, a family's disposable income would be greater than its earned income if its earned income were less than $16,000 per year.

_____ 11. Under welfare reform there is a lifetime cap of two years for receiving welfare.

_____ 12. Comparable worth looks at whether women and men are receiving the same pay for doing the same job.

_____ 13. In the several years after welfare reform was passed in 1996, the number of people on welfare dropped by over 40 percent.

Multiple Choice

1. If a negative income tax is established whereby the government pays each family (of four people) an amount equal to $3,000 - 0.6I$, where I is earned income (in dollars), and families who receive no such payment must pay taxes, the break-even income is

   a. $9,000.
   b. $6,000.
   c. $5,000.
   d. $3,000.
   e. none of the above.

2. If the negative income tax in the previous question were adopted, a family below the breakeven income that increased its earned income by $1 would net

   a. nothing.
   b. $0.40.
   c. $0.60.
   d. $1.
   e. none of the above.

3. The Social Security system is

    a.   an ordinary insurance system.
    b.   mandatory, not voluntary.
    c.   financed by a regressive tax on earnings.
    d.   all of the above.
    e.   b and c.

4. In 2001, it was estimated by the Social Security Administration that to be just above the poverty line, an urban family of four needed an annual income of

    a.   less than $4,500.   d.   between $4,500 and $6,000.
    b.   between $6,000 and $9,000.   e.   about $18,000.
    c.   between $9,000 and $15,000.

5. Which of the following kinds of families is most likely to be poor?

    a.   A white family with six members.
    b.   A nonwhite family with two members.
    c.   A nonwhite family with six members.
    d.   A white family with two members.
    e.   All of the above are equally likely to be poor.

6. Which of the following is not a progressive tax?

    a.   Inheritance tax   d.   Payroll tax
    b.   Federal income tax   e.   All of the above
    c.   Estate tax

7. Suppose that each year each family must pay either $500 or 5 percent of its income (whichever is greater) to support local schools. This tax is

    a.   regressive for families with incomes under $10,000.
    b.   proportional to income for families with incomes over $10,000.
    c.   both a and b.
    d.   more progressive than the federal income tax.
    e.   none of the above.

8. Suppose that each family in nation A receives $1,000 in benefits from federal highways and pays $500 plus 10 percent of its income in taxes to pay for the maintenance of these highways.

    a.   This government program provides more benefits to families with incomes under $4,000 than they pay for.
    b.   Families with incomes over $6,000 pay more for this program than the benefits are worth to them.
    c.   Families with incomes under $555 have negative disposable incomes.
    d.   All of the above.
    e.   Both a and b.

Discussion and Extension Questions

1. How well do you think welfare reform is working? Defend your position. What kind of changes would you make to the system and why?

2. Suppose that over the next generation or so, we have more older people who live longer and fewer younger people. How will this alter the Social Security program, from both the cost and benefit sides?

3. Should the prize money at professional tennis tournaments be distributed equally between men and women players? Why might the men be paid more? When should the women be paid more?

4. Generation-skipping trusts are one device the wealthy have used to avoid estate taxes. As put by one expert, "You provide income to your child for life, then to your grandchildren who are living today, with principal to their children at age 21." What are the gains and costs to society of allowing the use of such trusts? Are you for or against permitting their use?

5. "Since one cannot make interpersonal comparisons of utility (or satisfaction) there is no way to tell whether progressive taxes are really to be preferred over regressive ones." Comment and evaluate.

6. Is a sales tax progressive or regressive? Why? Is the personal income tax progressive or regressive? Why?

7. Suppose that the amount paid for a particular tax is related to the income of the taxpayer in the following way:

Income (dollars)	Tax (dollars)
1,000	50
10,000	600
100,000	7,000

Is this tax progressive or regressive?

8. What are some of the salient characteristics of poor families in the United States? What is meant by a negative income tax? Do you favor or oppose such a scheme?

Problems

1. Suppose that the breakeven income under a negative income tax is $8,000. This is the income at which a family of four neither pays nor receives taxes. Suppose that such a family receives 50 percent of the difference between its income and the breakeven income, if its income is below the breakeven income, and it pays 25 percent of the difference between its income and the breakeven income if its income exceeds the breakeven income.

a. In the table, indicate how much a family at each income level would receive or pay in taxes. All amounts are in dollars.

Family income	Payment received	Taxes paid
4,000	_____	_____
6,000	_____	_____
8,000	_____	_____
10,000	_____	_____
12,000	_____	_____
14,000	_____	_____
16,000	_____	_____
20,000	_____	_____
40,000	_____	_____

b. What incentive is there for an unemployed person heading a family with an income of $4,000 to get a job?

2. Suppose that the demand and supply curves for unskilled labor in a perfectly competitive labor market in the land of Canam are as shown in the graph.

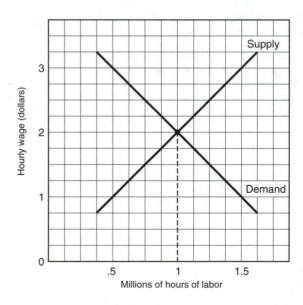

a. If a minimum wage of $2.50 per hour is established, what is the effect on the total employment of unskilled labor?
b. What is the effect on the total income received by unskilled labor?
c. Does the minimum wage solve the poverty problem in Canam?

3. a.   Suppose that the amount of tax paid by a person with income equal to X is given by the formula

$$T = 0.3X,$$

where T is the amount of the tax. Is this tax progressive or regressive? Why?

   b.   Suppose that the formula is

$$T = 0.2X + 0.1X^2.$$

Is the tax now progressive or regressive? Why?

4. Nation X's tax system exempts the first $5,000 of a person's income and taxes away 50 percent of the rest.

   a.   Suppose that Mr. Poor's before-tax income is $10,000 and Ms. Smith's before-tax income is $50,000. Ms. Smith's before-tax income is five times Mr. Poor's. What is the ratio of Ms. Smith's after-tax income to Mr. Poor's?
   b.   Is it true that, if any person has five times as much before-tax income as another person, the former person's after-tax income is less than five times as much as the latter person's? Why or why not?
   c.   Does nation X's tax system tend to reduce the inequality of income? Is the tax system progressive or regressive? Why?

5. Nation Y is considering three alternative tax systems. The first would exempt the first $5,000 of a person's income and tax away 50 percent of the rest. The second would exempt the first $8,000 of a person's income and tax away 70 percent of the rest. The third would exempt the first $10,000 of a person's income and tax away the rest. Nation Y's government assumes that the nation's total output is the same regardless of which tax system is adopted. Do you agree? Why or why not?

6. Nation Z changes its tax system. After the change, the first $5,000 of a person's income is exempted and 50 percent of the rest is taxed away. Before the change, the first $2,500 of a person's income was exempted and one-third of the rest was taxed away. John Jameson worked 2,000 hours at a wage rate of $5 per hour before the change.

   a.   If he continues to work as much as before the tax change, does his after-tax income change?
   b.   Assuming that he could vary the number of hours he worked, is an extra hour of leisure worth more or less than $3.33 to him before the change in the tax system? Why or why not?
   c.   Is an extra hour of leisure worth more than $2.50 to him after the change in the tax system? Why or why not?

7. This table shows how much, according to the Family Assistance Plan proposed by President Nixon in 1969, a family would receive in welfare payments, given that its earned income was a particular amount. All amounts are in dollars.

Earned income	Welfare payment
500	1,600
1,000	1,460
2,000	960
3,000	460

a. Assuming no taxes have to be paid on earned income under $3,000, what percentage of an extra dollar of earned income would a person keep if his or her income were $600?

b. What percentage of an extra dollar of earned income would a person keep if his or her income were $1,500?

c. What percentage of an extra dollar of earned income would a person keep if his or her income were $2,500?

d. In evaluating the Family Assistance Plan, why would the answers to previous parts of this question be relevant?

Answers

Completion Questions

1. one-half   2. $4,000, $4,000, no   3. negative income tax   4. progressive, regressive   5. Social Security, social insurance, unemployment, 47   6. different from, different from   7. $9,000, $3,000, $3,000   8. $1,000, $10,000, $30,000

True-False

1. True   2. False   3. False   4. True   5. False   6. True   7. False
8. False   9. True   10. True   11. False   12. False   13. True

Multiple Choice

1. c   2. b   3. e   4. e   5. c   6. d   7. c   8. d

Problems

1. a.

Payment received	Taxes paid
2,000	—
1,000	—
0	—
—	500
—	1,000
—	1,500
—	2,000
—	3,000
—	8,000

   b. He or she keeps 50 cents of every extra dollar earned, since the payments he or she receives decline by 50 cents for every extra dollar earned.

2. a. Employment declines from 1 million to 0.75 million hours of labor.
   b. Income declines from $2 million to $1.875 million.
   c. No.

3. a. It is neither regressive nor progressive, since the amount of the tax is proportional to income.
   b. Progressive, because $T/X = 0.2 + 0.1X$, which means that T/X increases as X increases.

4. a. 3.67 to 1.
   b. No. If one person has a before-tax income of $5,000 and another has a before-tax income of $1,000, the former person's after-tax income is not less than five times as much as the latter person's.
   c. Yes. Progressive because the proportion of income going for taxes rises with income.

5. No. In the third tax system, there would be no incentive to earn more than $10,000. In the second tax system, the incentive to earn more than $8,000 would not be very strong.

6. a. No.
   b. More, because if this were not the case, he would work an extra hour before the change in the tax system. After taxes, he would receive $3.33 for each extra hour he worked.
   c. More, because if this were not the case, he would work an extra hour after the change in the tax system. After taxes, he would receive $2.50 for each extra hour he worked.

7. a. 72 percent.
   b. 50 percent.
   c. 50 percent.
   d. Because it is generally believed that a welfare program should contain incentives for welfare recipients to increase their income and get off welfare.

CASE 4

The Well-Paid Receptionist

ROLAND B. COUSINS[1]

Harvey Finley did a quick double take when he caught a glimpse of the figure representing Ms. Brannen's salary on the year-end printout. A hurried call to payroll confirmed it. Yes, his receptionist had been paid $127,614.21 for her services last year. As he sat in stunned silence, he had the sudden realization that, since his firm was doing so well this year, she would earn at least 10 to 15 percent more money during the current fiscal year. This was a shock, indeed.

With a second call to payroll, Harvey found out that Ms. Brannen's salary had been approximately $112,000 the year before last and $100,000 the year before that. She had been well paid for some time, he concluded.

Background

Harvey began his career as a service technician for a major manufacturer of copy machines. He received rather extensive technical training, but his duties were limited to performing routine, on-site maintenance and service for customers. After a year's experience as a service technician, he asked for and received a promotion to sales representative. In this capacity, he established many favorable contacts in the business community of Troupville and the surrounding towns. He began to think seriously about capitalizing on his success by opening his own business.

Then, seven years ago, he decided to take the plunge and start his own firm. He was tired of selling for someone else. When he mentioned his plan to his friends, they all expressed serious doubts; Troupville, a city of approximately 35,000 people located in the deep South, had just begun to recover from a severe recession. The painful memories of the layoffs, bankruptcies, and plummeting real estate values were too recent and vivid to be forgotten.

Undeterred by the skeptics, Harvey was optimistic that Troupville's slow recovery would soon become a boom. Even though his firm would certainly have to be started on a shoestring, Harvey thought his sales experience and technical competence would enable him to survive what was sure to be a difficult beginning. He was nervous but excited when he signed the lease on the first little building. A lifelong dream was either about to be realized or dashed forever. Troupville Business Systems was born.

While he had managed to borrow, rent, lease, or subcontract for almost everything that was absolutely necessary, he did need one employee immediately. Of course, he

[1]Roland B. Cousins is professor of business administration and economics at La Grange College. This case appeared in the spring 1992 issue of the *Case Research Journal*. Management cooperated in the field research for this case, which was written solely for the purpose of stimulating student discussion. All individuals and incidents are real, but names and data have been disguised at the request of the organization.

hoped the business would expand rapidly and he would soon have a complete and competent staff. But until he could be sure that some revenue would be generated, he thought he could get by with one person who would be a combination receptionist/secretary and general assistant.

The typical salary for such a position in the area was about $14,000 per year; for Harvey, this was a major expense. Nevertheless, he placed what he thought was a well-worded ad in the "Help Wanted" section of the local newspaper. There were five applicants, four of whom just did not seem quite right for the position he envisioned. The fifth applicant, Ms. Cathy Brannen, was absolutely captivating.

Ms. Brannen was a 27-year-old divorcée with one small child. Her resume showed that she had graduated from a two-year office administration program at a state university. She had worked for only two employers following graduation, one for five years and the most recent for two years. Since returning to her hometown of Troupville two months ago, following her divorce, she had not been able to find suitable employment.

From the moment she sat down for the interview, Harvey and Ms. Brannen seemed to be on exactly the same wavelength. She was very articulate, obviously quite bright, and most important, very enthusiastic about assisting with the startup of the new venture. She seemed to be exactly the sort of person Harvey had envisioned when he first began to think seriously about taking the big plunge. He resisted the temptation to offer her the job on the spot, but ended the hour-long interview by telling her that he would check her references and contact her again very soon.

Telephone calls to her two former employers convinced Harvey that he had actually underestimated Ms. Brannen's suitability for the position. Each one said without equivocation that she was the best employee he had ever had in any position. Both former employers concluded the conversation by saying they would rehire her in a minute if she were still available. The only bit of disturbing information gleaned from these two calls was the fact that her annual salary had risen to $15,900 in her last job. Although Harvey thought that the cost of living was probably a bit higher in Houston, where she had last worked, he wasn't sure she would react favorably to the $14,000 offer he was planning to make. However, he was determined that, somehow, Cathy Brannen would be his first employee.

Ms. Brannen seemed quite pleased when Harvey telephoned her at home that same evening. She said she would be delighted to meet him at the office the next morning to discuss the position more fully.

Cathy Brannen was obviously very enthusiastic about the job as outlined in the meeting. She asked all of the right questions, responded quickly and articulately to every query posed to her, and seemed ready to accept the position even before the offer was extended. When Harvey finally got around to mentioning the salary, there was a slight change in Cathy's eager expression. She stiffened. Since Harvey realized that salary might be a problem, he decided to offer Cathy an incentive of sorts in addition to the $14,000 annual salary. He told her that he realized his salary offer was lower than the amount she had earned on her last job. And, he told her, he understood that a definite disadvantage of working for a new firm was the complete absence of financial security. Although he was extremely reluctant to guarantee a larger salary because of his own uncertainty regarding the future, he offered her a sales override in the amount of 2 percent of sales. He explained that she would largely determine the success or failure of the firm. She needed to represent the firm in the finest possible manner to potential customers who telephoned and to those who walked in the front door. For this reason, the sales override seemed to be an appropriate addition to her straight salary. It would provide her with incentive to take an active interest in the firm.

Cathy accepted the offer immediately. Even though she was expecting a salary offer of $16,000, she hoped the sales override might make up the difference. "Who knows," she thought, "two percent of sales may amount to big money someday." It did not, however, seem very likely at the time.

Troupville Business Systems began as a very small distributor of copy machines. The original business plan was just to sell copy machines and provide routine, on-site service. More extensive on-site service and repairs requiring that a machine be removed from a customer's premises were to be provided by a regional distributor located in a major city approximately 100 miles from Troupville.

Troupville Business Systems did well from the start. Several important changes were made in the services the firm offered during the first year. Harvey soon found that there was a greater demand for the leasing of copy machines, particularly the large expensive models which he originally planned to sell. He also soon discovered that his customers wanted to be able to contract directly with his firm for all of their service needs. Merely guaranteeing that he could get the machines serviced was not sufficient in the eyes of potential customers. In attempting to accommodate the market, he developed a complete service facility and began to offer leasing options on all models. These changes in the business all occurred during the first year. Growth during that year was steady but not spectacular. While sales continued to grow steadily the second year, it was early in the third year that Harvey made what turned out to be his best decision. He entered the computer business.

Harvey had purchased a personal computer soon after Troupville Business Systems was founded. The machine and its capabilities fascinated him, although he knew virtually nothing about computers. He was soon a member of a local users club, was subscribing to all the magazines, and was taking evening computer courses at the local university—in short, he became a computer buff. Harvey recognized the business potential of the rapidly growing personal computer market, but he did not believe that his original business was sufficiently stable to introduce a new product line just yet.

During his third year of operations, he decided the time was right to enter the computer business. He added to his product line a number of personal computers popular with small businesses in the area. This key decision caused a virtual explosion in the growth of his firm. Several key positions were added, including that of comptroller. By the fourth year of operations, computers produced by several other manufacturers had been added to Harvey's product line, and he had developed the capability of providing complete service for all products carried. His computer enterprise was not limited to business customers, because he quickly developed a significant walk-in retail trade. Rapid growth continued unabated.

During the first seven years of the company's existence, Cathy Brannen had proven truly indispensable. Her performance exceeded Harvey's highest expectations. Although her official position remained that of secretary/receptionist, she took it upon herself to learn about each new product or service. During the early years, Harvey often thought that she did a better job than he did whenever a potential customer called in his absence. Even after he acquired a qualified sales staff, Harvey had no concerns when Cathy had to field questions from a potential customer because a regular salesperson was not available. The customer never realized that the professional young lady capably handling all inquiries was "only" the receptionist.

Cathy began performing fewer sales functions because of the increased number of professional salespersons, but her secretarial duties expanded tremendously. She was still Harvey's secretary, and she continued to answer virtually every telephone call coming into the business. Since her office was in an open area, she still was the first to greet many visitors.

Cathy took a word processing course at a local business school shortly after joining the firm. As she began working with Harvey's first personal computer, she, too, developed into a computer aficionado and became the best computer operator in the firm.

The Current Situation

Harvey was shaken by the realization that Cathy Brannen had been paid over $127,000 last year. As he wondered what, if anything, should be done about her earnings, he began to reflect on the previous seven years.

Success had come almost overnight. It seemed as thought Troupville Business Systems could do no wrong. The workforce had grown at a rate of approximately 15 percent per year since the third year of operations. Seventeen people were now employed by the firm. While Harvey did acknowledge that some of this success was due to being in the right place at the right time, he also had reason to be proud of the choices he made. Time had proven that all of his major decisions had been correct. He also could not overestimate Cathy's contribution to the success of the firm. Yes, certainly, one of the most important days in the life of the firm was the day when Cathy responded to his ad in the newspaper.

Success had brought with it ever-increasing demands on his time. He had never worked so hard, but the rewards were certainly forthcoming. First there was the new Jaguar, then the new home on Country Club Drive, the vacation home on the coast, the European trips—Yes, success was wonderful.

During these years Cathy, too, had prospered. Harvey had not thought much about it, but he did remember making a joking comment the first day she drove her new Mercedes to work. He also remembered commenting on her mink coat at the company banquet last December. Cathy had been dazzling.

Now that Harvey realized what he was paying Cathy, he was greatly disturbed. She was making over twice as much money as anyone else in the firm with the exception of himself. The best salesman had earned an amount in the low sixties last year. His top managers were paid salaries ranging from the high forties to the mid-fifties. The average salary in the area for executive secretaries was now probably between $22,000 and $25,000 per year. A good receptionist could be hired for under $20,000, and yet Cathy had been paid $127,614.21 last year. The sales override had certainly enabled Cathy to share in the firm's success. Yes, indeed.

As Harvey thought more and more about the situation, he kept returning to the same conclusion. He felt something had to be done about her compensation. It was just too far out of line with other salaries in the firm. Although Harvey was drawing over $200,000 per year in salary and had built an equity in the business of more than

$1 million, these facts did not seem relevant as he pondered what to do. It seemed likely that a number of other employees did know about Cathy's compensation level. Harvey wondered why no one ever mentioned it. Even the comptroller never mentioned Cathy's compensation. This did seem quite odd to Harvey, as the comptroller, Frank Bain, knew that Harvey did not even attempt to keep up with the financial details. He relied on Frank to bring important matters to his attention.

With no idea of how to approach this problem, Harvey decided to begin by making a list of alternatives. He got out a piece of paper and, as he stared at the blank lines, overheard Cathy's cheerful exchange with a customer in the next room.

Discussion Questions

1. Was Cathy Brannen a typical receptionist or secretary? Why or why not?

2. Were her services an input to Troupville Business Systems? If so, what was the marginal product of her services?

3. Was she being paid the value of the marginal product of her services? Can you tell? Why or why not?

4. If she could make no more than $40,000 in another job, was her pay equal to the opportunity cost of her services? Why or why not?

5. Is it always sensible for a firm to give an employee a bonus of a certain percentage of sales? Why or why not?

CHAPTER 25

Economic Growth

Chapter Profile

Economic growth is measured by the increase of per capita real gross domestic product, an index that does not measure accurately the growth of economic welfare but is often used as a first approximation.

One factor that may influence a country's rate of economic growth is the rate at which its population grows. In Malthus's view, population growth, unless checked in some way, ultimately meant economic decline, since output could not grow in proportion to the growth in population. The law of diminishing marginal returns ensured that, beyond some point, increases in labor, holding the quantity of land constant, result in smaller and smaller increments of output. However, Malthus underestimated the extent and importance of technological change, which offset the law of diminishing marginal returns.

Another factor that determines whether per-capita output grows rapidly or slowly is the rate of expenditure on new plant and equipment. Without technological change, more and more of this sort of investment results in decreases in the profitability of investment in plant and equipment, as Ricardo pointed out. But because of technological change, this has not occurred. According to the available evidence, a country's rate of economic growth seems directly related to its rate of investment in plant and equipment.

To a considerable extent, economic growth here and abroad has resulted from technological change. A change in technology, when applied for the first time, is called an *innovation,* and the firm that first applies it is called an *innovator.* Innovation is a key stage in the process leading to the full evaluation and utilization of a new process or product. Unless knowledge is used, it has little effect on the rate of economic growth.

Another factor with an important effect on a country's rate of economic growth is the rate at which it invests in human capital. The United States invests in human capital on a massive scale, even more than in physical capital in the twentieth century. These enormous and rapidly growing investments have unquestionably increased the productivity, versatility, and adaptability of our labor force.

Still another set of basic factors influencing the rate of economic growth is the conomic, social, and political climate of the country. Some societies despise material welfare, are subject to violent political upheavals, and are governed by corrupt groups. Such societies are unlikely to have a high rate of economic growth.

Finally, the rate of economic growth is also affected by the extent and behavior of the gap between actual and potential GDP. However, once a country gets to full employment, it cannot grow further by reducing this gap.

Concepts for Review

economic growth	human capital	innovator
population growth	technological change	diffusion process
capital formation	innovation	entrepreneurs
capital-output ratio	David Ricardo	Club of Rome
Thomas Malthus		

Completion Questions

1. Ricardo and Malthus thought that the marginal product of labor would (increase, decrease) _____ as the labor force increased.

2. _____ occurs when an economy adds to its plant, equipment, structures, and inventories.

3. A(n) _____ is a change in technology when applied for the first time.

4. The _____ process, in which the use of an innovation spreads, begins once a change in technology has been applied for the first time.

5. The technological lead of the United States over other countries was due partly to superior _____.

6. The additional output resulting from the addition of an extra person-year of labor is called the _____.

7. A country's output under full employment is its _____.

8. The two most common measures of the rate of _____ growth are the rate of growth of a country's _____, which tells us how rapidly the economy's total real output of goods and services is increasing, and the rate of growth of _____ _____, which is a better measure of the rate of increase of a country's standard of living.

9. To achieve a more rapid rate of growth, consumers frequently must be willing to give up some _____ now so that they can have (more, less) _____ goods and services in the future. A country's potential output increases when its production possibilities curve shifts (inward, outward) _____.

10. Although the U.S. economy spent a great deal of money on new plant and equipment, the productivity of new investment opportunities (has, has not) _____ been exhausted or even reduced. The _____ on investment in new plant and equipment has not fallen.

11. If the capital-output ratio is 2, full-employment GDP will increase by $50 billion as a consequence of _____ billion of investment.

12. *Human capital* refers to investment in _____,
_____, and _____.

True-False

_____   1. In the United States, the total investment in the education of the population has grown much more rapidly in this century than total investment in plant and equipment.

_____   2. The rate of investment in plant and equipment is directly related to a country's rate of economic growth.

_____   3. National governments under peacetime conditions have few opportunities to push actual output close to potential output.

_____   4. The bulk of the long-term increase in per capita output in the United States has been due to increases in the capital-labor ratio.

_____   5. A country's rate of economic growth is influenced by its social and religious climate, as well as by technological change and changes in its educational level.

_____   6. The greater the percent of GDP a society devotes to investment, the greater is the increase in its full-employment GDP.

_____   7. The law of diminishing marginal returns makes it difficult to increase output even when there is a proportional increase in all inputs.

_____   8. Malthus believed that the population tends to grow at a geometric rate.

_____   9. Technological change has shifted the marginal-product-of-labor curve to the right.

_____   10. There has been a tendency for growing populations to push hard against food supplies in some of the countries of Africa, Latin America, and Asia; and the Malthusian model can explain important elements of the situation.

_____   11. A country's rate of economic growth is not influenced by the rate at which it invests in human capital.

_____   12. How rapidly an innovation spreads depends heavily on its economic advantage over older methods or products. The more profitable is the use of the innovation, the more rapidly it spreads.

_____   13. Joseph Schumpeter, Harvard's distinguished economist and social theorist, stressed the important role played by the innovator in the process of economic growth.

_____ 14. Until the twentieth century, technology seldom was built on science. Even today, many technological advances rely on little in the way of science.

_____ 15. Productivity in the United States slowed down in the late 1990s as people wasted more time on the Internet.

Multiple Choice

1. Country X, which has an average propensity to consume that is the same for all levels of disposable income (and no government or net exports), wants to establish a constant rate of growth of GDP. To do so, investment expenditure must

   a. increase at a faster rate than GDP.
   b. increase at a slower rate than GDP.
   c. increase at the same rate as GDP.
   d. be the same each year.
   e. none of the above.

2. In 2000, suppose that $MP_K = 300 - 100K$, where MP_K is the marginal productivity of capital and K is the amount of capital (in billions of dollars). In 2005, suppose that $MP_K = 400 - 100K$. If the marginal product of capital is the same in 2005 as in 2000, the amount of capital increased between 2000 and 2005 by

   a. nothing.   d. $100 billion.
   b. $1 billion.   e. none of the above.
   c. $5 billion.

3. In country X the capital-output ratio is 3, whereas in country Y it is 2. If the proportion of GDP saved (and invested) is the same in the two countries, country X's rate of growth of GDP is

   a. 50 percent greater than country Y's.
   b. 1/2 of country Y's.
   c. 2/3 of country Y's.
   d. 1/3 greater than country Y's.
   e. none of the above.

4. In country A, the proportion of GDP saved (and invested) is 0.15, whereas in country B it is 0.10. If the capital-output ratio is the same in the two countries, country A's rate of growth of GDP is

   a. 50 percent greater than country B's.
   b. 5 percentage points greater than country B's.
   c. $33^{1}/_3$ percent greater than country B's.
   d. the same as country B's.
   e. none of the above.

5. When between 3 and 4 million hours of labor are used, the marginal product of labor is two bushels per hour. If the average product of labor is three bushels per hour when 3 million hours are used, what is the average product of labor when 4 million hours are used?

   a. Three bushels per hour
   b. Two bushels per hour
   c. Two and a quarter bushels per hour
   d. Two and a half bushels per hour
   e. Two and three-quarters bushels per hour

6. Which of the following is *not* an advance in technology?

   a. A new industrial process
   b. A new type of hybrid corn
   c. A new surgical procedure
   d. A new educational technique
   e. A new house of old design

7. The law of diminishing marginal returns

   a. applies to cases where there is a proportional increase in all resources.
   b. is an empirical generalization that holds in the real world.
   c. assumes that technology is variable.
   d. all of the above.
   e. none of the above.

8. A country's rate of economic growth depends on

   a. its rate of technological change.
   b. the extent of the changes in the amounts of various inputs used.
   c. the rate at which it invests in human capital.
   d. all of the above.
   e. none of the above.

9. Malthus's most important mistake was to

   a. underestimate population growth in industrialized countries.
   b. underestimate the extent and importance of technological change.
   c. be too optimistic concerning the relationship between the rate of population increase and the rate of economic growth.
   d. assume that population increase was unimportant.
   e. feel that capital formation would solve the problem of poverty.

Discussion and Extension Questions

1. Some studies seem to indicate that what matters most to people is their income relative to others around them rather than the absolute level of their income. Would this fact tend to reduce the importance of growth as a means of helping the poor?

2. "Growth is merely an illusion, since no generation can experience the difference between its own living standard and that of previous times. We may be better off than the ancient Greeks, but we cannot really appreciate that fact since we cannot

trade places with them. What really counts is how a person's lot compares with that of his or her contemporaries." Discuss and evaluate.

3. "Anyone who prefers more to less should be in favor of economic growth and should vote for government measures to encourage economic growth." Comment and evaluate.

4. What are the defects in the rate of economic growth as a measure of the rate of increase of economic welfare?

5. State the law of diminishing marginal returns. Is this law applicable if technology changes? Why or why not?

6. To what extent have Malthus's views concerning the effects of population increase on economic growth been confirmed by history? To what extent have Ricardo's views concerning the effects of capital formation on economic growth been confirmed by history? What factor did both Malthus and Ricardo underestimate?

7. What factors determine the rate of technological change and the rate at which changes in technology are applied and spread?

8. Can economic growth be stimulated by reducing unemployment? Explain.

Problems

1. Suppose that in a highly industrialized economy, the relationship between hours of labor and production of steel (both in millions) is as follows:

Hours	Tons of steel
1	2
2	4
3	7
4	9
5	10
6	9

a. At what point does the marginal product of labor decline? At what point does the average product of labor decline?

b. Suppose that an advance in technology allows this economy to obtain twice as many tons of steel (as shown in the table) for each number of hours of labor. Under these conditions, what is the marginal product of labor when between 4 and 5 million hours of labor are used? What is the average product of labor when 6 million hours are used?

c. If the economy produced 4 million tons of steel before the technological advance and 8 million tons after the technological advance, by what percentage did labor productivity (output per hour of labor) increase?

d. Plot the average product curve for labor, before the technological change in the following graph.

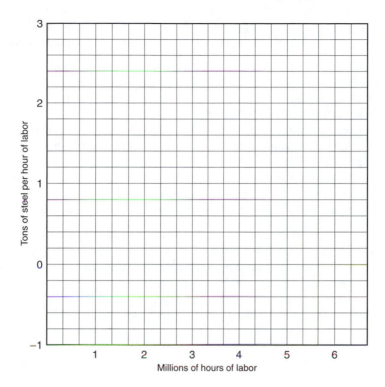

2. Suppose that the relationship between output per worker and the quantity of labor in Bangladesh is as follows.

a. Suppose the current labor force is such that the quantity of labor is $0Q$. If the subsistence level of output per worker is $0B$, what would the Malthusian theory predict about the change in population in Bangladesh?

    b.   Suppose that Bangladesh's labor force is $0R$ rather than $0Q$. What would the Malthusian theory predict about the change in population in Bangladesh?

3. a.   If the capital-output ratio is 3 in Bangladesh, what effect does $10 million in investment have on Bangladesh's full-employment GDP?

    b.   If Bangladesh saves 5 percent of GDP and if the capital-output ratio is 3, what is the rate of growth of full-employment GDP?

    c.   Under the circumstances described in part b, what is the effect on the rate of growth of full-employment GDP if Bangladesh saves 10 percent (rather than 5 percent) of GDP?

    d.   If Bangladesh's population increases by 4 percent per year, what is the rate of increase of per-capita full-employment GDP under the circumstances described in part b? Under the circumstances described in part c?

4. Assume that the capital-output ratio is 2 in a certain developing country and its full-employment GDP is $20 billion. For simplicity, assume that there is no government or foreign trade. The consumption function CC' is plotted in the graph below.

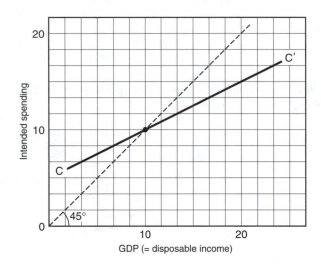

    a.   How much investment must there be this year if there is full employment?

    b.   If there is full employment this year, what is the full-employment value of GDP next year?

    c.   Next year, how much investment must there be to maintain full employment? (Hint: The marginal propensity to consume is $1/2$.)

5. The following table shows the output of an economy where various amounts of capital are employed. The amounts of all other resources used are held constant. Fill in the blanks.

Amount of capital (billions of dollars)	Total output	Average product of capital	Marginal product of capital
0	0	_____	
1	100	_____	_____
2	210	_____	_____
3	310	_____	_____
4	400	_____	_____
5	480	_____	_____
6	540	_____	_____

6. Some economists regard the optimal population as the population where output per worker is a maximum.

   a. Prove that the optimal population *cannot* be at a level where the marginal product of a worker increases as more workers are employed (and where this is true at all employment levels lower than this as well).

   b. Prove that the optimal population *cannot* be at a level where the marginal product of a worker is greater than the average product of a worker.

   c. Prove that the optimal population *cannot* be at a level where the marginal product of a worker is less than the average product of a worker.

7. In economy R, investment and consumption are the only components of aggregate demand. The average propensity to consume is 0.8 and the capital-output ratio is 2. Fill in the blanks. Assume that economy R remains at full employment during this period.

Year	GDP (billions of dollars)	Saving (millions of dollars)	Investment (millions of dollars)	Change in full-employment GDP (millions of dollars)
2004	1	_____	_____	_____
2005	_____	_____	_____	_____
2006	_____	_____	_____	_____
2007	_____	_____	_____	_____

Answers

Completion Questions

1. decrease   2. Capital formation   3. innovation   4. diffusion
5. management   6. marginal product of labor   7. potential output
8. economic, real gross domestic product, per capita real gross domestic product
9. consumption, more, outward   10. has not, rate of return
11. $100   12. education, training, public health

True-False

1. True   2. True   3. False   4. False   5. True   6. True   7. False   8. True
9. True   10. True   11. False   12. True   13. True   14. True   15. False

Multiple Choice

1. c   2. b   3. c   4. a   5. e   6. e   7. b   8. d   9. b

Problems

1. a. Beyond 3 million hours of labor, the marginal product falls. The average
        product of labor increases up to 3 million hours of labor, then falls.
    b. 2 tons of steel per hour of labor. 3 tons of steel per hour of labor.
    c. It doubled; that is, there was a 100 percent increase.
    d.

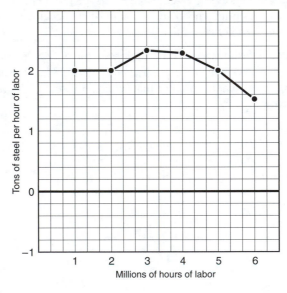

2. a. Population would increase until output per worker tended toward the sub-
        sistence level, 0B.
    b. Population would decrease until output per worker tended toward the
        subsistence level, 0B.

3. a. It will increase full-employment GDP by $3.33 million.
   b. 1.67 percent per year.
   c. The growth rate will be 3.33 percent per year.
   d. –2.33 percent per year. –0.67 percent per year.
4. a. $5 billion.
   b. $22.5 billion.
   c. If GDP is $22.5 billion, consumption expenditure will be $16.25 billion. Thus investment must be $6.25 billion.

5.

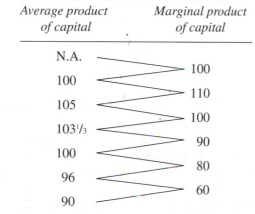

Average product of capital	Marginal product of capital
N.A.	100
100	110
105	100
103⅓	90
100	80
96	60
90	

6. a. If the marginal product of a worker increases as more workers are hired, output per worker must increase and thus is not at a maximum.
   b. So long as the marginal product of a worker exceeds the average product of a worker, the average product of a worker (output per worker) must increase and thus is not at a maximum.
   c. So long as the marginal product of a worker is less than the average product of a worker, the average product of a worker (output per worker) must decrease and thus this is not at a maximum.

7.

GDP (billions of dollars)	Saving (millions of dollars)	Investment (millions of dollars)	Change in full-employment GDP (millions of dollars)
1	200	200	100
1.1	220	220	110
1.21	242	242	121
1.331	266.2	266.2	133.1

CHAPTER 26

Public Goods and the
Role of the Government

Chapter Profile

To a considerable extent, the government's role in the economy has developed in response to the limitations of the price system. There is considerable agreement that the government should redistribute income in favor of the poor, provide public goods, and offset the effects of external economies and diseconomies (to some degree). Also, it is generally felt that the government should establish a proper legal, social, and competitive framework for the price system.

Beyond this, however, there are wide differences of opinion on the proper role of government in economic affairs. Conservatives tend to be suspicious of "big government," while liberals are inclined to believe that the government should do more.

Basically, the amount that the government spends on various activities and services must be decided through the country's political processes. Voting by ballots must be substituted for dollar voting.

Just as the price system suffers from limitations, so does the government. Special-interest groups sometimes gain at the expense of society as a whole. Government agencies sometimes have little incentive to increase efficiency. Citizens find it difficult to be selective in their choice of goods and services in the public sector. In recent years, economists seem to have put more emphasis on these (and other) limitations of the public sector.

It is generally agreed that people who receive more in benefits from a certain government service should pay more in taxes to support it. It is also generally agreed that people should be taxed so that the result is a socially desirable redistribution of income and equals should be treated equally. But these general principles, although useful, cannot throw light on many of the detailed questions a real-life tax code must answer.

The personal income tax is a very important source of federal revenue, the sales tax is an important source of state revenue, and the property tax is an important source of local revenue. These vary in their efficiency and impact on households of differing income levels. Sales taxes are regressive and property taxes are expensive to gather not to mention subject to inequitable application.

Concepts for Review

rules of the game	public good
income redistribution	personal income tax
external diseconomy	marginal tax rate

external economy   property tax
benefit principle   sales tax
ability-to-pay principle   tax incidence

Completion Questions

1. The government often tries by establishing _____ to control the activities of firms in markets where competition cannot be expected to prevail.

2. _____ are those that the government must provide, since there is no way that the market mechanism will provide them in the proper amounts.

3. Public goods are generally paid for by _____.

4. At the federal level, the biggest money raiser is the _____ tax.

5. Some _____ cannot be provided through the price system

   because there is no way to _____ a citizen from consuming

   the good. For example, there is no way to _____ a citizen from benefiting from national expenditures on defense, whether she

   or he _____ money toward defense or not. Consequently,

   the _____ cannot be used to provide such goods.

6. A(n) _____ is said to occur when consumption or production by one person or firm results in uncompensated benefits to

   another person or firm. A good example of a(n) _____ exists where fundamental research carried out by one firm is used by another firm.

7. Where external economies exist, it is generally agreed that the price system will

   produce too (little, much) _____ of the good in question and

   that the government should _____ the amount produced by private enterprise. This is the basic rationale for much of the

   government's huge _____ in basic science.

8. A(n) _____ is said to occur when consumption or production by one person or firm results in uncompensated costs to another

   person or firm. A good example of a(n) _____ occurs when a firm dumps pollutants into a stream and makes the water unfit for use by firms and people downstream.

True-False

_____   1. The research activities of industrial firms often result in external economies.

_____ 2. Tickets to a concert by the Chicago Symphony Orchestra are an example of a public good.

_____ 3. The government should impose taxes on goods that result in external economies to promote an optimal allocation of resources.

_____ 4. Public goods frequently are sold in the private market.

_____ 5. The government relies on the legitimate and systematic use of force.

_____ 6. Prices determined in noncompetitive markets provide incorrect signals regarding what consumers want and how scarce resources and commodities are.

_____ 7. The price system cannot be used to handle the production and distribution of public goods.

_____ 8. The government should tax higher-income households at a lower rate according to the ability-to-pay principle.

_____ 9. Government expenditures in the United States have grown much more rapidly than total output in this century.

_____ 10. At the federal level, the personal income tax brings in almost half of the tax revenue collected by the federal government. The next most important taxes at the federal level are the social security, payroll, and employment taxes and the corporation income tax.

Multiple Choice

1. A public good

   a. cannot be provided to one person without making it available to others as well.
   b. costs nothing (or essentially nothing) to produce and thus is provided by the government at a zero price.
   c. can never be provided by a nongovernmental organization.
   d. generally results in substantial external diseconomies.
   e. all of the above.

2. The functions of taxes are

   a. to reduce the amount of resources at the disposal of firms and individuals.
   b. to increase the amount of resources at the disposal of the government.
   c. to raise money needed to finance government expenditures.
   d. to redistribute income.
   e. all of the above.

3. An economic activity that would be unlikely to be financed or subsidized by the government is

   a. basic scientific research.
   b. the development of new weapons systems.

c. the development of new smog-control devices.

d. the development of improved varieties of corn.

e. none of the above.

4. Which of the following is *not* a public good?

a. National defense   d. Blood donated to the Red Cross

b. The services of the U.S. Army   e. The Apollo space program

c. A smog-free environment

5. If government activities could be made more efficient, this would permit

a. an increase in the output of public goods only.

b. an increase in the output of private (nonpublic) goods only.

c. an increase in either the output of private goods or the output of public goods or both.

d. no increase in output since the added efficiency would be offset by higher wages for government workers.

e. none of the above.

6. If a tax of 10 cents per gallon is imposed on gasoline, all the tax is paid by consumers if the

a. supply curve for gasoline is vertical.

b. supply curve slopes upward.

c. demand curve for gasoline is vertical.

d. demand curve slopes downward.

e. demand curve is horizontal.

7. The property tax

a. tends to discriminate against the poorer property owners.

b. is not very flexible.

c. typically is based on an assessed value, which is markedly different from actual value.

d. all of the above.

e. none of the above.

8. An example of a tax that relies very heavily on the benefit principle of taxation is the

a. personal income tax.   d. inheritance tax.

b. gasoline tax.   e. sales tax.

c. estate tax.

9. If a tax of $1 per gallon is imposed on gasoline in the United States,

a. the equilibrium price of gasoline increases by $1.

b. there is a shortage of gasoline if the price of gasoline is frozen at its pretax equilibrium level.

c. more gasoline is supplied.

d. all of the above.

e. none of the above.

10. The supply curve of good Y is a horizontal line. A tax of $1 per unit is imposed on good Y. The increase in the price of good Y due to the tax is

    a. greater if the demand curve is vertical than if it slopes downward.
    b. less if the demand curve is vertical than if it slopes downward.
    c. the same if the demand curve is vertical as if it slopes downward.
    d. zero.
    e. infinite.

11. In the circumstances described in the previous question, the reduction in the output of good Y due to the tax is

    a. greater if the demand curve is vertical than if it slopes downward.
    b. less if the demand curve is vertical than if it slopes downward.
    c. the same if the demand curve is vertical as if it slopes downward.
    d. zero.
    e. infinite.

Discussion and Extension Questions

1. Former President Gerald Ford has been quoted as saying that, "A government big enough to give you everything you want is a government big enough to take from you everything you have." Do you agree? Why or why not? How relevant do you think this statement is for the determination of public policy?

2. What are the principal limitations of the price system? It is generally agreed that government must establish the "rules of the game." What does this mean? It is also agreed that the government must see to it that markets remain reasonably competitive. Why?

3. Describe the rationale for the government's efforts to redistribute income. Do all government programs transfer income from rich to poor? Explain.

4. It is generally agreed that the government should discourage the production of goods and services that entail external diseconomies. What are external diseconomies? Give some examples.

5. Why are government expenditures so much bigger now than 50 years ago?

6. In 2001, Congress passed a bill to start a phaseout of the estate tax. Relate this idea to the tax principles discussed in this chapter. What is your position and why? In 2003, Congress started a similar reduction of the dividend tax with many urging its eventual elimination. Does your position change when two tax phaseouts are involved?

Problems

1. The paper industry has the demand and supply curves shown below.

Price of paper (dollars per ton)	Tons demanded	Tons supplied
2	80	40
3	70	50
4	60	60
5	50	70

   a. Suppose that this industry results in substantial external diseconomies. What can be said about its optimal output rate?

   b. In the following graph, draw the supply and demand curves for paper. Does the supply curve reflect the true social costs of producing the product? If not, does a supply curve reflecting the true social costs lie above or below the supply curve you have drawn?

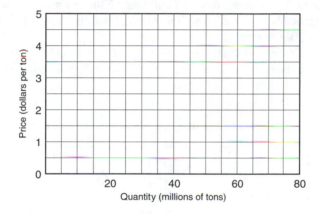

   c. What is the equilibrium price of paper? From the point of view of reflecting the true social costs, is this price correct, too low, or too high?

2. The town of Lucretia is faced with a serious smog problem. The smog can be dispelled if an air treatment plant is installed at an annual cost of $1 million. There is no way to clean up the air for some but not all the town's population. Each of the town's families acts independently, and no single family can afford to carry out the project by itself. Why doesn't a private firm build the air treatment plant and sell its services to the town's families (acting individually)?

3. Indicate the economic rationale for the government's carrying out the following functions:

   a. Regulating the sale and development of drugs
   b. Maintaining an army
   c. Granting aid to families with dependent children
   d. Supporting agricultural experiment stations
   e. Establishing the Antitrust Division of the Department of Justice

    f.   Imposing an income tax

    g.   Establishing unemployment insurance

4. In the United States, what processes are used to reallocate resources from the private sector (firms and individuals) to the government?

5. In addition to its smog problem, the town of Lucretia has a transportation problem, which it hopes can be solved by building a new road through the center of town. Three types of roads can be built, their annual costs and benefits to the townspeople being as follows:

Road	Total cost (millions of dollars)	Total benefit (millions of dollars)
No road	0	0
Road 10 miles long	5	8
Road 20 miles long	12	16
Road 30 miles long	20	20

    a.   What is the extra annual cost of building a 20-mile road rather than a 10-mile road? What is the extra annual cost of building a 30-mile road rather than a 20-mile road?

    b.   What is the extra annual benefit from building a 20-mile road rather than a 10-mile road? What is the extra annual benefit from building a 30-mile road rather than building a 20-mile road?

    c.   Should the town build one of these roads? If so, which one?

6. Suppose that the demand and supply curves for good X are as follows:

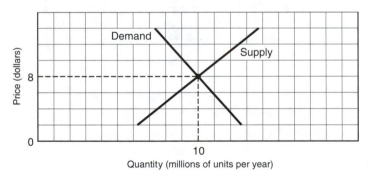

    a.   If the market for good X is in equilibrium, how much are consumers willing to pay for the last unit of good X?

    b.   The supply curve shows the extra cost of producing an extra unit of good X. If the market for good X is in equilibrium, how much does it cost to produce the last unit of good X?

    c.   If the social costs of producing good X *exceed* the private costs, is the social cost of producing the last unit of good X equal to the amount consumers are willing to pay for this unit? If not, is the social cost of the last unit greater or less than the amount consumers will pay for it? Why?

    d.   Under the circumstances described in part c, indicate why the socially optimal output of good X is less than 10 million units per year.

e.   If the social benefit of producing good X were more than the private benefit, indicate why the optimal output of good X would be more than 10 million units per year.

7. Suppose that a tax of 20 cents per pack is imposed on cigarettes. The tax is collected from the sellers. The before-tax supply curve for cigarettes was

Price (cents per pack)	Quantity supplied (millions of packs)
50	90
60	100
70	120
80	140

a.   After the tax, how much is supplied when the price is 80 cents per pack? 90 cents per pack?

b.   If the demand curve for cigarettes is as shown in the following table, what is the equilibrium price of cigarettes before and after the tax?

Price (cents per pack)	Quantity demanded (millions of packs)
50	110
60	100
70	100
80	100
90	90

c.   Suppose that the demand curve in part b no longer is valid. Instead, suppose that the demand curve for cigarettes is a horizontal line at 70 cents per pack. What is the equilibrium price of cigarettes before and after the tax? Draw the relevant demand and supply curves in the following graph:

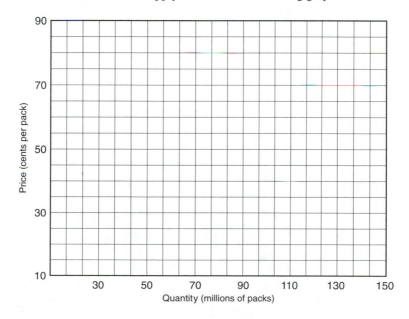

Answers

Completion Questions
1. regulatory commissions   2. Public goods   3. taxes   4. personal income
5. goods and services, exclude, prevent, pays, price system   6. external economy,
external economy   7. little, supplement, investment   8. external diseconomy,
external diseconomy

True-False
1. True   2. False   3. False   4. False   5. True   6. True   7. True   8. False
9. True   10. True

Multiple Choice
1. a   2. e   3. e   4. d   5. c   6. c   7. d   8. b   9. b   10. c   11. b

Problems
1. a.   It is less than 60 million tons.
   b.   The supply curve does not reflect the true social costs. A supply curve
        reflecting these costs would be above and to the left of the one shown
        here:

   c. $4. Too low.
2. If any family buys smog-free air, it automatically buys it for others too,
   regardless of whether the latter pay for it. And, since no family can afford the
   cost, so long as families act independently, it will be unprofitable for a private firm to carry out this project.
3. a.   The government must make sure that goods like drugs are properly
        labeled and reasonably safe.
   b.   National defense is a public good.
   c.   The redistribution of income is an accepted concern of government.
   d.   There are external economies from such research.
   e.   The government must try to maintain reasonably competitive markets.
   f.   The redistribution of income is an accepted concern of government.

g. The redistribution of income and economic stabilization are accepted concerns of government.

4. Taxes and borrowing are used for this purpose.

5. a. $7 million. $8 million.

   b. $8 million. $4 million.

   c. Yes. The 20-mile road, because the extra benefit from the 30-mile road is less than the extra cost.

6. a. $8.

   b. $8.

   c. No. It is greater than the amount that consumers are willing to pay for it, since consumers are willing to pay only $8 for it but its social cost exceeds $8.

   d. The optimal output of good X is less than 10 million units per year because the optimal output is at the intersection of the demand curve with the supply curve reflecting social costs. Because this supply curve lies to the left of the industry's supply curve (in the diagram), the optimal output must be less than 10 million units per year.

   e. If the social benefit of producing good X were more than the private benefit, the demand curve reflecting social benefit would lie to the right of the industry's demand curve. Therefore, the intersection of the demand curve reflecting social benefit with the supply curve would be at an output exceeding 10 million units per year.

7. a. 100 million packs. 120 million packs.

   b. 60 cents before the tax, 80 cents after the tax.

   c. 70 cents both before and after the tax.

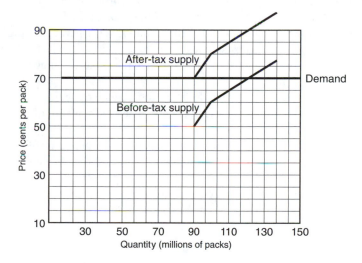

CHAPTER 27

International Trade

Chapter Profile

International trade permits specialization, and specialization increases output. This is the advantage of trade, for both individuals and countries.

Country A has an absolute advantage over country B in the production of a good when country A can produce a unit of the good with fewer resources than country B. Trade can be mutually beneficial even if one country has an absolute advantage in the production of all goods.

Country A has a comparative advantage over country B in the production of a good when country A can produce the good with a lower loss of alternative output. Specialization and trade depend on comparative, not absolute, advantage. Trade can result in higher worldwide production when countries export the goods for which they have comparative advantage and import the products for which they do not.

If markets are relatively free and competitive, producers are automatically led to produce in accord with comparative advantage. If a country has a comparative advantage in the production of a certain good, it will turn out (after the price of the good in various countries is equalized and total world output of the good equals total world demand) that this country is an exporter of the good under free trade.

A tariff is a tax imposed by the government on imports, the purpose being to cut down on imports to protect domestic industry at the expense of the general public, and in general, a tariff costs the general public more than the protected industry (and its workers and suppliers) gains.

Quotas are another barrier to free trade. They, too, reduce trade, raise prices, protect domestic industry from foreign competition, and reduce the standard of living of the country as a whole.

Tariffs, quotas, and other barriers to free trade can sometimes be justified on the basis of national security and other noneconomic considerations. Moreover, tariffs and other forms of protection can sometimes be justified to protect infant industries, prevent a country from being too dependent on only a few industries, and carry out other national objectives. But many arguments for tariffs are fallacious.

Concepts for Review

exports	tariff
imports	prohibitive tariff
absolute advantage	quotas
comparative advantage	NAFTA
export subsidies	infant industry
terms of trade	consumption possibilities curve

Completion Questions

1. If the United States exports corn to France, this results in a(n) (increase,

   decrease) _____ in the price of corn in the United States and

   a(n) (increase, decrease) _____ in the price of corn in
   France. If France exports wine to the United States, this results in a(n)

   (increase, decrease) _____ in the price of wine in the

   United States and a(n) (increase, decrease) _____ in the price
   of wine in France.

2. In the absence of trade, suppose that wheat would sell for $3 per bushel in
   the United States and £2 in England and that cloth would sell for $2 per yard in
   the United States and £.5 in England. If 1£ = $2.25, the United

   States (exports, imports) _____ wheat because U.S.

   wheat can be bought for £_____ by the English. England

   (exports, imports) _____ cloth because English cloth

   can be bought for $_____ by Americans.

3. Trade permits specialization, and specialization increases _____.

4. Specialization and trade depend on _____ advantage between
   countries.

5. Assuming for simplicity that only two countries exist, the price of a good tends
   to settle at the level where the amount of the good that one country

   exports (equals, is unequal to) _____ the amount that the other
   country imports.

6. Both a(n) _____ and a(n) _____
   generally increase the price of an imported good. Two ways in which
   governments try to help protect their domestic industries are by

   _____ and_____.

7. One country has a(n) _____ advantage over another when it
   can produce one unit of a good with fewer resources than the other country.

8. Suppose that one country has a comparative advantage in producing one good
   and another country has a comparative advantage in producing another good.
   Then, if each country specializes in producing the good in which it

   (has, has not) _____ the comparative advantage, each

   (can, cannot) _____ benefit from trade.

9. _____ indicate whether a country has a comparative advantage or disadvantage in producing a commodity. If it has a comparative advantage, after the price of a good in various countries is equalized and total world output of the good equals total world demand for it, a country (exports, imports)

_____ the good under free trade and competition.

10. Specialization can reduce production costs to a lower level than would be possible if each country tried to be _____.

11. Country A can produce a bushel of wheat or a ton of steel with one unit of resources. Country B can produce three bushels of wheat or $1\frac{1}{2}$ tons of steel

with one unit of resources. Country A (has, does not have) _____ a comparative advantage in the production of wheat, and it (has, does not

have) _____ a comparative advantage in the production of

steel. Country B (has, does not have) _____ a comparative advantage in the production of wheat, and it (has, does not have)

_____ a comparative advantage in the production of steel.

Country A has an absolute advantage in the production of _____.

Country B has an absolute advantage in the production of _____.

True-False

_____ 1. If Brazil could produce every good and service with 80 percent as much of each input as Argentina, Brazil would have a comparative advantage over Argentina in all goods and services.

_____ 2. If country A has an absolute advantage over country B in the production of every good, then trade would be beneficial for country A but not for country B.

_____ 3. If the United States has relatively bountiful supplies of land relative to Japan, Japan has relatively bountiful supplies of labor relative to the United States, and the production of electronic goods requires relatively little land and large amounts of labor, while the production of grain requires relatively little labor and large amounts of land, Japan is likely to export electronic goods.

_____ 4. Even though one country may be more efficient than another at producing two commodities, both countries may benefit if each pecializes and trades.

_____ 5. Under free trade, a country's economic welfare is always lower than under a tariff.

_____ 6. Quotas can be even more effective than tariffs in keeping foreign goods out of a country.

_____ 7. International differences in resource endowments and the relative quantity of various types of human and nonhuman resources are important bases for specialization.

_____ 8. The purpose of a tariff is to cut down on imports to protect domestic industry and workers from foreign competition.

_____ 9. Tariffs or other forms of protection are sometimes justified to foster the growth and development of young industries.

_____ 10. If country A uses 20 percent less of all inputs to produce every good and service than country B, there may be no advantage in two-way trade between these two countries.

_____ 11. More open trade between the United States and Mexico under NAFTA has cost the United States a large number of jobs.

Multiple Choice

1. If a country wishes to protect an industry that is young or necessary to its security,

   a.   a subsidy is likely to be preferable to a tariff.
   b.   a subsidy is likely to be preferable to a quota.
   c.   both a and b.
   d.   a quota is likely to be preferable to a subsidy.
   e.   none of the above.

2. Country C can produce a ton of food or 4 tons of coal with one unit of resources. Country D can produce 2 tons of food or 5 tons of coal with one unit of resources.

   a.   Country C exports food and imports coal.
   b.   Country D exports food and imports coal.
   c.   Country C neither imports nor exports food.
   d.   Country D neither imports nor exports coal.
   e.   None of the above.

3. If France exports wine to Britain and Britain exports textiles to France, an increase in the price of wine (relative to the price of textiles) means

   a.   an improvement for France in the terms of trade.
   b.   an improvement for Britain in the terms of trade.
   c.   no change in the terms of trade.
   d.   all of the above.
   e.   a and b.

4. The purpose of a tariff is

    a.   to reduce imports to protect domestic industry and workers from foreign competition.

    b.   to produce revenue to pay for shipping costs.

    c.   to reduce costs.

    d.   all of the above.

    e.   none of the above.

5. One difference between tariffs and quotas is that only tariffs

    a.   reduce trade.

    b.   raise prices.

    c.   provide the government with revenue.

    d.   reduce the standard of living of a country as a whole.

    e.   none of the above.

6. In addition to national defense, tariffs and other forms of protection are sometimes defended on the grounds that they

    a.   promote growth and development of young industries.

    b.   protect domestic jobs and reduce unemployment.

    c.   prevent overdependence of a country on only a few industries.

    d.   improve a country's terms of trade.

    e.   all of the above.

Discussion and Extension Questions

1. According to the U.N.'s World Economic and Social Survey 2003, "While . . . the costs of protection, can be difficult to gauge, there is a great deal of cross-country and sometimes controversial evidence that documents a positive relationship between a liberal trade regime and GDP growth." "Countries with well-functioning markets and a better human capital base benefit more from trade reforms." How could more-open trade lead to greater GDP growth, and why might this depend on the nature of the markets and human capital?

2. "It is a foolish and dangerous thing for U.S. firms to export their technology since this will result in foreign firms' imitating our products and beating us in foreign markets." Discuss and evaluate.

3. In an emergency, people frequently are called on to carry out tasks far removed from their normal occupations. Suppose that four people escape from a shipwreck and are marooned on a desert island. One member of the group, a college graduate, is given the job of sweeping the floor. He complains that this is a poor use of his talents. Using the theory of comparative advantage, explain why he may be wrong.

4. Is it better to "buy American" because we then have both the goods and the money? Explain.

5. If the free flow of goods leads to an increase in world output, should we also press for a free flow of people across countries (i.e., no immigration restrictions)?

Problems

1. Suppose that the demand and supply curves for transistor radios in the United States are as follows:

Price (dollars)	Quantity demanded (millions)	Quantity supplied (millions)
5	5	2
10	4	3
15	3	4
20	2	5

Further suppose that the demand and supply curves for transistor radios in Japan are

Price (expressed in dollar equivalent of Japanese price)	Quantity demanded (millions)	Quantity supplied (millions)
5	2.5	1
10	2.0	3
15	1.5	5
20	1.0	7

   a. Suppose there is free trade in transistor radios. What is the equilibrium price?
   b. Which country exports transistor radios to the other country?
   c. How large will be the exports?
   d. Suppose that the United States imposes a tariff of $10 per transistor radio. What happens to exports and imports?

2. Suppose that the United States can produce three computers or 3,000 cases of wine with one unit of resources, while France can produce one computer or 5,000 cases of wine with one unit of resources.

   a. Does specialization increase world output?
   b. Is this an example of absolute or comparative advantage or both?

3. Suppose that labor is the only input and two countries, Argentina and Brazil, can produce the following amounts of two commodities, bananas and nuts, with a day of labor:

	Bananas (pounds)	Nuts (pounds)
Argentina	10	3
Brazil	5	4

a. For both countries to gain from trade, between what limits must the ratio of the prices lie?

b. Suppose there is free trade and the price of bananas increases relative to the price of nuts. Is this change in the terms of trade to the advantage of Argentina or Brazil?

4. Countries A and B are neighbors and produce only food and machines. Both countries' production possibilities curves are straight lines. Country A has 500 units of resources, while country B has 200 units of resources. In country A, a unit of resources can produce 22 units of food or 11 units of machinery. In country B, a unit of resources can produce 15 units of food or 10 units of machinery. Before there was any international trade, output in the two countries was

| | Output | |
Country	Food	Machinery
A	8,360 units	1,320 units
B	2,250 units	500 units

a. What is the price of a unit of machinery (in terms of food) in each country when they do not trade with each other? Explain.

b. Can the two countries benefit from international trade? If so, explain why.

c. Find the total production of food and machines in the two countries together both before and after trade. What did we gain?

d. Between what limits will the ratio of the price of machinery to the price of food be once international trade begins?

5. Countries D and E have not traded with each other because of political differences. Suddenly, they reconcile their political differences and begin to trade. Cigars are relatively cheap, but beef is relatively expensive in country D. Beef is relatively cheap, but cigars are relatively expensive in country E.

a. When these countries begin to trade, is the demand for cigars produced in country D increase or decrease? Does the price of cigars increase or decrease in country D?

b. Does the demand for cigars produced in country E increase or decrease? Does the price of cigars increase or decrease in country E?

c. Does the demand for beef produced in country D increase or decrease? Does the price of beef increase or decrease in country D?

d. Does the demand for beef produced in country E increase or decrease? Does the price of beef increase or decrease in country E?

e. Does the demand for resources used to produce cigars in country D increase or decrease? Does the demand for resources to produce beef used in country E increase or decrease?

f. Does the demand for resources used to produce cigars in country E increase or decrease? Does the demand for resources used to produce beef in country D increase or decrease?

6. The following graph shows the production possibilities curves for country X and country Y.

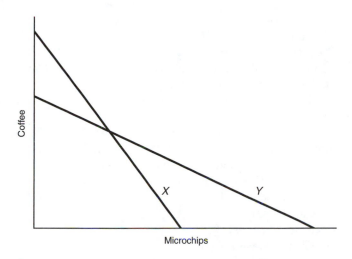

a. Which country has the comparative advantage for coffee? Which country has the comparative advantage for microchips?
b. Draw in the consumption possibilities curve.

Answers

Completion Questions

1. increase, decrease, decrease, increase   2. exports, $1^1/_3$, exports, $1^1/_8$
3. output   4. comparative   5. equals   6. tariff, quota, tariffs, quotas
7. absolute   8. has, can   9. Market forces, exports   10. self-sufficient
11. does not have, has, has, does not have, neither, both

True-False

1. False   2. False   3. True   4. True   5. False   6. True   7. True   8. True
9. True   10. True   11. False

Multiple Choice

1. c   2. b   3. a   4. a   5. c   6. e

Problems

1. a. $10.
   b, c.   Japan will export 1 million transistor radios to the United States.
   d.   Exports and imports drop.
2. a.   Yes.

    b.   The United States has an absolute and comparative advantage in computers; France has the same in wine.

3. a.   The price of a pound of bananas must be between $^3/_{10}$ and $^8/_{10}$ of the price of a pound of nuts.

    b.   Argentina.

4. a.   The price of machinery is double that of food in country A and 1.5 times that of food in country B, because of the relative costs of machinery and food in each country.

    b.   Yes, because country A has a comparative advantage in food and country B has a comparative advantage in machinery.

    c.   Before trade, food production = 8360 + 2250 = 10,610. Before trade, machine production = 2250 + 500 = 1820. After trade, food production = $500 \times 22 = 11,000$. After trade, machine production = $200 \times 10 = 2000$. We gained 390 units of food and 10 units of machinery.

    d.   The ratio is between 1.5 and 2.

5. a.   Increase. Increase.

    b.   Decrease. Decrease.

    c.   Decrease. Decrease.

    d.   Increase. Increase.

    e.   Increase. Increase.

    f.   Decrease. Decrease.

6. a.   Country X has the comparative advantage for coffee and Country Y has the comparative advantage for microchips.

    b.

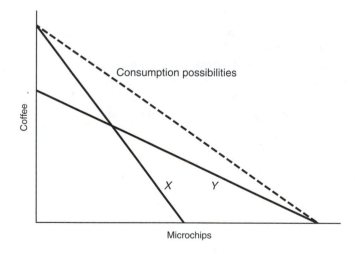

CHAPTER 28

Exchange Rates and the

Balance of Payments

Chapter Profile

An important difference between international business transactions and business transactions within a country is that international business transactions involve more than one currency. The exchange rate is the number of units of one currency that exchanges for a unit of another currency.

Under a system of flexible exchange rates, the market for foreign exchange functions like any other free market: It is determined by supply and demand. Under such a system, exchange rates tend to move in a way that removes imbalances among countries in exports and imports. The price of a country's currency tends to fall (rise) if its inflation rate and growth rate are relatively high (low) or its interest rate is relatively low (high).

Until 1973, when exchange rates became more flexible, most exchange rates were fixed by government action and international agreement. They were allowed to vary slightly, but only slightly, about the official rate.

If exchange rates are fixed, the amount of a foreign currency demanded may not equal the amount supplied. To maintain exchange rates at the official levels, governments enter the market and buy and sell their currencies as needed. They also intervene by curbing imports, limiting foreign travel, and other measures.

Under a system of fixed exchange rates, a country has a balance-of-payments deficit if its currency is overvalued and a balance-of-payments surplus if its currency is undervalued. A balance-of-payments deficit is the difference between the quantity demanded and the quantity supplied of the currency.

The United States experienced a chronic balance-of-payments deficit during the 1950s, 1960s, and 1970s. This deficit was the result of the growing productivity of other economies, our large investments abroad, and our military and foreign aid expenditures abroad. In 1973, the system of fixed exchange rates was abandoned, as many countries adopted flexible exchange rates with some government intervention. While these flexible exchange rates have worked well in some respects, there have been periods of exchange rate volatility, even crises.

The European Union tried more recently to tie its currencies together, even introducing a new currency, the euro, to eventually replace local currencies. By adopting one currency, the EU reduced transaction costs for businesses, improving productive efficiency as well as improving the fiscal performance of member governments. However, one currency translates into one monetary policy, and there is concern that the European Central Bank could run a monetary policy too tight for struggling economies or too loose for overheating economies.

Concepts for Review

exchange rate	fixed exchange rates
gold standard	balance-of-payments deficit
flexible exchange rates	balance-of-payments surplus
appreciation	International Monetary Fund
depreciation	gold exchange standard
devaluation of currency	euro

Completion Questions

1. If the U.S. economy grows more rapidly than other economies, U.S. (exports, imports) _____ are likely to grow more rapidly than its (exports, imports) _____. Therefore, U.S. demand for foreign currency grows (more, less) _____ rapidly than the amount of foreign currency supplied. Consequently the dollar is likely to

   _____.

2. If the rate of inflation in the United States is higher than in Britain, the pound _____ relative to the dollar, and the dollar

   _____ relative to the pound.

3. If the rate of interest is higher in Japan than in the United States, investors sell _____ and buy _____ to switch from the lower-yielding U.S. securities to the higher-yielding Japanese securities.

   Consequently, the dollar tends to _____ relative to the yen.

4. When exchange rates are allowed to fluctuate freely, they are determined by

   _____.

5. Under the gold standard, when a country increases the price of gold, this is called a(n) _____.

6. When country A's currency becomes more valuable than country B's currency, country A's currency is said to _____ relative to that of country B, and country B's currency is said to _____ relative to that of country A.

7. Representatives of the Allied governments met in Bretton Woods, New Hampshire, in _____ to work out a more-effective monetary system for the postwar era. It was generally agreed that competitive _____, such as occurred in the 1930s, should

be avoided. The _____ was set up to maintain a stable

system of _____ exchange rates and ensure that, when

exchange rates had to be changed because of significant trade _____,
disruption would be minimized.

8. Suppose that Spain's currency is overvalued. If so, the quantity of its currency

supplied (exceeds, is less than) _____ the quantity demanded.

The difference is called Spain's _____.
To make up the difference, Spain's central bank must give up some of its

_____.

True-False

_____ 1. Under the gold standard, exports and imports tended toward balance, because as a country's gold stock declined, its price level fell, and as its gold stock increased, its price level rose.

_____ 2. If there is a "run" on the dollar, speculators sell the dollar because they are convinced its price will fall and they do not want to experience losses by holding it, with the result that the price of the dollar does indeed fall.

_____ 3. The gold standard was abandoned because wages and prices fluctuated too much.

_____ 4. From 1950 to 1970, the United States showed a chronic deficit in its balance of payments.

_____ 5. During the latter part of the nineteenth century, the gold standard seemed to work very well, but serious trouble developed after World War I.

_____ 6. Throughout the 1960s our gold stock increased substantially.

_____ 7. A country might change its general price level to restore equilibrium in its balance of payments.

_____ 8. A country might adopt various types of controls to interfere with market forces to restore equilibrium in its balance of payments.

_____ 9. In 2003, the dollar appreciated significantly against most major currencies.

_____ 10. If the United States exports more goods to Europe, it increases the demand for the dollar and increases the supply of the euro.

_____ 11. In 1999, all European Union members adopted the euro to eventually replace their local currencies.

Multiple Choice

1. If the U.S. dollar appreciates from 150 yen to 200 yen, the dollar price of a CD player selling in Japan for 45,000 yen

   a. falls by $100.
   b. falls by $75.
   c. falls by $50.
   d. increases by $75.
   e. none of the above.

2. To support its currency, a government would be least likely to

   a. enter the market and buy its own currency.
   b. increase defense expenditures abroad.
   c. limit the travel abroad of its citizens.
   d. curb imports.

3. Exchange rates from 1975 to today usually were

   a. on a crawling peg basis.
   b. determined by the gold standard.
   c. fluctuating.
   d. none of the above.
   e. fixed.

4. The only factor listed here that did *not* contribute to the chronic deficit in our balance of payments in the 1960s and 1970s was

   a. recovery of European and Japanese economies.
   b. the amount we spent abroad for military uses and foreign aid.
   c. U.S. firms' investment abroad.
   d. increased foreign demand for some of our major exports.
   e. none of the above.

5. A shift to the right in the demand for Canadian dollars occurs if

   a. Canadian interest rates are relatively high and Canadian inflation is relatively low.
   b. Canadian interest rates are relatively low and Canadian inflation is relatively high.
   c. both Canadian interest rates and Canadian inflation are relatively low.
   d. both Canadian interest rates and Canadian inflation are relatively high.
   e. none of the above.

6. A country's balance-of-payments surplus tends to become greater if

   a. it reduces its interest rates.
   b. it allows its inflation rate to increase.
   c. it increases its economic growth rate.
   d. all of the above.
   e. none of the above.

7. Spain decides to use controls over trade to reduce its balance-of-payments deficit, with the result that there is a decrease in

   a. the rate of inflation.
   b. the growth rate.
   c. Spain's exports.
   d. Spain's imports.
   e. the balance of merchandise trade.

8. Under a regime of fixed exchange rates, if the rate of inflation is higher in Japan than elsewhere, Japan's

   a. exports and imports fall.
   b. exports and imports rise.
   c. exports rise and imports fall.
   d. exports fall and imports rise.
   e. balance-of-payments surplus becomes larger or its balance-of-payments deficit becomes smaller.

Discussion and Extension Questions

1. Late in 1999 and during 2000, the European Central Bank raised key interest rates over 2 percent, while the Federal Reserve in the United States cut key interest rates. What effect do you think these policies had in the market for the dollar and the euro?

2. "Under floating exchange rates, a deficit in our balance of payments is not a measure of pressure on the dollar, as it was under fixed exchange rates." Comment and evaluate.

3. The Bretton Woods agreements established a system of fixed exchange rates. What happened if the amount demanded of a currency did not equal the amount supplied?

4. What does a country's balance-of-payments deficit or surplus measure? What factors were responsible for the chronic deficit in the U.S. balance of payments?

5. What are some of the ways that a country with a deficit can try to restore equilibrium in its balance of payments?

6. Why and how might a country increase the value of its currency as the United States did in the mid-1990s? Why and how might a country decrease the value of its currency as the United States did in the middle to late 1980s?

7. During the Asian crisis of the late 1990s, problems in the banking and asset markets of several Asian countries led to rapid drops in their currencies. Foreign exchange speculators were blamed by many for the financial crisis. Comment.

Problems

1. The supply curve for Japanese radios to the U.S. market is shown in the following graph for two periods of time.

    a.   One curve is before a depreciation of the dollar relative to the yen; one curve is after it. Which curve is which? Why?

    b.   What is the effect of the depreciation on the dollar price of Japanese radios?

    c.   What is the effect on U.S. expenditures (in dollars) for Japanese radios if the demand for them in the United States is price elastic?

    d.   What is the effect on U.S. expenditures (in dollars) for Japanese radios if the demand for them in the United States is price inelastic?

2. Suppose that the demand curve in Japan for U.S. computers is as follows.

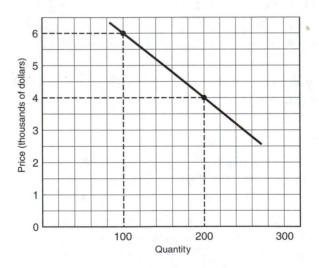

    a.   If the Japanese yen depreciates relative to the U.S. dollar, does the quantity of computers sold in Japan at a dollar price of $4,000 rise or fall?

    b.   Under these circumstances, does the demand curve rise or fall?

    c. Under these circumstances, do the dollar expenditures on U.S. computers in Japan rise or fall?

3. a. Suppose that people in Switzerland want to import a product from the United States. If the product costs $5 in the United States, how much will it cost in Switzerland if the exchange rate is 3 Swiss francs = 1 dollar? If the exchange rate is 4 Swiss francs = 1 dollar? If the exchange rate is 2 Swiss francs = 1 dollar?

    b. Suppose that the quantity of the product (in part a) demanded in Switzerland is related to its price (in Swiss francs) in the way indicated in the table. The table shows the desired expenditure by Swiss on this product at various levels of the exchange rate. Fill in the blanks.

Exchange rate	Dollar price of good	Swiss price of good (Swiss francs)	Quantity demanded	Total desired expenditure (in dollars)
4 francs = 1 dollar	5	_____	500	_____
3 francs = 1 dollar	5	_____	1,000	_____
2 francs = 1 dollar	5	_____	1,200	_____

    c. Plot the relationship between the price of a dollar (in Swiss francs) and the quantity of dollars demanded by the Swiss to buy the product in parts a and b.

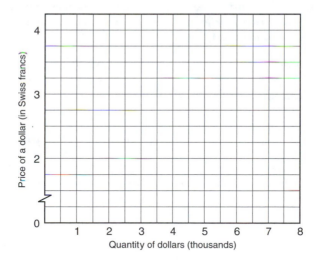

4. a.　Suppose that people in the United States want to import a product from Switzerland. The following table relates to the demand for this good in the United States. It shows the desired expenditure on this product by Americans at various levels of the exchange rate. Fill in the blanks.

Exchange rate	Swiss price of good (Swiss francs)	Dollar price of good	Quantity demanded	Total desired expenditure (in dollars)
4 francs = 1 dollar	12	_____	2,000	_____
3 francs = 1 dollar	12	_____	1,250	_____
2 francs = 1 dollar	12	_____	500	_____

　b.　Plot in the graph in problem 3c the relationship between the price of a dollar (in Swiss francs) and the quantity of dollars supplied by Americans to buy the product in part a.

　c.　If the only international trade between Switzerland and the United States is that described in the table, what is the equilibrium exchange rate?

　d.　In the situation described in the table, would there be a shortage or surplus of francs if exchange rates were fixed and the exchange rate for the Swiss franc was $0.30?

5. Assume that both countries X and Y are on the gold standard and a unit of country X's currency is worth $1/40$ of an ounce of gold, and a unit of country Y's currency is worth $1/8$ of an ounce of gold.

　a.　How much is a unit of country X's currency worth in terms of country Y's currency?

　b.　How much is a unit of country Y's currency worth in terms of country X's currency?

　c.　If a unit of country Y's currency suddenly begins to sell for 3 units of country X's currency, what forces will push the exchange rate back toward equilibrium?

6. The demand and supply curves for the Swiss franc are as follows:

Price of Swiss franc (dollars)	Millions of Swiss francs demanded	Millions of Swiss francs supplied
0.80	300	400
0.70	320	370
0.60	340	340
0.50	360	310
0.40	380	280

　a.　What is the equilibrium rate of exchange for the dollar?

　b.　What is the equilibrium rate of exchange for the Swiss franc?

　c.　How many dollars are exchanged for Swiss francs?

　d.　How many Swiss francs are exchanged for dollars?

7. The demand curve for British pounds is as follows:

Price of British pound (dollars)	Millions of pounds demanded
2.00	200
2.10	190
2.20	180
2.30	170
2.40	160
2.50	150

   a. Suppose that the British government sets the exchange rate at $2.40 and the quantity of pounds supplied at this exchange rate is 180 million pounds. Does the British government have to buy or sell pounds? If so, how many?

   b. If the British government has to buy pounds with dollars, where does it get the dollars?

Answers

Completion Questions

1. imports, exports, more, depreciate   2. appreciates, depreciates   3. U.S. dollars, Japanese yen, depreciate   4. supply and demand   5. devaluation of its currency   6. appreciate, depreciate   7. 1944, devaluations, International Monetary Fund, fixed, imbalances   8. exceeds, *balance-of-payments deficit,* reserves

True-False

1. True   2. True   3. False   4. True   5. True   6. False   7. True   8. True
9. False   10. True   11. False

Multiple Choice

1. b   2. b   3. c   4. d   5. a   6. e   7. d   8. d

Problems

1. a. The higher curve is the one following the depreciation. Because of the depreciation, it takes more dollars to elicit the same supply as before.
    b. It increases the price.
    c. It reduces expenditures.
    d. It increases expenditures.
2. a. It falls.
    b. It falls.
    c. They fall.
3. a. 15 Swiss francs. 20 Swiss francs. 10 Swiss francs.

b.

Swiss price of good (Swiss francs)	Total desired expenditure (in dollars)
20	2,500
15	5,000
10	6,000

c.

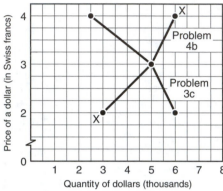

4. a.

Dollar price of good	Total desired expenditure (in dollars)
3	6,000
4	5,000
6	3,000

  b. See answer to problem 3c.

  c. 3 Swiss francs = 1 dollar.

  d. More Swiss francs would be demanded than supplied. There would be a shortage of Swiss francs.

5. a. A unit of country X's currency is worth one-fifth as much as a unit of country Y's currency.

  b. A unit of country Y's currency is worth five times as much as a unit of country X's currency.

  c. People in country Y can exchange a unit of their currency for $\frac{1}{8}$ ounce of gold and ship it to country X, where it can be exchanged for five units of country X's currency. Therefore, people in country Y will not accept only three units of country X's currency for one unit of country Y's currency.

6. a. A dollar sells for $1\frac{2}{3}$ Swiss francs.

  b. 60 cents.

  c. 340 million francs × 60 cents = 204 million dollars.

  d. 340 million francs.

7. a. Buy. 20 million pounds.

  b. From its reserves.

CASE 5

The Benefits of a Global Economy

COUNCIL OF ECONOMIC ADVISERS[1]

Trade economists have long recognized the benefits of specialization in production and of access to markets. When a country produces and exports those goods and services that it can produce relatively inexpensively, and imports those that are relatively inexpensive to produce abroad, trade improves standards of living on both sides of the transaction. For example, the United States can produce financial services at lower cost, relative to other products that it might produce, than most developing countries can. Costa Rica, by comparison, can produce coffee at lower cost, relative to other products, than can most industrialized countries. In this example, the United States would likely benefit from producing and exporting financial services and importing coffee. The reverse is true of Costa Rica. Through freer trade and specialization, a country's resources can be directed more efficiently to those uses in which they generate the most economic value, thereby raising income.

Access to larger markets can also reduce costs and increase the returns to innovation. Producing such goods as automobiles and airplanes requires building large plants and installing complex and costly equipment. By adding exports to their domestic sales, manufacturers can lower their unit costs by extending production runs and spreading overhead costs more broadly. Moreover, the ability to spread fixed research and development costs may allow globally competitive firms to be more innovative than those confined to selling in domestic markets.

Domestic production can expand when firms export, drawing workers into jobs in the economy's most productive and internationally competitive sectors. Recent studies find a substantial wage premium—on the order of 15 percent—in U.S. jobs supported by goods exports. Moreover, opening up to trade means giving consumers and firms greater freedom of choice about what inputs to purchase and what goods to consume. For consumers, the availability of less expensive and more varied products increases the real purchasing power of domestic wages. Some of the benefits of market opening are quantifiable. For example, a study of the costs of protection in the United States found that tariffs and quantitative import restrictions in place in 1990 cost American consumers about $70 billion. Since 1990, these costs to U.S. consumers have fallen, as trade barriers have been reduced on some products. At the same time, import competition creates incentives for U.S. businesses to price their products more competitively.

Access to international capital markets can also improve living standards. International capital mobility allows portfolio diversification and improved risk sharing. It allows investments to take place where they offer the highest returns, thereby improving global resource allocation. And it allows a country to smooth its consumption by consuming today more than it produces today, paying for the difference by borrowing

[1]*Economic Report of the President* (Washington, DC: Government Printing Office, 2000), pp. 213–225.

abroad. Therefore, global investment, like trade, yields benefits to both sides of the transaction. Capital goes to those who are best able to make productive use of it, and the suppliers of that capital receive a higher return for a given level of risk than they could get elsewhere. These benefits may be particularly pronounced in the case of FDI. Too large a volume of short-term capital flows, by contrast, may in some cases make an economy more vulnerable to crisis, as discussed later.

Trade and investment activities can be mutually reinforcing. For example, FDI by U.S. companies can help pave the way for U.S. exports. It may create demand for U.S.-produced inputs, possibly from the parent operations. It may also offer U.S. companies a foothold in foreign markets from which they can further expand sales. In many cases, investment in distribution and other essential services increases a supplier's ability to export into a market. Trade between firms and their foreign affiliates, so-called intrafirm trade, can be an efficient means of doing business over-seas, particularly when firms need substantial information about suppliers, clients, or markets abroad in order to operate effectively. Over a third of U.S. merchandise exports and about two-fifths of U.S. merchandise imports are estimated to be intrafirm; worldwide, intrafirm trade's estimated share is about a third. Trade may also expand capital flows. For example, the growth of trade has created a need for more trade-related financing and, as noted previously, for tools to hedge risk.

Globalization and Growth

Although causality may be hard to establish, simple measures of the correlation between the openness of an economy and its growth suggest a mutually supportive relationship. For example, ample evidence demonstrates that countries that actively participate in international trade tend to have higher incomes than those that do not. They also experience more rapid growth and productivity improvements. Studies also suggest that countries that have adopted outward-oriented economic policies since the early 1970s experienced significantly higher annual growth of GDP per capita over the next two decades than countries that remained inward-oriented.

Exposure to foreign competition gives domestic firms an incentive to raise their productivity—and these gains recur. Once competition is introduced, it leads to a cycle of productivity improvements and quality enhancements that continue to benefit the economy indefinitely. Studies of the United States and Japan find a positive relationship between import growth and productivity growth. Furthermore, evidence suggests that openness can induce higher average productivity through access to a greater range of intermediate inputs and, within a given industry, through faster growth of those firms that achieve the highest productivity.

Increased trade and FDI can also boost productivity growth by improving the flow of knowledge and the transfer of technology. Traded manufactures, like all manufac-tures, embody knowledge and technology and, in the case of information and com-munications technology for example, may boost countries' ability to innovate. Besides providing funding, direct investors can bring international best practices, including managerial, technical, and marketing know-how, to the recipient, which can then spill over into the rest of the economy. In turn, the direct investors may also benefit from the expertise of the recipient firms. The flow of knowledge and transfer of technology also occur through local research and development (R & D). Expenditure on R & D performed by foreign affiliates in the United States accounted for about 12 percent of the R & D performed by all U. S. businesses in 1997. The ratio of R & D expenditure to gross product for these affiliates was 5 percent, twice the ratio for all U.S. businesses.

In short, increased globalization benefits the United States and other economies. Globalization yields gains from trade, through specialization and through realization of scale economies in production. And by allowing capital to flow across borders, it lowers the cost of financing investment in the recipient country, increases the return to saving, and allows for portfolio diversification in the country providing the funds. Both trade and investment contribute to the flow of knowledge and transfer of technology.

The Challenges of Globalization

The United States has long sought to extend the benefits of trade and investment as widely as possible, both within and among countries, but significant challenges remain. The United States is committed to expanding trade and investment opportunities around the world. It is also committed to putting a human face on the global economy, in part through greater consideration of labor and environmental concerns and more openness in WTO proceedings. For all the evidence that trade raises living standards, some U.S. industries and their workers may face difficulties adjusting to more open markets. Economists attribute only a small share of worker dislocation (roughly 10 percent or less) to trade, but crafting sound domestic policy to help ease the transition for those affected poses another important challenge. The emerging market financial crises of 1997–99 highlight yet another challenge: the risk that sudden reversals in capital flows can in some cases be destabilizing. Finally, the growing U.S. trade deficit raises the challenge of ensuring not only that the United States remains an attractive location for investment, but also that Americans are saving enough for the future.

Spreading the Benefits of Trade
The United States has sought to open markets, extend the rule of law, and encourage economic growth internationally through bilateral, regional, and multilateral trade agreements. The multilateral trading system, consisting originally of the GATT and more recently the WTO, is at the core of these efforts. Although its achievements have been considerable, this system remains a work in progress. The recent difficulty in establishing a mandate for a new round of WTO negotiations, and the public protest accompanying the WTO Ministerial in Seattle, give a sense of the challenges that lie ahead.

Many countries continue to maintain high trade barriers, especially in agriculture and services, but institutional concerns, such as those relating to the WTO's accessibility and transparency and to its relationships with international labor and environmental organizations, have come increasingly to the fore. Much work also remains to be done to ensure that developing countries—particularly the least developed—enjoy improved market access and obtain the technical assistance they need to realize the benefits that international trade can afford. At the same time, the United States must also address legitimate concerns about the adjustment of domestic industries and workers. On balance, trade does raise living standards, but there are those within an economy who may suffer losses when more-open markets shift resources from one use to another.

Opening Markets More Fully

The United States gains when it lowers its trade barriers, but it gains most when other nations also lower theirs. Indeed, as one of the world's most open economies, the United States has a particular interest in promoting liberalization abroad. The Uruguay Round, which lasted from 1986 to 1994, brought agriculture and textiles and clothing more fully into the GATT and took the first steps toward liberalizing trade in those sectors. It also brought service trade into the multilateral system by creating the General Agreement on Trade in Services. A series of post-Uruguay Round negotiations have yielded additional market access commitments in financial services, basic telecommunications services, and information technology, opening up new opportunities in areas where the United States is believed to be highly competitive. Yet room for improvement remains, as many countries continue to maintain significant tariff and nontariff barriers.

Agriculture provides a stark example. Bound tariff rates (maximum rates to which countries commit themselves in trade negotiations) on agricultural products average about 50 percent around the world, compared with less than 10 percent in the United States. Moreover, even after the European Union and Japan fully implement their Uruguay Round commitments, they will be free to provide as much as $78 billion and $35 billion, respectively, in trade-distorting domestic support to their farmers each year. By comparison, the United States will be limited to about $19 billion. Partly because of these policies, average prices for food and related goods are 34 percent higher in the European Union and 134 percent higher in Japan than in the United States.

To help meet the challenges of market opening, the United States is seeking additional market access in agriculture, services, and certain industrial products in the WTO. Notwithstanding the difficulty in establishing a negotiating mandate during the Seattle Ministerial, the WTO's built-in agenda calls for further negotiations on agriculture and services to have begun by January 2000. In agriculture the United States has proposed eliminating export subsidies and reducing tariffs and trade-distroting domestic supports. In services the United States has sought commitments for more openness in key sectors such as finance, telecommunications, and construction. In other areas—chemicals, energy products, environmental products, fish, forest products, jewelry, medical and scientific equipment, and toys—the United States has sought accelerated tariff liberalization.

Strengthening Rules and Institutions

Credibility and predictability are essential components of the trading system. For firms to undertake the investments necessary to serve foreign markets, they need to believe that new barriers will not be raised and that old ones will not reassert themselves. To rely on foreign suppliers, buyers need to believe likewise that market access will not be disrupted. Traders need assurance that commitments will be binding and that markets will remain open even if circumstances change. And the rules of the trading game should ensure that governments play fair—that they neither seek advantage for favored interests by subsidizing their producers, nor pass regulations that unnecessarily distort international trade, nor otherwise circumvent international commitments.

In setting these rules and encouraging compliance with them, the WTO has tried to strike an appropriate balance between the needs of the trading system and those of sovereign nations. Its agreements do not preclude the United States or other countries from establishing, maintaining, and effectively enforcing their own laws, nor do they prevent the United States from setting and achieving its environmental, labor, health, and safety standards at the levels it considers appropriate.

By and large, countries participating in the GATT and later the WTO have adhered to their commitments. The trend toward market liberalization since World War II, and the maintenance of commitments not to raise barriers even in the face of international financial crises, stand in sharp contrast to the trade policy experience of the interwar period. The multilateral trading system has played a critical role in maintaining and expanding economic ties, helping make the last half century one of historically unprecedented economic growth for the United States and many of its trading partners.

Nevertheless, the rules of the WTO and the ways in which they are administered can be improved. The dispute settlement process, although much strengthened, is opaque and sometimes slow. During the Seattle Ministerial, the United States led the call for greater public access and participation. The United States has sought to open the WTO's dispute settlement procedures to the public and to allow nongovernmental organizations to file amicus briefs. The drawn-out pace of settlement proceedings has also caused dissatisfaction. Ordinarily, a case should not take more than a year (15 months if it is appealed), but in practice the dispute settlement process can continue to drag on even after the WTO has adopted a ruling.

Promoting Growth Internationally

The United States has long advocated the use of the multilateral trading system to promote economic growth internationally, often with considerable success, but not all countries are well positioned to reap the benefits that trade can afford. Steps can be taken to help ensure that developing countries, including the least developed, obtain the market access and technical assistance they need to benefit more fully.

Developing countries have increasingly come to appreciate the value of the multilateral trading system. The system not only provides them opportunities to trade on the basis of their comparative strengths but also reinforces market-oriented development strategies where they have been adopted. Originally dominated by the industrial countries, the system has witnessed growing participation as other nations have sought inclusion. Today the WTO counts 135 members, with over 30 nations, including China, seeking accession. This allure of the trading system supports the conviction that international trade is not a zero-sum game: Both the United States and its trading partners reap the benefits.

Developing countries have come to account for an increasingly large share of world trade, but some have moved ahead more rapidly than others. Developing countries' total trade (exports plus imports) rose at an annual rate of 9.9 percent between 1989 and 1997, exceeding the 7.6 percent growth rate of trade worldwide. Over this period their share of world trade rose from 29.1 percent to 34.7 percent. Among developing countries, the trade of those that are WTO members grew slightly faster, at an annual rate of 10.5 percent. The 48 least developed countries have, as a group, done less well. For these countries, many of which are also WTO members, trade grew at an annual rate of only 6.1 percent through 1996.

As these data suggest, not all WTO members are well equipped to use the trading system effectively. Some of the least developed members lack the necessary domestic institutions and infrastructure to reap the full benefits of trade. For them, capacity building and technical assistance, coupled with additional market opening, could help spread those benefits. Through the WTO, the international community can make more progress in liberalization in certain priority areas, such as agriculture and services. But developing countries, including the least developed, can also take their own actions. In addition to participating in multilateral initiatives, they can benefit from increased unilateral liberalization, as free trade promotes the movement of labor and capital into their more productive uses, strengthens competitive forces, facilitates innovation, and raises living standards.

The United States has proposed measures for the WTO to provide developing countries with technical assistance in implementing trade policy. The United States will also work to give the least developed countries greater access to global markets, as it is already doing through the U.S. Generalized System of Preferences (GSP) program. However, lapses in authorization of the program, which have occurred several times over the past five years, have tended to detract from its efficacy, by creating uncertainty for investors and importers.

Addressing Concerns about Adjustment

As markets become more open, some domestic industries will expand while others may contract. Although globalization provides benefits overall, the adjustments that businesses and workers in shrinking industries may undergo can be costly and painful. Although, as noted above, economic studies typically find that trade is a small factor in U.S. job displacement, some workers may face short-term unemployment, and others may even face permanent wage reductions if they are unable to find comparable jobs in expanding sectors.

Trade, like other sources of economic growth, therefore presents challenges at home. But the fact that trade produces additional income means that, in principle, resources are available to help those who are hurt—either to adapt by becoming more productive and competitive at what they are already doing, or to switch activities. One way to help in the transition is to develop programs that directly address the problems of dislocation. Another is to encourage trade while limiting the pace at which change occurs, as the United States has done by phasing in provisions of the WTO agreements and applying safeguard measures. Such gradualism may be desirable under certain circumstances, but trying to prevent liberalization altogether would be counterproductive. Permanent protection inevitably costs more, in terms of benefits forgone, than it saves. The key lies in maintaining an economy that is sufficiently flexible and vibrant to meet the challenges of reaping those benefits.

To address problems of worker dislocation, regardless of cause, the Administration has developed new programs to assist in job search and training. These programs add to the assistance already available to displaced workers through the Federal Trade Adjustment Assistance program. The Workforce Investment Act of 1998 retains a funding stream for dislocated workers and promotes customer access to services and information, as well as customer choice, through a One-Stop delivery system and through Individual Training Accounts. The Administration is also acting to ensure that Lifetime Learning tax credits and scholarships are available to assist workers in preparing for new jobs. Federal job and talent banks are meanwhile providing mechanisms for helping millions of U.S. workers find new jobs. For example, on a single day in January 2000, America's Job Bank listed over 1.5 million jobs.

The WTO agreements and U.S. trade laws also provide a cushion during periods of adjustment. For example, key features of the Agreement on Agriculture and the Agreement on Textiles and Clothing phase in gradually over periods of 6 to 10 years. Moreover, the WTO agreements allow countries to use certain forms of safeguards to protect themselves temporarily against import surges that seriously injure or threaten to seriously injure a domestic industry. The United States has invoked its own safeguard provisions three times since the creation of the WTO, in cases involving corn brooms, wheat gluten, and lamb meat.

Addressing Concerns about Core Labor Standards and the Environment

During the Seattle Ministerial, some participants and observes raised important questions about the relationships between trade and labor and between trade and the environment. The Administration is committed to ensuring that the benefits of trade are shared broadly and do not come at the expense of core labor standards or the environment. Economic evidence, presented below, suggests that trade can support labor and environmental objectives rather than obstruct them.

Over time, the United States has developed strategies to address international labor and environmental considerations through a variety of means. For example, preferential U.S. trade programs contain criteria for workers' rights: Legislation for the U.S. GSP program states that the President shall not designate any country a beneficiary developing country if "such country has not taken or is not taking steps to afford internationally recognized worker rights to workers in the country. . . ." The North American Free Trade Agreement contains side agreements on labor and the environment. At the same time, the United States has sought to promote core labor standards and environmental goals through multilateral institutions such as the International Labor Organization and the United Nations Environmental Program. During negotiations in Seattle, the United States proposed to strengthen the WTO's links to these and other relevant international organizations. The United States is also seeking to create a working group on trade and labor in the WTO, to better understand the linkages between them. And just before the Seattle Ministerial, the President issued an executive order for the United States to conduct environmental reviews of certain kinds of trade agreements.

Economic evidence suggests that trade can support both labor and environmental objectives, in part through its positive effect on economic growth. For example, analysis using wage, employment, and income data to study the relationship between economic development and working conditions in Hong Kong, the Republic of Korea, Singapore, and Taiwan has found that these conditions generally improved as the economies developed. Studies of the relationship between pollution and income per capita are also revealing: In several cross-country analyses of emissions patterns of air and water pollutants, emissions seem to increase with income at low incomes and fall with income at high incomes. As countries become wealthier, they may eventually become cleaner, perhaps because of increased demand for environmental protection. Recognizing that trade and environmental objectives can be mutually supportive in even more direct ways, the United States is seeking to eliminate fishery subsidies that contribute to overfishing and to eliminate tariffs on environmental goods.

Nevertheless, international trade occurs in the context of domestic policy. Although sovereign nations bear responsibility for adopting sound domestic policies, the international community can contribute its expertise. In this regard, the United States has proposed measures in the WTO to provide technical assistance on implementing trade policy and on strengthening institutions in developing countries responsible for trade, labor, environmental, and other policies that influence the gains to living standards from trade.